Literacy at all levels

Literacy at all levels

Proceedings of the eighth annual study conference of the United Kingdom Reading Association, Manchester 1971

Editor Vera Southgate

United Kingdom Reading Association.

Ward Lock Educational

372.4
U57 L

ISBN 0 7062 3099 X

First published 1972

Set in 10 on 11 point Linotype Plantin
by Willmer Brothers Limited, Birkenhead
for Ward Lock Educational
116 Baker Street, London WIM 2BB
Printed in England

Contents

Contributors

Introduction

The theme of the eighth annual study conference of the United Kingdom Reading Association, held at the University of Manchester in July 1971, was 'Literacy at all levels.' This particular theme was chosen because it was considered that the time was ripe for reaffirming our belief on two important points: first, that reading should not and indeed cannot be separated from the related skills of speaking, listening and writing; second, that the teaching of reading and the other language skills should be regarded as a matter which concerns all teachers of pupils of all ages from nursery schools to college and university level.

Adequate coverage of such a wide theme at a conference obviously demanded not only lectures on topics of general interest but also opportunities for delegates with common interests and problems to work together for continuous periods in homogeneous groups. Two contrasting kinds of meeting were therefore included in the five-day programme. In seven plenary sessions papers were presented to the entire conference assembly by well-known reading experts from Austria, Britain, Canada and the USA. In addition there were six sessions in which simultaneous meetings were timetabled for seven different groups, catering for inexperienced teachers of beginning reading, experienced infant teachers, teachers in junior and secondary schools, remedial teachers, college and university lecturers, overseas delegates and educationists with a general interest in reading and the language arts. In the study groups, under the guidance of their convenors, members were able to benefit from continuing programmes of talks, discussions and workshop sessions directly related to the practical issues of the work in which they are normally engaged. The complete programme of forty-nine sessions was based on contributions from a team of seventy-nine speakers and tutors.

A programme of such breadth made editing and selecting papers for inclusion in the published conference proceedings rather difficult. It was clear that all seventy-nine contributors could not be asked to provide written papers for publication, otherwise the resulting book would be enormous and far too expensive. Furthermore, many of the study group sessions consisting of discussions and workshops could not be covered by written papers. Accordingly, twenty-seven papers and reports were selected to form the contents of this book. The majority of these contributions are papers delivered at plenary and general sessions; the remainder are reports by convenors of the work undertaken in their study groups and papers or notes prepared by contributors to study groups. Therefore this book does not represent the entire conference proceedings; invaluable contributions to the programme were made by a large number of people whose names do not appear in the list of contributors. Our thanks are due to many speakers who are not mentioned, as well as to those whose papers form this book.

Published conference proceedings can never hope to give the reader even a small fraction of the stimulation and inspiration experienced by members of an international conference who have listened to and shared experiences with other educators from at home and abroad. Nevertheless, it is hoped that the selected contributions will convey some feeling of the full flavour of the conference, as well as present certain ideas to help the reader (whatever his educational position might be), to improve the literacy training in which he is engaged, and thereby contribute to a general raising of literacy standards.

Vera Southgate

Part one Improving literacy standards in the UK and the USA

1 Literacy at all levels

Vera Southgate

Introduction

Had the theme of this conference been, for example, 'Teaching infants to read', the programme would necessarily have been restricted in terms of both the subject matter and the people for whom it had relevance. Instead, the theme of 'Literacy at all levels' was deliberately selected to emphasize the breadth of the subject matter and its relevance for all educators concerned with children of all ages and adults.

In this paper I shall begin by examining briefly the meaning of literacy and noting how its various aspects are applicable at different levels. I shall then attempt a critical appraisal of literacy training in the United Kingdom, followed by an outline of certain differences between the British and American approaches to this subject. I shall conclude by listing a number of proposals whereby we in Britain might more nearly approach the goal of 'literacy at all levels'.

What do we mean by literacy?

First I must emphasize that by 'literacy' I do not just mean reading. In 1950 the Ministry of Education, while defining as 'illiterate' those with reading ages below seven and as 'semiliterate' those with reading ages between seven and nine, were certainly just as aware as we are that being literate implies more than being able to read at the level of an average nine year old. *The Concise Oxford Dictionary* defines literacy as 'the ability to read and write'. If we add to this the ability to speak our native language concisely and fluently and to listen effectively to others speaking it, we should be nearer to the broader meaning of literacy which many of us now hold: the mastery of our native language in all its aspects, as a means of communication. Through listening to the spoken word or reading the printed word we are exposed to the thoughts and ideas of others; we use language in our own thinking processes; and finally, we communicate our thoughts to others by means of either speech or writing. It is impossible to segregate reading from the other three aspects of language development—listening, speaking and writing. Clearly the concept of literacy can also be extended to include languages other than our native tongue and, in the case of immigrants, mastery of the language of the new country assumes paramount importance.

In aiming for higher standards of literacy we should be involved in a continual striving towards the fullest possible extension of each individual's mastery of these four aspects of language. Even accepting that the optimum level will not be the same for each individual, we have a long way to go before these levels are reached. This statement is equally as applicable to ourselves as to those whom we seek to teach.

Whom does literacy training concern?
Who are the people who require training in the skills of literacy and who should be engaged in the training? Mastery of the language skills begins in babyhood, concerns school children of all ages, and should continue throughout higher education and on into adulthood.

We ourselves, as more or less educated adults, are consciously engaged in improving our own reading and writing skills every time we look up the meaning or spelling of a word in a dictionary or redraft a letter or lecture. Yet on occasions we still feel inadequate. For example, preparing advance information for a conference or directions to accompany census forms does not constitute a simple exercise in written expression. And how often do we find such directions ambiguous when we have to complete application forms, census forms, tax returns etc? Communication through reading and writing is not easy even between educated adults. We also suffer from deficiencies in speaking and listening skills.

If we accept that mastery of these four interrelated skills of literacy is likely to be a long-term process, an extensive programme of training at all age levels is necessary. This programme should be the responsibility of, among others, parents, teachers of children of all ages, teachers of all subjects, college and university lecturers, librarians, publishers, educational advisers, inspectors, psychologists, linguisticians and speech experts. The membership of this conference indicates that an increasing range of people are concerning themselves with literacy. We have representatives from all the categories mentioned but not, as far as I know, experts in spoken English.

Literacy training in the United Kingdom

Three important general points
Three features of literacy training in the United Kingdom are particularly important. First, we do not have a broad concept of literacy training. Neither the word 'literacy', in the terms used here, nor the phrase 'language arts' as it is used in the USA are in common

use. I myself prefer the phrase 'language skills', but in any event in Britain we concentrate mainly on the skill of reading. Certainly many infant teachers are well aware that the four literacy skills are inter-related and they act accordingly. But in teachers' initial and in-service training courses and in books, articles and lectures, only a modest amount of attention is given to written expression and even less to speech education, while the skills of listening are almost entirely disregarded at every level. The lack of training in efficient speech is particularly unfortunate as this is our most common form of com-munication, employed much more frequently than the skills of read-ing and writing. Almost equally depressing is our neglect of training in listening, especially as most people spend more time listening to each other talking than they do reading; also our addiction to radio and television is increasing, so that people's main intake of ideas and information comes from listening rather than from reading.

Second, although our interest in literacy is concentrated on teaching reading we take a narrow view of the subject, limited almost entirely to beginning reading skills. We have barely begun to analyze the many subskills which make up the total skill of reading. In the upper classes of primary schools, in secondary schools, and in higher educa-tion establishments, we have given scant attention to the improvement and extension of comprehension skills, study skills or recreational reading skills. Teaching reading is regarded as a subject concerning only those who teach infants and older retarded pupils, and those responsible for training such teachers.

This narrowly defined concept of reading leads directly to my third point: in Britain the subject of reading lacks status. There is an educational convention, accepted also by the community at large, that the ability and status of any teacher or other educator is directly related to the age and ability of those for whom he carries responsi-bility. Some educationists would hotly deny this but I am certain that most infant teachers and many teachers of backward readers would agree with me. For example, the head of the science department in a secondary school is undoubtedly considered more important than the teacher in charge of backward readers, even though both might possess similar qualifications. The same principle holds good in higher education.

If these three points are accepted as valid, we might, with advantage consider changing the title of the UKRA. Even the substitution of the word 'language' for 'reading' might give a clearer indication of our wide interest in literacy. As our links with the International Reading Association make similarity of titles desirable, this is a question to which I should like the executive committees of our two associations to give future consideration. I should also like to see closer links established between the UKRA and other associations concerned with literacy, for example the National Association for the Teaching of English.

Details of our strengths and weaknesses

Against this background let us now examine some of the strengths and weaknesses of literacy training in the United Kingdom. Neither is absolute: in certain of our strengths there lurk dangers; on the other hand, where deficiencies exist there are some encouraging signs of awareness of the gaps and embryonic movements towards filling them. As my list of suggested improvements is rather long, I shall begin with what I consider to be the most notable feature of our work in the field of literacy.

One of our greatest strengths is the flexibility of our education system, which allows headteachers a large measure of freedom of choice regarding the school syllabus, organization, timetabling and methods. The permissiveness of our system is well illustrated by the fact that in England and Wales it is not even specifically laid down that children should be taught to read and write. Despite this, I have not come across any primary school in which the teachers do not make some attempt to help children to read and write! In addition, in many nursery and primary schools the opportunities for experimenting have resulted in informal, stimulating educational environments, with an emphasis on motivation, individuality and discovery methods of learning. In such schools many children have developed wider interests and made more rapid progress than teachers ever imagined possible.

Our nursery schools and classes provide excellent communities for the development of language, especially in their encouragement of speaking and listening skills. At the same time, positive attitudes towards reading and writing are being established by the availability of attractive books, by teachers who read stories aloud and encourage children's creative work. Yet sadly nursery education is only available for one child in nine (Palmer 1971).

The advent of informal primary schools has also heralded an increased emphasis on communication. As children move about, talk to each other and to their teachers, they really discuss ideas and problems, in contrast to the older more formal question and answer teaching techniques. In so doing, children learn to express themselves in speech and to listen to and evaluate what others are saying. At the same time, most children who are actively exploring the world around them soon become eager to read and write. They see others enjoying reading and writing and they realize that interesting information can be gained from books. They want to dip into the story books and information books on the nearby shelves. In such schools children's written expression has also flourished noticeably.

I appreciate that permissiveness in education can be accompanied by certain dangers regarding learning to read. For instance, it is easy to assume that because the absence of motivation is a serious handicap to learning, its presence precludes the need for some teaching. In this context, Cane and Smithers (1971), reporting on the recent NFER's investigation, note that in the permissive school which was most successful in teaching reading, the teachers emphasized phonics and rejected the idea of waiting for reading readiness to appear.

I think it is advantageous that schools are free to choose any medium, method or reading materials they prefer, as experimenting with new techniques or equipment rarely fails to inspire the teacher and so benefit the children almost regardless of the nature of the innovation. Although I have seen classes dampened by the lack of sparkle in teachers who were themselves dulled by the dreariness of repetitive routines with old and familiar reading schemes, I have not come across children whose reading has suffered when their teacher was filled with enthusiasm by the stimulus of experimenting.

However, both freedom for schools to experiment with new reading materials and opportunities for children to read widely from personally selected books depend on sufficient money being available to buy reading materials. Yet in the financial year 1969–70, the average *per capita* allocation for textbooks and library books in primary schools in England and Wales was only 93p in county boroughs and £1.32 in counties (the range extended from 45p to £3.06). For secondary schools the average figures were £2.17 in county boroughs and £2.62 in counties. In view of the rising cost of books, these amounts are quite inadequate; the figures at the lower end of the range are deplorable, as the Educational Publishers Council has been quick to point out. As teachers we too should condemn these figures, despite the indubitable yet almost incredible fact that not all schools spend their total allocation.

Apart from recent developments in primary education in the United Kingdom, some notable work in reading is being undertaken by dedicated teachers in remedial educational services, special schools, classes for handicapped children, and classes for adult illiterates and non-English-speaking immigrants. Yet all such provision is still patchy, and most areas require more skilled help.

Viewing this short list of praiseworthy points against the framework of the total field exposes many gaps in literacy training in this country. As the achievements of children and students correlate highly with the abilities and knowledge of their teachers, which is in turn related to the expertise of their tutors and advisers, we should first examine the available provision for studying the language skills at an advanced level. In contrast to the practice in many universities in Canada, the USA and certain European countries, no British university has a department devoted to reading and the language arts, and consequently no chair in these subjects exists. At the majority of universities the subject of reading is rarely considered to merit serious attention. For example, when a proposal that reading and the language arts should be included as a subject of study at master's degree level was recently rejected by a university committee of advanced study, a typical comment against the proposal was 'but reading is not a discipline!' Well, neither is brewing but it is still possible to study it at a higher degree level. Whilst I realize that in Britain brewing good beer is considered extremely important, it would seem reasonable to suggest that producing literate adults might merit at least the same level of study.

It is true that at certain of our universities reading has for many years been offered as a subject in various diploma courses for experienced teachers and other educators. Opportunities have also existed for submitting theses based on reading research as the total or partial requirement for higher degrees. In addition, the Institute of Education of London University introduced an optional course on the psychology of literacy at the level of a master's degree. (Unfortunately, this course will have been discontinued by 1972). Courses on reading, lasting one term at Reading University and Mather College, Manchester, and one year at Edge Hill College, Ormskirk, are also now being offered. Nevertheless, facilities for advanced study of language skills are still woefully inadequate.

One encouraging sign is the growing desire of lecturers and advisers to increase their own expertise in the subject of literacy. I have had ample evidence of this in courses for lecturers in English and education which I have arranged at Manchester University during the past few years. This UKRA conference affords another example. Approximately one-third of the delegates are lecturers in colleges, polytechnics and universities and they form the largest of our study groups.

As a result of the current paucity of provision for advanced training, we have too few people with the necessary expertise to act as lecturers, advisers, consultants, heads of reading centres, remedial centres and remedial departments within schools. Thus there are serious weaknesses in the areas of both initial and in-service teacher training.

If we look at teacher training, we find that in university departments of education where most graduates receive their training, the study of language skills is rarely included, except for the few graduates intending to teach in primary schools. In colleges of education, usually only students expecting to teach in primary schools study reading and maybe glance at the other language skills. Even so, the total course may be as short as eight hours and is unlikely to extend beyond thirty-six hours. Students planning to teach children older than nine or ten frequently receive no training whatsoever in teaching the language skills, although we know that a large proportion of teachers do not eventually teach the age range on whom their training was concentrated. In this context, one of the proposals I have made (Southgate 1971) to the James Committee is that *all* teachers in training should be expected to take at least one basic course in reading and the language arts, as well as additional selected courses.

The strengths and weaknesses of initial teacher training courses are reflected in the work of the schools. When newly qualified teachers have only a minimum of knowledge and experience in teaching the language skills, it is hardly surprising that headteachers are continually complaining on this score. When few college lecturers or experienced teachers are knowledgeable about the development of the skills of literacy *after the initial stages,* it is to be expected that pupils of eight to fifteen rarely receive effective tuition in extending the skills. Indeed, after the age of about eight, reading rarely appears as a regular subject on the timetable for all pupils. It is thus inevitable that secondary school pupils and students in higher education establishments will lack essential literacy skills and be unable to express themselves coherently in either speech or writing.

However, just as lecturers and advisers are anxious to increase their proficiency, so also are both newly-trained and more experienced teachers. Although many in-service courses on reading are provided by local authorities and other educational bodies, teachers still express the need for more. The national survey of in-service training undertaken by Manchester University School of Education a few years ago, showed (Department of Education and Science 1970) that teachers' requests for courses on reading outnumbered those for any other subject and far exceeded the provision being made. Bolam (1971) also reports a similar strong demand for reading courses from teachers in their probationary year. The growth of an association such as the UKRA confirms this trend.

Appraising interest in literacy at local authority level reveals some points which not only reflect our lack of language arts specialists, but also support my contention that reading lacks status. First, it is noticeable that while many of the larger authorities have advisers or inspectors in subjects such as physical education, music, art and mathematics, few have advisers specializing in reading and the language arts. Second, the recent upsurge of interest in the new mathematics has caused many local authorities to open mathematics centres, often staffed and equipped at great expense. I am not suggesting that mathematics is unimportant but merely that mastery of one's native language is perhaps even more important. Yet few authorities have opened special reading centres concerned with the total development of reading for all pupils at every age, although certain authorities have had remedial reading services in existence for many years.

However, some of the new local teachers centres are concerning themselves with reading, although not usually with the extension of reading skills beyond the beginning stages. Other encouraging signs of a growing interest in literacy are an increase in articles and letters on this subject in the press, the introduction of a number of television

B

programmes on reading and the news that the Open University is to offer a course on reading from March 1973. Further interest in the spoken language is illustrated by the introduction of examinations in oral English in the Certificate of Secondary Education and by optional examinations arranged by certain General Certificate of Education Boards. The subject of the 1971 Reith Lectures by Professor Richard Hoggart was 'communication' or as he puts it 'The way we talk to each other.'

My final points on neglected aspects of literacy training concern testing and research. In this country we are not test-orientated. Teachers' assessments of children's progress are often intuitive and incidental; procedures which are rarely adequate. I believe that effective learning needs to be planned on the results of skilled diagnosis, designed to reveal gaps and deficiencies which can form the core of future tuition. Diagnostic testing is certainly an area requiring additional attention.

In the field of research, money available for investigation into the language skills is meagre. We are further handicapped by lack of co-ordination in reading research and the language skills, with the results that some aspects are heavily researched while others, which might be of more benefit to the teacher and the learner, are neglected. The Schools Council has done something to redress the balance of research towards questions of practical importance to teachers, and the various surveys undertaken by the National Foundation for Educational Research and the Department of Education and Science have also been useful in this respect.

Comparing and amalgamating British and American approaches to literacy training
The targets for standards of literacy, and consequently the practices in common use in different countries, show wide variations. Most countries have features of which they can be proud, as well as others in which they lag behind. Even if we were all agreed on our ultimate objectives, there is little reliable evidence available on which systems produce the best results in the long run. Nevertheless, I am certain we can all learn from each other, and an international conference provides us with an invaluable opportunity to do so. It is unlikely that any nation will want to copy exactly another's procedures, even if these were appropriate, but a study of different practices can stimulate reappraisal of one's own.

Although we have delegates from fifteen countries, the majority come from either Britain or the USA. Accordingly, I propose to examine some of the differences in literacy training in our two countries. However, I am aware that in both countries there is a wide range of beliefs and practices, and that by mentioning differences I may not be doing justice to the overlaps which undoubtedly exist.

There are five differences of which I am most conscious; the size of the populations concerned, the money available, the definition of the task, the means whereby the task is approached and the training of staff.

The first two are interrelated. Unfortunately, I have been unable to collect data to supply us with comparative figures on a *per capita* basis. Not only is the population of the USA greater but it is probable that, especially in the large cities, the percentage of pupils with literacy problems is also larger. Also the USA is prepared to spend more money on the inculcation of literacy than Britain. For example, the recent announcement of the US Office of Education's $10 million budget for the Right To Read Program in 1971 certainly fills me with some envy. (As Alton Raygor points out in chapter 2 of this book, this $10 million budget merely covers the administrative cost of 'The Right To Read' office for one year: the office itself will actually be co-ordinating the expenditure of some $460 million).

My third comparison relates to definitions of the task. The American conception of the language arts is more extensive than the British. In the USA, reading is regarded as a developmental process extending from infancy to adulthood and it is accepted that at every age and stage there are specific skills to be mastered. American lecturers and writers have analyzed these subskills, enumerated and labelled them in different ways, to form a vast framework which leaves me lost in admiration. In this respect I am certain that British educators could learn much from their American counterparts. Greater consideration has also been given to the skills of listening, speaking and writing in the USA.

The fourth comparison concerns ways of tackling the task, for example the methods, materials and procedures employed. Americans have taken this huge, itemized master plan of the whole task, devised teaching strategies and produced detailed pupils' books and teachers' manuals, whereby *teachers* may *teach* every minute particle of it. Probably all teachers do not get through all this with every pupil, but I think the majority aim to do so. When visiting schools and establishments of higher education in the USA, I have always been struck forcibly by the fact that the friendly relationships displayed between teachers and pupils rarely caused teachers to waver from their conviction that learning to read is a serious and important business. A topic such as 'How do I schedule my pupils' time?' (meaning reading time) as mentioned in a recent IRA newsletter, is one to which many American teachers do give serious consideration. In contrast, in the more permissive British primary schools, the question would never arise as timetables are either nonexistent or extremely flexible. Moreover, in such schools, British teachers tend to be less earnest about children learning to read and write, as they believe that motivation and interest are more important than serious teaching.

Yet one should not leave the contrast in these bald terms. I have visited American schools where teachers are feeling their way towards greater individual freedom for children. At the same time, a large number of British schools are still run on lines which many advisers and inspectors would consider too formal. As Goodacre (1967) has reported, the majority of British infant schools follow a reading scheme fairly closely, although these schemes are comparatively simple affairs compared with American schemes. Indeed, most British teachers would not like to work under the constraints imposed by the use of the massive American basal reading schemes and explicit teachers' manuals, although less experienced teachers might find some of these helpful.

Perhaps a fair summary of the position would be to suggest that in the USA there is a tendency to emphasize teaching, while the current movement in the United Kingdom is towards placing priorities on learning, but that in both countries there are examples of schools at each end of this continuum. As I have pointed out elsewhere (Southgate 1970), both these approaches have dangers. When teachers pin their faith on instruction the danger is that they may assume that what has been taught has been learned. In contrast, when the emphasis is on learning, it is tempting to assume that in the right environment all children will learn to read almost automatically without specific instruction.

One ought to question whether, even if teachers could by persistent teaching ensure that all children acquired mastery of the relevant sub-skills in reading, many of these pupils after progressing through intensive categorized reading programmes would *want* to go on reading afterwards for relaxation and pleasure. On the other hand, one might query the usefulness of fostering high motivation to read, write and use the other language skills in infant classes, if this is not backed up at every level by a certain amount of actual teaching of language skills, accompanied by ample opportunities and encouragement to utilize these skills functionally and pleasurably.

Finally, the fifth contrast I mentioned was in the training of staff. The majority of American teachers appear to be better equipped to deal with literacy training than their British counterparts. Not only do more American teachers undertake longer courses on reading and the language arts during their initial training, but more opportunities are open to them for advanced study in these subjects. The New York State Education Department has ruled that as from January 1972, all candidates requiring certification as elementary school teachers must have completed at least the equivalent of a full year's course in the teaching of reading (i.e. ninety hours instruction) and will be required to demonstrate their competence in it.

I believe that standards of literacy in both countries might be improved if we could effectively combine our two approaches to literacy training. We might begin by drawing on American expertise to ensure that all teachers acquire a broad background knowledge of the total subject of literacy, as well as a more detailed knowledge of the parts comprising the whole. Then we might adopt certain of those features of British primary schools in which strong motivation induces ideal learning situations. To arrange for eventual mastery of all the relevant skills, without jeopardizing the desire to use them, would require an amalgamation of ideas and expertise from both countries. Diagnostic devices would certainly need improving so that teachers could discover and record children's progress in the light of the master plans. Finally there would be—that overworked word— the 'challenge' of helping children towards mastery of the higher sub-skills, in such a way that individual choice, momentum and spontaneous pleasure were not quenched by dull, repetitive exercises and meaningless restrictions. Such a goal would require a pooling of the best ideas and techniques from both sides of the Atlantic.

Improving literacy in Britain in the 1970s
If during the 1970s we in Britain are to increase our progress towards the highest possible levels of literacy for all, urgent action should be taken on the following proposals.

1 Departments of language arts should be established in a number of geographically dispersed universities. They should be staffed by people knowledgeable about all aspects of language skills and should include psychologists, linguisticians, researchers and teachers, as well as experts in reading, speech and English. Such departments would offer advanced courses at diploma and higher degree levels, thereby contributing to the further training of lecturers, advisers, consultants and experienced teachers. These language departments would also be concerned with coordinating and undertaking research and with the dissemination of results, not only in the form of erudite research reports but also in brief pamphlets, written in nontechnical language, and containing pointers to the practical implications of the findings.
2 In establishments for the training of teachers, lecturers in English, education and psychology should combine with tutor-librarians to form language departments, concerned with promoting an increase in students' own literacy standards, as well as providing them with the necessary knowledge and techniques for improving the standards of their future pupils.
3 In the initial training of teachers, all students should be required to undertake a minimum basic course of forty hours study on teaching the language arts, in addition to one or two optional courses of similar length.
4 Extensive programmes of in-service training should be put into operation, not just for teachers of infants and older failing readers

but for teachers of normal classes in junior and secondary schools, and especially for many of those specialist teachers who have not previously considered it their function to extend the skills of literacy of their pupils. (The UKRA has an important part to play in this programme.)

5 In schools and all establishments concerned with higher education, the extension of the skills of listening, speaking, reading and writing should be planned as developmental programmes extending to include all ages and abilities of children and students. All teachers should participate in the work of ensuring the continued improvement of these skills.

6 The money generally available for books should be greatly increased. It might even be advisable to impose a central directive laying down minimum *per capita* allowances, far in excess of the niggardly amounts now being expended by a small number of local authorities. Such a directive would not deprive local authorities of their freedom to spend generously on books, as some now do.

I suggest that the implementation of these proposals during the 1970s would bring Britain nearer to the goal—a higher standard of 'literacy at all levels'.

References

BOLAM, R. (1971) Guidance for probationer teachers in *Trends In Education* no. 21, 41-48 London: HMSO

CANE, B. and SMITHERS, J. (1971) *The Roots of Reading* Slough: National Foundation For Educational Research

DEPARTMENT OF EDUCATION AND SCIENCE (1971) *Statistics of Education Special Series no. 2 Survey of In-Service Training of Teachers 1969* London: HMSO

GOODACRE, E. J. (1967) *Reading in Infant Classes* Slough: National Foundation for Educational Research

MINISTRY OF EDUCATION (1950) *Reading ability: Some Suggestions For Helping the Backward* (Pamphlet no. 18) London: HMSO

PALMER, R. (1971) *Starting School: A Study in Policies* London: University of London Press

SOUTHGATE, V. (1970) The importance of structure in beginning reading in Gardner, K. (ed.) *Reading Skills: Theory and Practice* London: Ward Lock Educational

SOUTHGATE, V. (1971) *Reading and the language arts* (Memorandum and recommendations on the content of courses provided in colleges of education) Unpublished paper presented as written evidence to the James Committee—Inquiry into Teacher Training

2 The right to read

Alton L. Raygor

Like almost every other nation in the world, the United States has not been able to produce universally high levels of performance in reading. Various surveys have shown the extent of the reading problem. For example, according to the National Centre for Educational Statistics, one out of every four eleven year old children in the United States reads at or below the level of an average nine year old child. About seven million public school pupils in the United States (about 16 per cent of school enrolment) require special instruction in reading. In those schools in which at least half of the pupils come from poor homes, more than one fifth of the elementary and more than 40 per cent of the secondary pupils require special instruction in reading. It is estimated by the Bureau of the Census that when literacy is defined as the ability to read and write a simple message in English or some other language, there are more than three million adult illiterates in the United States.

These and other statistics and the experience of educators has made us aware of the fact that more of the resources of our society need to be put into the educational process, particularly with regard to reading.

In the light of the information given above it was appropriate for the then US Commissioner of Education to announce as the 'moonshot' goal for United States education for the 1970s, a massive national effort designed to reach the goal that 'no one shall be leaving our schools without the skill and the desire necessary to read to the full limits of his capability'.

Since September 1969 when Dr Allen announced that goal, many things have happened. First, he discovered that he had captured the imagination and the desire of the nation; response from the public and educators was immediate and supportive.

Before describing the planning and efforts involved in the Right to Read campaign, some comments about education in the United States are necessary. First of all the locus of responsibility for the schools is in the hands of local agencies. Educational control is extremely decentralized. On the other hand there is widespread support of educational programmes by the federal government, but always using money that is controlled at the local level. Ultimately the responsibility for educating the people is in the hands of the several states. This means that one cannot talk about a federal programme of education in the same way one can in a country in which the control is centralized. It is important, therefore, to distinguish between a federal programme of support for public education and a federally controlled system of education.

The Right to Read effort is a national effort—a coordinated endeavour undertaken by all segments of society, public and private, professional and nonprofessional, to ensure that in the next decade Americans shall not be denied a full and productive life because of an inability to read effectively. This effort is not primarily a government effort or a single programme. It is a national effort, hopefully undertaken by everyone in the country. This national effort is being coordinated within the federal government by a Right to Read office funded by the federal government but without control over local educational institutions. Much of the support for the development of instructional systems will be provided by the government. The application of the new materials, techniques and organizational structures will be done at the local level.

The Right to Read effort is a campaign to persuade the American public, including the government, to put resources into a massive effort to improve the reading skills of our citizens. The purpose is to determine what changes are required to accomplish the goal, to persuade those who need to change to do so, to identify resources, public and private, which can be brought to bear on the situation, and to make additional resources available.

Planning for this national effort has taken place at several levels. First of all, a task force appointed by the Commissioner of Education developed an administration structure for involving the public and private sectors of the society in this national campaign. This task force resulted in the announcement by President Nixon on 31st July, 1970 of the formation of the National Reading Council. This council, composed of a cross-section of outstanding members of society, will help mobilize public support for the effort. The operating arm of the council is the National Reading Centre, whose activities will include coordinating the efforts of contributing public and private organizations, assisting in the utilization of volunteers, and in general, developing public support for the programme.

A Right to Read office was established in the US Office of Education and is responsible for coordinating efforts carried on by the federal government, and for providing national leadership for the effort. The Right to Read office will be funded at the level of approximately ten million dollars for the next fiscal year and will be coordinating the expenditure of some four hundred and sixty million dollars in reading and reading-related programmes.

Once the administrative structure had been created, a long-range, ten-year management plan for activities of the National Reading

Council and the Right to Read office was produced. A six-man planning team was convened in February 1970 and spent about a month in very intensive planning. The planning techniques used were a variation on the convergence technique, originally produced for application by medical research and development problems. The general idea is to take a goal and work backwards from it, determining what events and information need to exist in order for that goal to be met. A tentative plan was produced in that planning session for the ten-year Right to Read effort. There were three major areas of activities in addition to continuous planning. These areas were reading progress activities, information and coordination activities, and complementary activities. Each of these was divided into streams or sequences.

It must be emphasized that this plan was a management plan, not an instructional plan. It was a way of organizing the effort of many people to produce instructional systems that would meet the needs of all children. There was no assumption that any single method or technique would work on all children or that all teachers ought to be using the same materials or techniques. The business of this planning group was not to decide how children were to be taught to read but to decide how the efforts of the Right to Read effort were to be mobilized in order to meet the goal.

The general progression of events went from the design of instructional systems to the testing and assembly of instructional systems to the implementation of the plan in local agencies. This was, of course, a tentative plan. It will be constantly reviewed as the effort continues.

A more complete description of the plan with some explanation of the proposed activities will soon be published. Miss Julia Hamblet, Associate Director of the Right to Read effort, presented and explained the chart before the Twentieth Annual Meeting of the National Reading Conference held on 4th December, 1970 in St Petersburg, Florida and her discussion will be published in the forthcoming twentieth yearbook of the National Reading Conference. (Much of the information in this paper is from her report.)

In addition to the activities implied by this general management plan, the Right to Read effort is also going on in a variety of other ways. 'The Right to Read: target for the 70s' speech and poster have been distributed to all local school districts. To date 122,000 copies of that speech and 118,000 copies of the Right to Read poster have been distributed.

Publications such as the description of the Educational Research Information Clearing House bibliographies, the reports of various committees and commissions, and other publications have been very widely disseminated.

Several television programmes relevant to the Right to Read effort have been produced. Contracts have also been given for several commercials to be used in public service broadcasts on commercial television in the United States. The commercials will be offered to 800 television stations and to 5,000 radio stations across the nation for public service broadcasting. A film has been begun which will be available to organizations and to television outlets which describes the current reading problem in the United States.

Some travelling seminars have been organized and will be held in various parts of the country, utilizing the services of about 150 influential citizens, largely drawn from outside the educational community, to muster support for the Right to Read effort and to explore possibilities of bringing the resources of the local educational agency to bear on the problem.

A Speakers Bureau has been set up and will be coordinated through the Right to Read office.

For some time the information retrieval system supported by the United States Office of Education at Indiana University has been providing retrieval services in reading. Plans are being made now for seventy-eight resource centres so that information about reading will be available quickly in many parts of the country.

The highly successful television programme for children, *Sesame Street*, has been refunded through the Office of Education and a second season of this programme for preschoolers will be emphasizing more reading skills than it has in the past. In addition exploratory study is investigating the possibility of a new series on reading for children aged six to eleven.

Contracts have been given to identify and validate exemplary federally funded reading programmes and exemplary public library reading and reading-related programmes for children. Information about these programmes, once they are identified and validated, will be widely disseminated.

For several years in the United States a national assessment of educational progress has been in the planning stages and the measurement of national reading ability was planned for October 1971. This has been moved up to October 1970. The data have now been collected and reasonably soon there will be reports which will clearly indicate the level of reading skill on the part of American citizens aged nine, thirteen, seventeen, and adult.

In addition to the efforts listed above, many other things are happening. Professional groups concerned with reading instruction such as the International Reading Association, the American Library Association, the American Educational Research Association and many others are having meetings in an effort to determine what they can do that will be of assistance in the Right to Read effort. Teacher training institutions, adult basic education programmes, the Teacher Corp, various tutorial programmes, various other agencies in the federal government, public libraries and federally funded research and development laboratories are all extremely active in mobilizing their forces to meet this ten year goal.

The target for the total effort has been stated most recently in the following goal statement: 'By 1980, 99 per cent of the individuals in the United States sixteen years old and 90 per cent of those over sixteen years will be functional literates.' It is important to note that while the stated goal of the Right to Read effort is in terms of eliminating functional illiteracy, the ultimate goal is much broader. The hope is that functional literacy will only be a beginning and that the net result will be a great increase in the level of ability on the part of all citizens.

The inevitable question is 'Where does the money come from?' There has been considerable delay in answering that question. Finally ten million dollars have been allocated for the Right to Read office and its related activities. In addition it is expected that approximately four hundred and sixty million dollars will be spent on reading and reading-related research, development and support activities in the fiscal year of 1972. This level of support for public education in reading represents a tremendous increase in the commitment of the federal government to the Right to Read effort. In addition local and state agencies will be focusing more of their resources on the reading problem. The net result should be a really massive effort to eliminate reading problems in the United States.

Probably no one really expects that by 1980 it will be impossible to find a functional illiterate or a poor reader. However, because of these efforts we will be closer to that goal than we ever have been before.

Part two Initial mastery of language skills

3 Coordinating reading with the other language arts

Marion Monroe

Assessment of children's ability in all the language arts is vital if teachers are to achieve the goal of every child reading at the level of his true ability.

When a child enters school it is most important to assess his knowledge and ability to use the kind of language he will learn to read. In fact reading is one of the language arts, it is not an isolated skill.

There are four language arts, all of which interrelate and are part of communication, or the exchange of ideas. Through *listening* a child receives and learns to interpret the ideas of others. Through *speaking* he responds to the ideas received or makes known his own ideas, needs and wants. These two arts involve the skills of oral language. The listener and speaker are usually in close contact with one another, as in conversation, although with the telephone and radio the actual distance may be as great as that between the earth and the moon. Speech may be recorded by tape or other methods for delayed listening. Listening and speaking both require auditory skills and associations with experiences that give meaning to the sounds heard and spoken. In speaking, the motor mechanisms of producing sounds are involved and associated with the experienced meanings.

Oral language developed prehistorically, before there were any means of recording speech. However, along with oral communication, prehistoric man experimented with drawings and sculpture of animals and events. Some of the drawings became symbolic such as a picture of an animal hunt containing three suns, the suns representing three days. When a drawing or sign became a symbol, a big breakthrough towards recording oral speech began. A sign could represent not only an object but a sound. Written language developed when a phonetic alphabet was devised and reading the symbols for sounds was a natural outcome. Writing and reading, therefore, are skills intimately connected with oral language and its meaning. To try to teach reading without an appreciation of its connection with listening, speaking and writing often results in failure. *Reading* and *writing* involve all the associations the child has already made in learning oral language plus the visual and motor skills involved in the recognition, perception and production of visual symbols. Through *reading* the child receives the recorded ideas of others and through *writing* he expresses and records his own ideas.

Listening, speaking, reading, and *writing* have a common base of a language which may be English, German, Spanish or whatever. This common base is the grammatical system of the language used; the systematic arrangement of words in sentences for the purpose of communication. Oral language is often more abbreviated and informal than written language. For example, 'Where are you going?'; reply, 'to town.' The phrase 'to town,' is almost meaningless without recognizing that the phrase has sentence meaning, 'I am going to town.' The meaning is inferred from the preceding question.

Many children come to school quite competent in oral language. They have learned to use a tremendous number of words which they group together in phrases and sentences which follow the same grammatical patterns of syntax and have the same meanings as those used by parents, friends and adults in their community. They do not know that they are using grammar. They do not know the grammatical terms for the relationships of words they put together any more than they know the names of the muscles and nerves that they use when they hop, skip or jump, or when they breathe or digest their food. Yet they do all these acts easily.

The language children use when they come to school reflects the poverty or richness of their environment. It reflects the nature of their experiences and the concepts they have developed in their contacts with others. The language they use is largely oral and informal unless the child comes from a book-loving home where he has heard the book language of many stories read aloud. Sooner or later in the child's life he learns that the printed black marks in books represents the language he hears and speaks. The discovery of *visual language* is one of the most important discoveries a child will ever make. He finds that the printed marks in books cue his parents on what to say when they read the book aloud. He becomes curious about how this is done. He 'pretend reads' by looking at a book and repeating as much of the text as he can remember. He becomes familiar with the more formal sentences found in books. He discovers for example that although he may say 'I got a puppy', the book language will probably be 'I have a puppy'.

Learning to read will enable a child to educate himself. Children from homes in which there are little or no reading activities on the part of parents may not discover that print represents language until they go to school.

The four modes of language, although dependent upon one another, may develop at different rates. There are good speakers but poor listeners and vice versa; there are good readers but poor spellers and writers. The handwriting of some of our most brilliant people is sometimes illegible. Many good writers depend upon secretaries and editors to correct their spelling. Many of us develop preferred modes of language. One person may say that he 'never remembers anything until he writes it down'. Another may remark that he was glad the professor lectured on a certain theory because 'it didn't mean a thing to me when I read it in the book'. Even children have preferred modes of learning and the teacher who hopes to reach each pupil in her class may need to find the child's best perceptual and motor skills and stress these skills in teaching him to read.

The kindergarten and first grade teacher cannot do all the work in overcoming language deficiences in children. In the middle and upper grades the remnants of early language difficulties still colour the meaning students get from the printed page.

The meanings of words grow through experience with language. A young child may know two meanings of the word 'post', for example 'post a letter' or 'fence post', yet he may have trouble in understanding 'the soldier remained at his post.'

Figurative language also grows with experience. Young children usually take the literal meanings of figurative language, metaphors and the like. 'The bird ate insects while on wing' may give a child the idea that the bird ate the insects which were on its wing. Such expressions as 'Honey catches more flies than vinegar'; 'Don't give up the ship'; 'Hitch your wagon to a star,' and other maxims are often interpreted literally until the child has experience with abstractions. Words such as 'courage', 'justice', 'integrity', require a high type of language ability. One nine year old defined justice in this way: 'Well, justice means—you know—just as big or just as little as something.' It takes a great deal of living and growth in language to interpret the meaning of 'All the world's a stage'.

In conversational oral speech, it is normal to run words together, to elide sounds and even syllables, so that many children cannot identify the separate words within a sentence. When children begin to read they notice that words are printed with a space between each group of letters that forms a word.

An eighth grade boy was trying to write about going into hospital for an appendicitis operation. Suddenly he stopped writing, went over to the dictionary where he thumbed through the pages. At last he sat down again and crumpled up what he had written. 'Why, Steve, what's the matter? Didn't you find the word you wanted?' asked his teacher. 'Naw, I can't find anything in the dictionary. I wanted to find out how to spell 'pendicitis.'

The teacher looked at the dictionary which he had left open. He had been searching for 'appendicitis' among the words beginning with the letter *p*.

Steve's writing had been blocked by an inability to spell, which in turn was related to his inability to hear the elided first syllable of appendicitis. Being a poor reader perhaps he had never seen the word in a book, or if he had his visual memory of it was too vague to help him. Language grows not only through listening but also through reading, and through all of life's experiences.

Growth in language never stops; new words are constantly being added to our language and the meanings of old words are always undergoing change. Our hair may grow grey with age. Our reflexes may slow down. Our hearing and vision may dim. But if we stop enlarging our vocabularies and learning new meanings for old words we lose the ability to communicate with young people. The generation gap widens partly because we fail to keep open the paths of communication.

Because of the intimate interconnection of all the language communication skills it is both wise and economical to correlate the skills in every area. Some teachers may feel that if they teach children to decode the printed symbols for sounds into oral words they have done enough. A child may read every word in a passage with correct pronunciation and yet fail to get meaning. It isn't until the child derives a message from the printed page that communication takes place. And, hopefully, the message the child gets should be the same message that the author was trying to transmit. Sometimes we do not have enough experience with words and syntax to get a speaker's message. The only meaning we can get from listening to or reading a passage must be provided from our own store of experiences.

Written language presents problems of interpretation because the oral language that a child brings to school may be very different from the standard English he is about to read.

There are regional differences in American pronunciations, in word meanings and grammar that may be confusing. A child from the deep South may say he ate 'pone' and 'sop' for dinner while a Northern child would refer to the same meal as 'cornbread' and 'gravy'. A child from a Mexican home may speak of *tortillas* or *chili*.

Pronunciations are also regional. A child from Boston may insert the *r* sound at the end of words, such as 'Cuber'. Final sounds are omitted in some sections, such as 'lef' for 'left', 'des' for 'desk'. Not only may pronunciations differ, but grammatical syntax as well. Here are some examples of sentence structure in ghetto areas of American cities: Judy got hurts; Can I goes home now?; Pearl be late hers mother gone; He be crying; Nobody had no lunch; I tol im I dint do nothin; He six year ol; Them kids aint play fair.

A child whose oral speech contains the sentence, 'Them kids aint play fair', is likely to have difficulty in reading a sentence beginning with the words 'Those boys,' because he would never start a sentence that way himself.

In our schools there are often wide variations in the nature and maturity of oral language that children bring to school. Unless a class group comes from a community that shares the same dialect, the teacher may need to study the individual characteristics of each child's language in order to find a common base for communication. In general the varieties of language may be classified under four major categories.

First, many children enter school already speaking standard English. They have thousands of words in their vocabularies which they arrange in sentences using much the same syntax as the teacher does. They can immediately communicate with the teacher and she with them. They talk an almost adult language. They come from book-loving homes where parents have read aloud to them. They want to learn to read and are eager to begin. Some have already picked up the ability to recognize words. They know the names of many of the letters of the alphabet and can usually write their names.

For these children language instruction is simply broadening their interests and adding new words to their vocabulary as they need them. Through discussing stories read to them the teacher discovers that they understand and interpret well whatever they hear. They are superior in intelligence and information.

Second, some children come to school using language similar to the superior group but at a more immature level. They may retain infantile pronunciation of some words. Their sentences may be shorter and less mature. They have developed language at a slower rate than the other children and they may not have had as much contact with books.

For them, language instruction may go hand-in-hand with early reading activities. A classroom atmosphere designed to encourage talking, listening to stories, dramatization and play activities requiring conversation will help their language to grow. If there are specific difficulties in articulation a speech teacher may be helpful, but many minor articulation problems disappear with practice and many opportunities for listening and speaking.

Third, some children who enter school are learning English as a second language. Their parents may speak English with an accent and grandparents may speak only the foreign tongue. These children may show in their speech relics of the foreign accent of their parents. Their sentence structure may be more like that of the foreign language than that of English.

These children, if bright and socially active in the group, readily learn English just by being with English-speaking children. Before long they lose the foreign accent and syntax they were using. If the teacher can speak a little of their first language she may help them to feel at home and welcome. She may sometimes call on them to tell the others how to say 'pencil', 'school', and so on, in their first language. Intelligent children often learn two or more languages at an early age without difficulty.

Fourth, there are the children who speak English with the dialect and grammar of the region in which they live. The language problems of these children are more specific and more difficult to overcome than those of the previous group, because they continue to hear and use the language of their parents at home and neighbours in the community. If these dialects are referred to as 'illiterate' or 'bad grammar', the children may develop a feeling of shame or inadequacy which retards their development.

In helping these children the teacher must be especially tactful and sensitive. The child is simply imitating his parents and if he speaks the dialect fluently he deserves the same praise as the child who speaks the standard English he has learned in an educated home. The child should be praised for ideas, and his manner of speaking should be accepted. Gradually, after a relationship of friendly respect between pupil and teacher has been established, the teacher may suggest that there are many ways of saying the same thing. If a child says 'I ain't got no pencil' she kindly gives him one. She may ask the class, 'Is there anyone else who would like to have a pencil?' She gives the children an opportunity to hear a variety of speech patterns without becoming self-conscious about their own. She may say, 'There are many ways to ask for a pencil. How would you ask for one, Cecil?' She may call on volunteers who suggest such sentences as, 'Give me a pencil'; 'Pass the pencils'; 'My pencil done broke'; 'I haven't got a pencil' and so on. One child may suggest that a polite way to ask would be 'Please pass me a pencil'. The teacher welcomes each variation and after the children have exhausted their suggestions she says, 'I think *Please pass me a pencil* is a very good way to ask for one at school.' In this way children learn that language is flexible and ideas may be expressed in many different ways. They also learn a good way to ask for something at school using standard English. Yet no one feels embarrassed about his own language.

Children learn from one another through school experiences and through word and sentence games. In classes where most of the children speak standard English, the trend will be towards a common language for all the children—standard English. However, if most of the children speak nonstandard English with a regional dialect, the children who speak standard English may take on the dialect and grammatical syntax of the majority in the class. Parents are then likely to protest that their children's language has degenerated since they entered school.

In such a classroom it may be desirable to separate a group of youngsters from the rest of the class for more structured language training, working especially towards the goal of standard English. Standard grammar can then be taught almost in the same way one would teach a second language.

The teacher may read books aloud to these children to familiarize them with book language. She may need to search for stories which will appeal especially to the interests of these youngsters (there is a need for more good stories with urban settings familiar to our ghetto or inner city children). At the same time, through films, visual aids and field trips to the country or zoo, we can broaden their backgrounds of vocabulary and information about areas other than their own.

Introduction to reading should be based on the children's own experiences through individual and group creative writing. Using their own experiences the children may become involved with the adventures of characters like themselves.

One way to help prepare the child for visual and motor language is through his drawings. He communicates through his pictures. Ask him to show and talk about his picture. The teacher takes down his language verbatim or with a tape recorder. She then writes or types the story as he gave it. He may simply give the picture a title such as *My dog*. He may produce a sentence which can be used as a caption, 'My cat had kittens', or he may even create a short story. The title, caption or story can then be pasted by the picture. Individual booklets can be made by the pupils, or some of the drawings with stories may be bound into a class book.

Through combining drawing and language activities the children learn about the nature and design of written communication. They learn that

1   Whatever is said can be written.
2   Every spoken word has a written counterpart.
3   Spoken words are made of sounds; written words are made of letters; the letters stand for sounds.
4   There are two kinds of letters, capital and small letters.
5   The first word in each new idea begins with a capital letter. The rest of the words are usually written in small letters.
6   A person's name also begins with a capital letter.
7   The dot at the end of the idea is a full stop.
8   Writing goes across the paper from left to right and when you read you say the words from left to right too.
9   Before you write you try to think of a good way to say what you mean.

Armed with information about how stories are written and how books are made, the children now enjoy following the printed words in a book read aloud by the teacher. Such initial reading books should contain plenty of illustrations and a minimum of text on each page. As children become familiar with the books through frequent repetition they begin to 'play read' the books, retelling the story as they turn the pages. Many children begin to remember certain phrases and sentences verbatim using the more formal standard English of the text as they retell the story.

They are now ready to compare printed words, to scrutinize them for similarities and differences, and to learn the various strategies by which words can be recognized, including the letters that stand for initial sounds, vowels and final consonant sounds.

Above all, the children learn to search for meaning, using all the strategies they know—the illustrative pictures, the discovery of new words through context and sound-letter associations, and the completion of sentence-meaning. The transition from oral to written language now becomes a thrilling act of discovery for the child who has mastered the oral language needed to comprehend the text. There are few greater satisfactions to a teacher than to observe the ease with which well-prepared children can make the transition to reading when reading is coordinated with all the other language arts.

4 Spoken language and learning to read

Geoffrey R. Roberts

Introduction

The study group on which this paper is based was planned for experienced teachers and lecturers concerned with the early stages of learning to read. Its purpose was to examine ways in which the teacher can help the children and, in particular, to consider the relationship between spoken language and learning to read.

Language in schools

For many years in schools in the UK there has been a movement towards encouraging children to talk to one another about the things that interest them in the classroom. The justification has been that it would contribute to the social development of the children. However, the work of Piaget, Bernstein, Halliday and others has made the more perceptive teachers realize that this increased communication by means of the spoken word also has implications in terms of intellectual development. From Piaget (1959) comes the idea that language is the expression of inner thoughts and one of the tools with which the child attempts to master his environment. Bernstein (1970) points to the two broadly different categories of language which emerge from formal and informal contexts. Halliday (1969) takes the teacher a step further and defines the different ways in which language is used to achieve many objectives. These studies suggest that one of the aims of a teacher should be to provide facilities for the child to increase the range of uses of his language, so that he is better able to interpret the various nuances of meaning conveyed in the formal language of even the simplest school book. Hence there is a close relationship between the language teaching in school and the teaching of reading.

Only a person who has been totally cut off from the main stream of thought in primary education in the United Kingdom would fail to interpret language teaching in its broadest sense. It in no way implies the direct teaching of grammar as such, nor does it imply a formal system of instructor and recipient. Increased facility in spoken language can be achieved only within an engrossing environment in which the children *want* and *need* to communicate. Furthermore, we now know enough about language development to realize that merely allowing children to chatter, essential though this is, is not enough to prepare them to meet fully the demands of life and to appreciate language in its written form. Children must be placed in many different contexts, so that differing forms of language will be used to suit different situations.

The aims and objectives of reading

Reading enables people to participate in communication from which they obtain information and ideas, and which meets the needs of the individual. Broadly speaking these needs fall into two categories; practical needs, and emotional and intellectual needs. The tremendous concentration focused on comic strip books by the least educated people in our society, demonstrates the strength and ubiquity of the need to receive ideas in printed form.

The task of teaching children to read can be made so much easier if the children see some purpose in learning to read, and if they enjoy the task as it proceeds. We should therefore bear in mind these two main themes of purpose and enjoyment.

From the early stages reading should not only allow the child to follow the actions of others, in the form of characters in the book, but also involve the child himself in action. To give only one example, it is possible to follow activities with single word labels, by using on succeeding labels phrases and sentences which instruct the children to do simple tasks. There are many other ways in which the child can be involved in actions through reading games and exercises of this nature. Gradually many forms of communication in print between teacher and child and between children can be introduced, and soon these will begin to involve interclass and even interschool communication.

The second theme—enjoyment—should not be taken for granted. Teachers must not assume that because a child succeeds in reading a passage or book he is therefore enjoying the content. In the first place, enjoyment may be inappropriate if the child is reading for information. The enjoyment may come later when the child benefits from using the information. Hence the importance of providing pursuits which the child finds interesting. However, in the case of fiction enjoyment should form an essential part of the immediate task; this will only result from understanding and appreciation on the part of the reader. Thus the teacher's task includes training the children to appreciate stories by leading them towards greater insight into the content through evaluation of what is read, beginning in the early stages with such simple questions as 'Who or what did you like in that story?' 'Why did you like . . . ?' and progressively probing more deeply as the child improves. Such training will lead automatically to greater selectivity by the child as he becomes more aware of what he needs to read and what he wants or likes to read.

If these ideas are accepted, certain pertinent questions may be posed which are closely related to classroom practices. The first question is, 'Do I really plan the work of my classroom so that children *need* to read or are they merely engaged in reading to please me?' The second question is, 'Am I fully aware of the differences between children (Bernstein 1970) and the differences within the same child (Halliday 1970) in the range of uses of spoken language?' This is a crucial question because children will need to be familiar with the elaborated code, i.e. the type of language used by the teacher and in books. Such language will have a wider range of uses than that used by the majority of children in our schools. By contrast, if the children are learning to read on one of the popular and widely used schemes (which I prefer not to mention by name) they will come face to face with a type of language that is frequently sterile. Children in these circumstances will require a certain degree of flexibility. The third question is, 'Do I take the narrow view of reading which assumes that provided a child can decode the print he is progressing satisfactorily, or do I really place reading high amongst the great pleasures of life?' If the latter is the case, then it will be necessary to discuss the children's reading with them; to ask them about the story, the characters and their reaction, and so on. Such discussion can contribute to training in evaluation, the progressive establishments of standards and to fostering selectivity in reading.

Four contrasting views of language experience approaches
Dorothy Jeffree, in her consideration of a language experience approach, presented a teaching model which consisted of four interacting stages. First, there must be systematic observation of the children, their competencies and their foibles, within the learning situation. Second, the teacher must define her objectives and know what she is going to teach. Third, the teacher must plan the individual steps leading from the child's present competence towards her objectives. And fourth, the teacher must continually assess each child's progress towards these objectives, and reassess her method and media in the light of this knowledge.

The suggested model was implemented by emphasizing the necessity for proceeding from the known to the unknown and, in most cases, from the whole to the parts. A strong case was also made for dealing with many of the subskills in parallel rather than consecutively, so that the children are able to discover synthesis and witness their own increasing ability to read. The importance of fitting methods and media to each child rather than the reverse, and of arranging for adequate reinforcement at every stage, were stressed.

These general considerations were then applied specifically to the early stages of learning to read. The initial transfer from spoken to written language was regarded as crucial, and it was considered essential that the child should grasp the idea that what can be said can also be written and decoded. This idea may not come easily to the immature child and extra imaginative help with something like symbol accentuation may be necessary.

Edna Rodwell, describing the interesting work she has initiated in Stockport, began with the basic statement that 'Language is the verbalization of concepts.' The stimulation for the formation and verbalization of the concept has to be arranged by the teachers; language has to be taught. In the many cases of children coming from linguistically deprived homes, the school must attempt to make up for the inadequacies of the home training. In addition, children must be given insight into symbols.

Edna Rodwell's teaching method favours the idea of using a child's drawing as a vehicle for written text. Wherever the drawing contains human beings, the words they speak are placed in 'balloons', as in comic strips. The child supplies the words, the teacher writes them in, and the child reads them. This type of writing emphasizes the connection between spoken and written language in a way which the young child can really understand. When this procedure is repeated frequently, the child begins to grasp the nature of print and its connection with meaning.

To write down what a child dictates is not enough. There must be a carefully worked out sequence of training in spoken language proceeding from the fact that the egocentric phase—I have, I want—is predominant in the child in the early days of schooling. As the child passes through this stage, he must gradually be placed in situations where there is feeling between himself and those with whom he communicates, so that language becomes a vehicle for that feeling. In this way the child's social language develops.

Turning to reading, a strong plea was made that teachers should pay greater attention to sensory learning, and especially to tactile and kinaesthetic learning. It is impossible to teach only through what is seen. Effective learning takes place through the eye seeing what the hand is doing. Children should be encouraged to touch things, to manipulate them, and to examine all their properties.

Alongside these teaching techniques there is the equally important personal relationship between the child and his teacher. We must remember that the child has to learn to withdraw from his mother's protection and he must be helped to pass beyond the egocentric stage. It was also emphasized that true teaching goes deeper than mere techniques; consideration must be given to the general intellectual and emotional development of the children.

Evelyn Spache set up the following criteria for learning:

1 The material must be of significance to the learner.
2 It is necessary to build up each child's use of vocabulary and the range of his language patterns.

3 The teacher must be content with the child's experiential background and must build her teaching programme upon this basis.
4 The learner must be involved in the learning process.

An example was given of a child who brought her doll to school and said, 'I brung my doll to school. If anybody touches her I'm gonna bite 'em.' It would have destroyed the child's willingness to communicate strongly held feelings about her doll if the teacher had intervened to correct this language; thus the sensitive teacher accepts the incorrect form in the early stages of the programme. It is particularly important that where strong feelings are involved the teacher does not offend these feelings by a pedantic insistence upon formality. A boy who had accidentally hurt his friend, later wrote about the teacher on yard duty, 'She didn't have to tell me to say sorry. John was my friend. I *was* sorry.'

The first step is for the teacher to accept and record the child's language as it is spoken, thus reinforcing its usage and emphasizing its significance. Books about the child, his games, pets, and family etc can be compiled. The whole operation is made more exciting if the teacher types out the scripts using a large type face. Then the children can be asked to proofread to check her typing!

A group of children can listen to a child rereading his story. From this the teacher can develop some group work on language skills. Maybe each child writes only one story per week, but this can lead to work on the meaning of new words, new spelling, new phrases, as well as art and dramatic play, with its subsequent language development. The range of activities is infinite.

Phrase or sentence cards can be split into words by the child and a vocabulary box can be built up. Word lists can be constructed— words for my family e.g. daddy can be ... son, brother, grandfather, uncle. Substitutes can be woven into actual situations—my, I, they, them—so that the child experiences the relationships between these words.

Gradually the child will build up discrete categories of words: words that tell where, how, when; words that work with 'the', 'a', 'am'; words that end with *ly, s, ed, ing, er*; opposites, sound words, weather words, and words for how we move. These words should all be acquired in group discussions, or in individual work centred upon or starting from the child's own speech construction.

A profitable device is to write out lots of words encountered by the children on cards, and give a group of children varying numbers of cards. The teacher can then base phonic and visual practice on the word cards. For example, 'Have you words beginning with this letter?'; 'Have you any words beginning with the same sound as the word "boy"?'. The cards can also be used for mental arithmetic and number work by asking such questions as, 'How many of you have more cards than 5?'; 'How many have less than 9?' and so on.

This language experience approach makes it easy to develop ways of breaking down the communication barriers between child and teacher; it strengthens the child's recognition of printed material as real language; it extends his vocabulary and the range of his language patterns; it helps him to develop word recognition, phonic skills, and concepts of sentence structure, in ways that are meaningful to him. Furthermore, this method can be extended to include other curricula areas.

Joyce Morris postulated a very different approach to the teaching of reading. Whereas Evelyn Spache suggested that it is necessary to begin by using the child's own language, so that he is on familiar ground, and then to develop this language through a long series of discussions and practice sessions, leading eventually to the child becoming familiar with accepted English, Joyce Morris considered that this trend towards meeting the child on his own ground had gone too far and contained many hidden dangers.

Her emphasis was on organization for teaching. She pointed out the necessity for teachers to possess a knowledge of techniques appropriate to solving particular problems before actually facing these problems in teaching situations. Such knowledge depended on effective initial and in-service training.

Her critique of the language experience approach as it is normally practised began with an outline of several misconceptions and mis-leading ideas connected with the teaching of reading. The first mis-conception is the assumption that ability to read can be acquired naturally, and many of the books that are written about the teaching of reading, through tacitly accepting this assumption, fail to deal with every part of the process in detail. Thus begins a cycle whereby the teaching of the teachers of reading is deficient.

The second misconception is that a text for reading is only speech written down. Hall (1961), Haas (1970), Lefevre (1964), Fries (1962) and Withnall and Fry (1964) were quoted to show that in order to read the child has to learn many more things than simply how to recognize his own speech when it is encoded in the form of written symbols. He must learn to deal with the problems of linguistic meaning and symbolic representation. This means that he must acquire the ability to think in terms of symbols. For example, when he sees the printed word 'cat', he must have learnt to think of it as a word consisting of sounds which can be attached to its graphemic parts, rather than to think of it in the form of the animal to which it refers. The child must also become familiar with the fact that there are many different kinds of meaning—letters are meaningful in terms of the sounds they communicate, sounds lead to the formation of words,

words are meaningful in a different, semantic sense — and he must learn that the meaning of many words can vary according to the text which contains them.

The third misleading idea emanated from the objection to the stories contained in early primers: the type which consist of 'Look, look. Look Peter. See, see Janet.' Really we should be objecting to the fractured English that is being foisted upon the child. Books should not consist entirely of the language children use or of the language authors think they use. They should be written in a form which represents in a *reasonable* way the language of children, and their purpose should be to familiarize the children with written English in its accepted form.

Thus Joyce Morris presented a strong case for the necessity to look critically at the present popularity of language experience approaches to the teaching of reading. Her contention was that we must think very carefully about the reading materials to which children are exposed, and in doing so, we must consider the longer term effects of exposure to different forms of language and not be content solely to consider short term expediency.

Critical thinking and reading
Kathleen Clayton, in examining some of the semantic aspects of reading, began by quoting Stauffer and Cramer (1968): 'Reading, like thinking, is a mental process.... It requires a reader's use of his experience and knowledge.' Critical thinking should be fostered before the child starts formal reading, so that he becomes accustomed to behave in a critical manner.

Training children to read and think critically requires a specially prepared programme. This should contain provision for group instruction in which ideas can be communicated; there should be freedom to express ideas; there should be directed reading activities; there must be a general atmosphere of acceptance and assistance amongst the children.

Within the groups, common reading matter should be discussed and evaluated. From a free flow of ideas and the expression of opinions, new creative ideas will develop and the children will begin to use their critical powers with a growing degree of penetration.

Critical reading involves questioning the ideas expressed in the reading matter, evaluating them, and judging them. All of this fits into the pattern suggested in Russell's (1961) four reading levels:

1 word calling
2 reading for literal meaning
3 interpretation
4 thoughtful analysis or critical review

In Kathleen Clayton's view our teaching programmes are incomplete, unless there is specific attention to the fourth level.

Conclusions
Each of the speakers emphasized the central role of spoken language during the early stages of learning to read. There were various interpretations of this role, but no one doubted the benefits which accrued. These were that by paying attention to spoken language the teacher could help the child to understand how written language is constructed; she could base the instruction in reading upon the things the child was talking and thinking about, and so be sure that the reading matter was of interest to the child; and she could determine what compensatory teaching was necessary in order to acquaint the child with the types of written language that he would meet in his reading books.

References
BERNSTEIN, B. (1970) A critique of the concept of 'contemporary education' in Rubinstein, D. and Stoneman, C., *Education for Democracy* Harmondsworth: Penguin

FRIES, C. C. (1962) *Linguistics and Reading* New York: Holt, Rinehart and Winston

HAAS, W. (1970) *Phonographic Translation* Manchester: Manchester University Press

HALL, R. A. (1961) *Sound and Spelling in English* Philadelphia: Chilton

HALLIDAY, M. A. K. (1969) Relevant models of language in Wilkinson, A. *The state of language* in *Educational Review* 22, no. 1

LEFEVRE, C. A. (1964) *Linguistics and the Teaching of Reading* New York: McGraw-Hill

PIAGET, J. (1959) *Language and Thought of the Child* London: Routledge and Kegan Paul

RUSSELL, D. H. (1961) *Children Learn to Read* Waltham: Blaisdell

STAUFFER, R. G. (1969) *Directing Reading Maturity as a Cognitive Process* New York: Harper and Row

STAUFFER, R. G. (1969) *Teaching Reading as a Thinking Process* New York: Harper and Row

STAUFFER, R. G. (1970) *The Language Experience Approach to the Teaching of Reading* New York: Harper and Row

STAUFFER, R. G. and CRAMER, R. (1968) *Teaching Critical Reading at the Primary Level* Newark: IRA

WHITNALL, E. and FRY, D. B. (1964) *The Deaf Child* London: Heinemann

5 The language experience approach today: reappraisal and development

Ronald Morris

Problems of definition

Current nomenclature
The language experience approach to the teaching of reading is usually, but not invariably, associated today with the San Diego Reading Study Project and the writings of its senior worker, Roach Van Allen, in the early sixties. Van Allen argued forcefully for teaching reading in combination with other language arts, for relating reading to the child's experience and for insisting that the child's words written down should constitute the main source of his reading material (Allen and Halvorsen 1961).

Need for redefinition
There are many reasons for questioning the strict identification of the language experience approach to reading with the detailed teaching procedures most favoured by Van Allen and his coworkers. In fact there are two good reasons for thinking of language experience as anterior to the San Diego Project.

First, there is the evidence of Van Allen himself who stated that he used the term to express a range of practices already known to, and used by, schools involved in the Project. It was not the aim of the Project to make innovations either in nomenclature or practice but rather to make clear to the teachers the characteristic values of three main approaches, categorized broadly as 'basal', 'individualized', 'language experience', and to demonstrate that teachers who underwent special training in any one of these approaches could improve significantly the effectiveness of their teaching.

Second, one need only go back to the 1930s and 40s to find a period when curriculum builders were very deeply involved in designing and implementing teaching practices based on the experience of those being taught and on due recognition of their developing powers of linguistic expression (Lamoreaux and Lee 1943, Gans 1941, Gray 1944). Precursors of the language experience idea may be identified at even earlier dates (Farnham 1887, Huey 1908, Decroly in Hamaïde 1925, Jagger 1929).

Therefore, it can be argued that not only does language experience antedate the San Diego Project but also that it cannot be equated with it. In fact, there is not a strict language experience canon but rather a wide range of language experience ideas and practices. Emphases favoured by Van Allen may be excluded from some forms of language experience and the range may include practices not specifically included by Van Allen. Thus Stauffer (1969) discusses language experience extensively but without reference to the San Diego Project which was then less than ten years old. Again, the curriculum builders of the 30s and 40s who sought to base reading on the language and experience of the child often differed greatly from Van Allen by putting far less stress on writing down the child's own words as either the main source of reading matter or the main technique for acquiring reading skill. Similarly, the Breakthrough to Literacy Project (Mackay *et al* 1970), while basing its approach on the language and experience of the child, deliberately incorporates an introductory non-writing stage in the foundations of learning to read.

The need for reappraisal and development
Currently teachers of reading and their advisers have very little use for the language experience argument (Chall 1967). Perhaps the only exception to this generalization is the survival of the experience-chart as part of the readiness programme. Even in this small corner of the reading field the conditions are not always favourable. Experience-charts often come as part of a package deal, with the publisher 'anticipating' the language and experience of the child. Or perhaps the teacher makes her own charts with her own children and proceeds to use them in teaching as if they were the opening pages of a basal reading scheme.

Any deep analysis of the current failure of the language experience argument to advance beyond this position of a precarious hold on the experience-chart front would involve a comprehensive study of curriculum development over the past half century. Here it is possible to attempt nothing more than some brief notes on what may be called the boomerang effect of the San Diego Project.

Ironically, Van Allen's attempts to support the language experience position have resulted in its virtual destruction. It is not difficult to see how this has happened. As has been indicated above, the language experience tradition is older and wider than the special features which Van Allen so strongly emphasized at the beginning of the last decade. Not unnaturally, criticism was directed at these particular features and, in so far as these criticisms were valid, condemnation of Van Allen's variant of language experience became for many a condemnation of the whole language experience tradition. To particularize (e.g. Spache and Spache 1969) the following criticisms were levelled:

1 Failure to organize sufficiently for the systematic building of skills resulting in

i overvaluing of incidental learning

ii making excessive demands on teacher's powers to evaluate progress in a loosely-structured situation.

2 Restrictive content, confining child to the small circle of his own ideas.

3 Unjustified assumptions concerning

i the transfer of interest by the child from reading his own words to reading the words of others, and

ii tight linkage in mechanisms for vocabulary extension in the language arts. Expectancy of *pari passu* enlargement of speech, listening, reading and writing vocabularies.

It is not suggested that these criticisms of Van Allen's variant of the language experience approach are invalid criticisms of that variant. However, it is not equally valid to proceed, without further examination, to apply these criticisms to all forms of the language experience tradition as it has been developed over the years, and as it may be further developed in the immediate future. Had this point been more generally appreciated in the past decade, the language experience argument would perhaps stand in better credit today.

Some reappraisal is necessary to drive home the basic but forgotten truth that it is not difficult to find some form of the language experience tradition which does not:

1 put any special stress on the close linkage of reading and writing

2 confine the child's reading to the backyard of his own unstimulated and unenriched experience

3 exclude the possibility of systematic work on the consolidation of skills, provided always that the work can be seen to be related to the material and activities associated with the language and enriched experience of the child.

Yet another group of reasons suggests that the time is more than ripe for a reappraisal of the language experience argument.

In the first place, it is amazing to find that over a period of more than half a century there has been no abatement of the criticism that language experience approaches put too great a strain on the teacher, require her to be in too many places at once, to divide her attention between too many children all clamouring simultaneously for answers to questions arising from the diversity of their individual experiences and linguistic backgrounds. This criticism is voiced today in the 70s in the same vein and measure as it was in the 20s. Yet it should be obvious that the situation has been greatly changed in recent years by the development of many new resources for making more child-centred learning possible. It is not necessary here to confine one's attention solely to the autotelic responses of O. K. Moore and his elaborate computerized equipment (Gross and Murphy 1964). There are many quite simple devices e.g. Language Master and Audio Page, which can be very effective aids in a modern language experience approach. Perhaps the best, if abrupt, answer to critics who forget the existence of child-operated aids to learning, capable of linking sight and sound and yielding immediate knowledge of results, would be along Skinnerian lines. Any teacher who turns herself into an on-demand correction machine should be replaced by an on-demand correction machine (Skinner 1954 and Taylor 1971).

In the second place, in recent years, there have been many studies of structure of language and how children acquire language. This work certainly postdates the original work on language experience approaches in reading and it is doubtful whether followers and developers of the language experience tradition have fully assimilated this new knowledge and related it to teaching practice.

It is neither possible nor relevant within the limits of this paper to review more than one brief corner of the field of modern language study. Indeed, there is not yet a consensus on how to apply this growing body of knowledge either to a better understanding of the reading process or to translate it into terms of practical teaching. One point, however, is pertinent here. There has been not only a failure on the part of advocates of language experience to explore fully the new linguistic knowledge, but also a failure on the part of linguisticians to understand the language experience tradition sufficiently to see the relevance of their own contributions to improved practice in the teaching of reading.

This is the result of obscuring the function of context-support in the reading process. By context-support is meant the totality of devices which can be used to prime the mind of the reader, fully or partially, with the meaning of the text before it is encountered in written form. Experience-charts are a good example of giving the child one hundred per cent context-support in his first efforts to read. Sentence method and story method are also examples of context-support approaches. But curiously enough they are not always seen in this way. Rather are they categorized as approaches to the problem of word-recognition in which the unit to be recognized is longer than a single word. There is here a great confusion of thought. In recognition approaches the reader is expected to recognize what he sees in the text so that he can grasp the text's message. Sometimes the child is encouraged to perform this act of recognition by learning the skills of decoding: sometimes the emphasis is on other types of clues, perhaps the length or shape of the word, or by drill in matching word-wholes to picture clues or by many other devices. The difference between any form of recognition approach and any form of context-support lies in the timing. In context-support approaches to a greater or lesser extent the reader knows in advance the message contained in the text: in recognition approaches he does not; he is expected to read the words of the text to find out what it says.

The experience-chart, cited as an instance of context-support approach, must not be allowed to dominate the scene through being taken as the sole example. It is important to recognize that experience-charts constitute a form of context-support in which the support given by the context is complete. Progress in a context-support approach is measured by the rate at which the reader learns to cope with texts where the context-support is increasingly attenuated. Full context-support is only the beginning: the approach demands provision for gradual diminution of context-support. If desired this could be done in a systematic way with carefully structured materials.

If language experience approaches of many kinds are looked at from this point of view, it becomes clear that such varied techniques as experience-charts, confining reading to the child's own writing, teaching by story method, or the use of two-tier texts, all imply adherence to the principle of providing a gradient of advance in terms of gradual diminution of context-support rather than in terms of increased size of sight-vocabulary, increased knowledge of phonic or structural rules etc (Morris 1965, 1971).

There are many links that could be explored in relating the context-support rationale to the current state of knowledge in the field of language. Of special interest is the point that for a long time linguistic study has asserted the primacy of oracy and has emphasized too that in English meaning is conveyed not simply by the sounds of words and their position in sentences, but also by the clues supplied by the speaker as he modulates what he is saying in accordance with various conventions regarding emphasis, pitch and pausing to make the phrasing clear. In addition, meaning is conveyed by the speaker's stance, gestures and facial expression. The reader, if he comes to his text following a recognition approach, has no help from the spoken word. He must read into the text those aids to meaning which are either of the paralinguistic type (stance, gesture, facial expression) or of the suprasegmental phoneme type (stress, pitch, juncture). By contrast, the reader who encounters his text following a context-support approach is primed in these respects and has at his disposal a rich store of aids to grasping meaning. The importance of this kind of help should not be underrated. Critics of language experience have often commented that while the methods often seem impracticable, they do sometimes succeed in producing readers with a good grasp of meaning. This result is obtained not because the reader has been given abundant practice in reading his own words, or in writing his own words, but because he has been helped to make good use of the spoken word in his efforts to cope with the representation of words on paper. Some interesting experimental work is being done in this area under the auspices of the Institute of Education of the University of Newcastle upon Tyne (UNIE 1968).

Summary and conclusion

It has been argued that the familiar association between language experience approaches in the teaching of reading and the San Diego Reading Study Project of a decade ago has tended to present a rather limited view of language experience approaches, which have a much longer and more varied tradition. Thus much current criticism of language experience, while relevant to the 1960 variant, is not necessarily equally applicable to what went before and to what may emerge in the future.

In particular it has been shown that a wide range of language-experience approaches incorporate the principle of advance through diminution of context-support as contrasted with approaches that use a gradient of advance defined in terms of increasing powers of recognition.

The relationship between the context-support rationale and those aspects of linguistic study that are concerned with the primacy of oracy and with the aids to grasp of meaning that are provided by such factors as stress, pitch, juncture, stance, gesture and facial expression has been examined. Reference has been made to sources suggesting implications here for practical teaching.

Reappraisal of language experience is clearly overdue in the light of modern linguistic knowledge. Attempts at such reappraisal should include consideration of the rationale built into those language experience approaches that can be shown to advance along a gradient of gradual diminution of context-support.

References

ALLEN, R. Van and HALVORSEN, G. C. (1961) *The Language Experience Approach to Reading* Boston: Ginn and Company

CHALL, J. S. (1967) *Learning to Read: The Great Debate* New York: McGraw-Hill

FARNHAM, A. B. (1887) *The Sentence Method of Teaching Reading* New York: Syracuse

GANS, R. (1941) *Guiding Children's Reading Through Experiences* New York: Teachers College, Columbia

GRAY, W. S. (ed.) (1944) *Reading in Relation to Experiences and Language* Chicago: Proceedings of the Conference on Reading, volume 6

GROSS, R. and MURPHY, J. (1964) *The Revolution in the Schools* New York: Harcourt Brace

HAMAÏDE, A. (1925) *The Decroly Class* London: Dent

HUEY, E. B. (1908) *The Psychology and Pedagogy of Reading* New York: Macmillan

D

JAGGER, J. H. (1929) *The Sentence Method of Teaching Reading* Glasgow: Grant Educational

LAMOREAUX, L. A. and LEE, D. M. (1943) *Learning to Read through Experience* New York: Appleton, Century, Crofts

MACKAY, D, THOMPSON, B, and SCHAUB, P (1970) *Breakthrough to Literacy* London: Longmans

MORRIS, R (1965) *Success and Failure in Learning to Read* London: Oldbourne (reprinting in Penguin edition 1972)

MORRIS, R (1971) What children learn in learning to read in *English in Education* volume 5, no 2

SKINNER, B. F. (1954) The science of learning and the art of teaching in *Harvard Educational Review* 24, 86–97

SPACHE, G. D. and SPACHE, E. B. (1969) *Reading in the Elementary School* Boston: Allyn and Bacon.

STAUFFER, R. G. (1969) *Directing Reading Maturity as a Cognitive Process* New York: Harper and Row

TAYLOR, L. C. (1971) *Resources for Learning* Harmondsworth: Penguin

UNIE (1968) *My Book, My Friend* Newcastle: Institute of Education, University of Newcastle upon Tyne

6 The language arts in informal British primary schools

Margery Corlett

Introduction

As visitors from abroad are usually extremely interested in what is happening in some of the more informal British primary schools, a special study group for overseas visitors was arranged as part of the conference programme. Members of this group, in addition to visiting nearby schools, considered the rationale underlying the growth of such schools, listened to lectures and entered into discussions on various aspects of teaching, learning and organization within these schools.

The brief summary of points which follows represents certain of the principles and practices of modern informal primary schools which came under discussion. The general concepts of 'integration' and 'self-learning' were emphasized and examined, and particular attention was given to the language development of children.

Integration

The term 'integration' can be extended to include the following four aspects of primary education:

1 children—age groups, vertical grouping; classes, use of space, open plan building
2 teachers—cooperative and team teaching
3 subjects—integrated curriculum
4 time—unstructured timetable or free day

Thus integration seems to be largely an organizational concept to do with timetabling, grouping of children and the utilization of space. In an integrated day these factors interlock but it is possible to have some aspects without others; for example, a free day without vertical grouping or an integrated curriculum without an open plan building. Such organizations have evolved from our thinking about the aims of primary education, which have then been worked out in relation to the curriculum (subjects and contents) and the methods of teaching.

While it is vital for teachers to have a clear understanding of long-term aims, the aims themselves require interpreting in terms of practical procedure at classroom level. They need to be broken down into specific objectives, which in their turn must be worked out in relation to the required attitudes and changes in behaviour; and also the essential knowledge and skills which will enable children to learn and to discover knowledge for themselves. In addition, it is important to consider which fundamental concepts have to be acquired and the stages at which such learning would be appropriate. The teacher's task is to

1 clarify long-term aims
2 define stages in thinking
3 work out specific objectives
4 break down the objectives into observable behavioural changes
5 show how these behavioural changes can be brought about by the use of many different materials and in a variety of situations
6 gear the content either to the individual child or to a group of children, even though the ultimate objective may be the same for the entire class

Detailed work of this nature is now being undertaken in the Schools Council 5–13 Science Project.

What is meant by the integrated curriculum? The interpretation will be influenced by the age group under consideration. The very young child has an undifferentiated whole world view. For him knowledge is not artificially fragmented and therefore a global approach to learning is required. One of the teacher's tasks in the upper primary school is to begin to lead the child from his earlier global view to an awareness of different and distinct forms of understanding. It is also important to encourage the development of the child's awareness of the links between various areas of study, and his ability to assess the validity of the knowledge he acquires and the discoveries he makes.

Self-learning

The degree of choice in self-learning should be examined. There are areas where a definite sequence of content is essential because the logical development of the material is in-built; mathematics is the clearest example of this. Certain language skills, for example phonics, where a body of rules exists and where practice is required to master the skills, affords another example of the necessity for sequence. In other areas the exact sequence of topics is less important and opportunities exist for children's individual choices. Environmentally-based studies, as well as some scientific interests, where objectives can be achieved in a number of ways, fall into this category. The development of certain of the more general language skills also lend themselves to individual selection.

In the modern primary school the importance of the individual is stressed. The concern is not only for intellectual growth but for the development of the total personality. To cater for individual learning the teacher must be aware of each individual child's pace of progression as well as his interests. Knowledge of these will enable the teacher to help the child to determine the content of his work in those areas in which choice is practicable. Children's individual modes of thought and learning must be kept in mind, so that each child can work in the manner most suited to him. At the same time, as the child develops the teacher can encourage him to become aware of other approaches to learning problems. In order to establish efficient work habits, it is vital for the child to take increasing responsibility for organizing his own time, for selecting his work and for judging his own efforts.

There is a strong motivational value in individual self-direction and choice of work, but the teacher has an active and demanding role to play. He must observe the child's initial interest, be aware of the possibilities it engenders and lead the child to select profitable areas of experience. This demands from the teacher knowledge of:

1 the child as an individual and his learning processes
2 the underlying concepts involved
3 the skills and subskills required

Language development
On entry into school some children already possess an extensive vocabulary built upon wide and varied experiences. They have been encouraged to ask questions and are already curious about the world around them. Others have had only limited experiences and may be linguistically impoverished. Here the teacher's task is more difficult. She needs to extend experiences and to create a challenging environment. The teacher, through personal contact with children, can work to arouse interest, stimulate questioning, initiate discussion and help formulate problems. One aspect of this work will be vocabulary extension and the use of appropriate syntax.

Language develops out of experiences which provoke both the need for new words and their definition. A young child enjoys language and uses it to practise and test out his intellectual grasp of reality. One of its important functions is in his own thinking where its mastery helps him to group, classify and order his thoughts.

To influence the development of language skills the teacher needs to have a knowledge of the complexity of language structure and to be able to recognize the individual's needs. Teachers must take the opportunities that arise daily in conversation and discussion, individual and group enjoyment of literature, and the constant use and practice of the developing skills of reading and writing. Children need to have their interest in words and structures aroused and they need help in the selection of appropriate terms of expression. The teacher has to work to establish feedback so that the language passes into the functional vocabulary of the child.

Conclusions

At its best, modern, informal primary education is efficient—equipment and space are economically used; child-time and teacher-time is valued and not wasted; learning is sound and geared to the individual; the child is interested and well-motivated. However, this type of education makes heavy demands upon the school staff and requires able, well-informed and dedicated teachers. It is not sufficient merely to provide a suitable environment; the teacher will have to use a whole array of teaching skills—extending interests, structuring learning situations, posing problems, making information available and direct teaching of individuals, groups or the whole class where appropriate.

Bibliography

BLACKIE, J. (1967) *Inside the Primary School London*: HMSO

BEARD, R. M. (1969) *An Outline of Piaget's Developmental Psychology* London: Routledge and Kegan Paul

BREARLEY, M. (ed.) (1969) *Fundamentals in the First School* Glasgow: Basil Blackwell

DEARDEN, R. F. (1968) *The Philosophy of Primary Education* London: Routledge and Kegan Paul

WALTON, J. (1971) (ed.) *The Integrated Day in Theory and Practice* London: Ward Lock Educational

7 The significance of spelling patterns for beginning reading

Audrey Haslam

An important consideration in beginning reading must surely be the nature of the units which children are required to blend in the process of learning to read. Gibson (1967) points out that the relevant literature suggests that the unit for reading is not the single grapheme, and that the reader does not proceed sequentially from left to right, letter by letter, across the page. Using a fast tachistoscopic exposure, Cattell (1885) found that a skilled reader could perceive four unconnected letters, a very long word, and four or more words if they formed a sentence, while Dodge (1905) showed that perception occurs in reading only during fixations and not at all during the sequential jumps from one fixation to the next. (A tachistoscope is a piece of equipment which can be used to display unconnected letters, single words or groups of words, for a measured period of time. The interval of exposure can be decreased as the learner's speed of recognition increases.)

Miller's work (1956) on the importance of grouping and organizing the input sequence into units or chunks is also relevant. Using the jargon of information theory, he maintains that since the memory span is a fixed unit of chunks, we can increase the number of bits of information that it contains simply by building larger and larger chunks, each chunk containing more information than before. This process is called recoding. The input is given in a code that contains many chunks with few bits per chunk. This input is recoded into another code that contains fewer chunks with more bits per chunk. More simply, the input events are grouped, a new name is applied to the group and the new name is remembered rather than the original input events. In the process of reading, the input events are individual letters which are grouped or recoded into spelling patterns.

This is borne out in experiments by Newman (1963) which show that when a person is shown individual letters tachistoscopically, he reads with only the greatest difficulty. If he sees each letter for only a hundred milliseconds, he can read words of six letters with only 20 per cent accuracy, while if given three hundred and seventy-five milliseconds to view each letter, his probability of accuracy is still under 100 per cent, even though he has had over two seconds to look at each word. He also found that the overall rate of reading with a three-letter span is three times as great as with a single-letter span, because the chunk is three times as large, while the time per chunk is constant.

Gibson concludes from this that however graphemes are processed perceptually in reading, it is not a letter-by-letter sequence. She maintains that the smallest component units in written English are spelling patterns, by which she means a cluster of graphemes in a given environment which has an invariant pronunciation according to the rules of English.

The question which now arises, concerns the manner in which these spelling patterns can best be presented to children who are beginning reading to ensure maximum transfer in the reading of unfamiliar words. This would probably be within the context of words which are similar in structure, as this would help the children to make the necessary discriminations and also to form a learning set for the identification of words containing these patterns. 'Learning set' is the term used by Harlow (1949) for learning how to learn a kind of problem. He maintains that the acquisition and use of learning sets is very important in the development of intellectual organization.

The following experiment was carried out to determine the effect of teaching children to perceive groups of letters as spelling patterns within words and to transfer them to the reading of other, similar words. The spelling patterns selected consisted of pairs of initial consonants, pairs of final consonants, and final clusters comprising a vowel followed by a pair of consonants. These patterns were all presented within the context of four-letter, monosyllabic words; twelve words were selected for each of the three types of spelling patterns. One group of children was taught to respond to each letter in the words as a separate sound, while the other group was taught to respond to pairs of initial consonants, pairs of final consonants, and final clusters as spelling patterns. There were seventy-two children in the experiment aged from 6:0 to 6:11 years inclusive and they were all drawn from one infant school in Salford. They were taught in groups of six, consisting of three children of high and three of low ability, but they were tested individually with similar words to those used in the teaching sessions. They were again tested individually with the test words two weeks later.

The results of the experiment indicate that the children learned to identify words beginning and ending with a pair of consonants more easily if they were taught to respond to such consonants in similar words, as one phonemic unit or spelling pattern, than if they were taught to respond to such consonants as two separate sounds. This suggests that transfer of training is facilitated if these consonants are presented as spelling patterns within words.

Words beginning with a pair of consonants were identified more easily than words ending with a pair of consonants. This suggests that

54

perhaps more attention should be given in the teaching of reading to words ending with a pair of consonants.

Firm conclusions about the perception of these particular final clusters cannot be drawn from the experiment. This is due to interference from the common practice in infant schools of teaching children to blend the first two letters of words. This practice was reinforced by the teaching of a pair of initial consonants as one phonemic unit in the experiment, where it proved most effective. It was something of a stumbling block with the final clusters however, as the children preferred to read the word 'sand', for example, as 's/a/ sa,n/d, sand'. Different results might have been obtained if the children had not been taught previously to blend the first two letters of words. In some schools, for example, the children are taught to blend the initial letter with a known combination of sounds. Words such as 'bat', 'cat', 'fat', can be learned in this way if the word 'at' is already known. If the children in the experiment had been taught in this way, they would presumably have been more willing to try to read such words as 'lend', 'mend', and 'send' by blending the initial consonant with the word 'end', which was the method used in the experiment.

However, there are very good reasons for using the method of blending the first two letters of words. Perhaps the most important reason is that during the early stages of learning to read, the child has to learn to appreciate the part played by order and a left to right orientation because, unless he learns the significance of moving from left to right, he will find reading virtually impossible. There are of course instances when the strict left to right sequence must be broken, as in teaching the effect of the final e in such words as 'take', but there is no necessity to break it in teaching the words in the experiment. It seems that the children in the experiment had previously acquired a most effective learning set for blending the first two letters of words.

In information theory terms, the results of the experiment suggest that recoding two initial or two final consonants into a single chunk facilitates the identification of monosyllabic words containing these consonants. Further research into the effects of recoding three letters into a single chunk would be helpful. Future experiments might produce more conclusive results if clusters of three consonants rather than a vowel and two consonants were used. Longer words and older children than those used in the present experiment would then have to be selected.

The results of the experiment also indicated that more words were identified correctly on the delayed post-test than on the immediate post-test, even though no teaching took place in the interval as the children were on holiday. This suggests that short periods of direct teaching in small groups with the type of material used in the experiment eliminate the effects of forgetting, at least in the short-term. They also seem to facilitate the formation of a learning set which children can use on a later occasion, enabling them to identify more words correctly.

References

CATTELL, J. McK. (1885) The inertia of the eye and brain in *Brain* 8, 295–312

DODGE, R. (1906) Recent studies in the correlation of eye movement and visual perception in *Psychological Bulletin* 3, 85–92

GIBSON, E. J. (1967) Learning to read in Endler N. S., Boulter, L. R., and Osser, H. (eds) *Contemporary Issues in Developmental Psychology* London: Holt, Rinehart and Winston

HARLOW, H. F. (1949) The formation of learning sets in *Psychological Review* 56, 51–65

MILLER, G. A. (1956) The magical number seven, plus or minus two: some limits on our capacity for processing information in *Psychological Review* 63, 81–97

NEWMAN, E. (1966) Speed of reading when the span of letters is restricted in *American Journal of Psychology* 79, 272– 277

8 Psycholinguistic inferences for reading instruction

H. Alan Robinson

Introductory remarks

Psycholinguistics is a blend of two fields—psychology and linguistics. There is, and should be no psycholinguistic method of teaching reading. It is as foolish to speak of a *psycholinguistic method* as it is to speak of a *psychological method* of teaching reading. The same can be said of a *linguistic method*, although there are some who feel such a 'method' is the panacea for reading problems.

Any reputable system of teaching reading cannot help making use of some of the positive, basic tenets of linguistics and psychology. The amalgamation of the two disciplines adds dimensions of vital concern to the teacher and the learner. To quote Smith and Goodman (1971); 'The value of psycholinguistics lies in the insights it can provide into the reading process and the process of learning to read.'

At first this paper was given the title, 'Psycholinguistic implications for reading instruction'. But, as I reviewed the so-called implications, I realized that they were actually my own inferences based on information and implications contributed by others. The inferences which follow, therefore, are by no means agreed upon by all psycholinguists or reading experts. They have been generated from the oral and written discourse of psycholinguists and other educators, as well as from my varied experiences in the fields of reading and psycholinguistics over the past years. Some are broad concepts which would stimulate little or no argument; others are speculative and possibly controversial. Nevertheless, all are suggested as possibilities for implementation. The number of inferences stated is by no means inclusive or conclusive; they are limited by both my present thinking and the space allotted for this paper.

Inferences

First, *a learner's dialect should be respected*. Language is used (normally) to express meaning. The child comes to school with a remarkable knowledge of how to gain meaning from oral language. Specifically, he is adept at obtaining meaning from his language or dialect, that which he has heard and used in his environment prior to school entrance. If the school respects that dialect, the child will be able to express his thoughts. If the language is denigrated, he will stop using language almost completely in school, or will cease to use it for positive communication, and will look for ways of using it in negative behaviour. In any case, he will most likely make little conscious effort to learn the changes in the rules represented by standard English.

If the child is given many opportunities to use language to express meaning, and to search for meaning in the language of others, he will gradually learn to cope with standard English which is commonly used in the school and in school work, since it represents the dialect needed to gain upward mobility in society. Transitions to standard English usage must be made or the school is failing in its task. The teacher's role in promoting proficiency in standard English is to respect the dialect of the learner, respect the learner himself, and then capitalize on those times and places when differences in dialects can be noted and reviewed without harming the learner's self-respect.

Second, *initial reading experiences should capitalize on the learner's dialect.* The learner should recognize a need to transfer from oral to written language in order to receive a message of importance to him. Such an abstract, high-flung goal as 'you need to learn to read because it will help you all the way through school and life' is a feeble reason for most youngsters. Initial messages to be read, when prepared by the teacher, should parallel the learner's dialect—graphophonologically (the sounds written down), semantically (word meanings and interrelationships), and syntactically (language patterns or structure)—as much as possible. 'John opens box. John eats candy.' printed on a little box along with a drawing of a piece of candy is not a bad way of starting to learn to read—as long as the box contains a real piece of candy which can be eaten on successful comprehension of the message. It seems better than some of the nonsense too often found in a beginning reading book.

When the learner prepares a message to be read by having the teacher write it for him, that message should be transcribed intact—graphophonologically, semantically, syntactically. There will be plenty of time in the future to make a transition to standard written English. At present the learner must feel that his dialect is respected both at written and oral level.

Third, *instructional materials and recreational materials used in beginning reading programmes should be selected on the bases of significance and relevance—not for the teacher but for the learner.* Reading, particularly in beginning stages, should satisfy immediate goals. The messages should have significance and relevance in terms of solving problems, supplying enjoyment, enhancing ability. The material read should, as far as possible, satisfy the present interests and needs of the specific learners in given learning situations. Interests and needs should be evaluated by the teacher with the pupils; past studies of interests and needs will not provide sufficient information about the wants of today's learners. Too often our reading programmes have been largely literature programmes emphasizing literary and narrative aspects. Certainly part of the reading diet should be narrative, but the diet should be well balanced. In all probability, a large number of boys and even girls would gain more from beginning reading experiences if initial materials placed more stress on expository and utilitarian reading.

The style of the material should also be considered. At the outset, styles and syntactical structures should not be far outside the language experience backgrounds of the learners. In the past many preprimers and primers began with sentence structures and writing styles foreign to the learner. Although perhaps not as rhythmic, 'John sees Mary. Mary sees John.' is certainly a lot closer to the basic language patterns of most dialects than 'See, John, see. See, Mary, see.' Young readers learn rather quickly to contend with a variety of styles and structures if the transition period is carefully planned.

Fourth, *since most messages are transmitted through a series of interrelated words, sentences, or paragraphs, minimal attention in reading instruction should be placed on the recognition and analysis of individual, isolated words.* Maximum attention to phonic and structural analysis on individual words isolated from the rest of language is uneconomical and neeedlessly frustrating for many pupils. In this type of instruction the learner can only depend on one aspect of language, the graphophonological, rather than making use of syntactic and semantic aspects as well.

Large numbers of pupils have been prevented from learning how to read and enjoy reading by the word list method. Not only have they come to think of reading as a mechanical exercise, but they have also been kept from using cues represented within the total context of a message. They have only been equipped to decode words rather than language.

In all probability for some learners in some situations teachers do have to place emphasis on helping learners figure out phonemes and groups of phonemes. This inference is in no way a denunciation of such help; rather is it a plea for using more than just one aspect of language as a tool, particularly on words removed from their natural environments. There follows a suggestion for a strategy for using the many cues to figuring out a message represented by written symbols.

Fifth, *the learner develops and needs to be helped to develop strategies for unlocking the ideas found on the printed page.* Rather than place attention on absolute accuracy in reading the words in print, emphasis should be placed on utilizing the least number of cues to obtain the author's meaning. As a number of psycholinguists have implied or even stated, reading should be an intelligent guessing game, making use of whatever aspects of language are needed as the reader searches for the meaning. The learner should be encouraged to make errors in his search for meaning; this is how he learns. The teacher should understand, encourage, and delight in the miscues of his young charges as he helps them make use of such a strategy in search of meaning. According to Smith (1971):

> This readiness to take chances is a critical matter for beginning readers who may be forced to pay too high a price for making 'errors'. The child who stays silent (who 'misses') rather than risk a 'false alarm' by guessing at a letter or word before he is absolutely sure of it, may please his teacher but develop a habit of setting his criterion too high for efficient reading.

The 'guessing game' should become less chaotic as youngsters learn and teachers help in the development of strategies to use when parts of messages are confusing or unknown. The most essential strategy appears to be the utilization of context. The pupil should learn to search a given context intensively when he is stopped by a confusing or unknown message. The context which provides the answer may be a phrase, clause, sentence, group of sentences, paragraph, or group of paragraphs. Often the reason for not understanding the message will be an unknown word or two, or a new use of known words. An inspection of interrelationships among words and the function of the word or words within the structure of a sentence will often result in the unlocking of the message. This is characteristic of the reading behaviour of the mature reader, and emphasis should be placed on the use of context strategy right from the very beginning of reading instruction.

When context alone is not sufficient, the reader should be encouraged to use the strategy of looking at the beginning of the word or words. He should be helped to relate this inspection of initial graphemes to the context again. These combinations of strategies will frequently permit the reader to interpret the message. (Obviously if the reader keeps meeting words with the same initial graphemes and cannot read them, the teacher will develop a lesson to assist him, interrelating the phonographological cue with context cues.)

In some cases readers will want to and need to inspect the final grapheme in a word, or divide a long word into parts as they try to figure out the word in relation to context. By the time they resort to this strategy the message either becomes clear rather promptly or they are forced to resort to the help of the dictionary or some other outside authority.

Whatever the strategy or group of strategies learned and/or employed, the important point is that the teacher should be available to help the learner marshall what he already knows about language, and what he is learning, into useful procedures for unlocking ideas in print.

Sixth, *reading tasks are dictated by the nature of the language user, the purposes to be met, and the nature of the material.* There is no specific sequence of skills to be taught in reading instruction. Sequences of skills to be learned in various reading programmes have most frequently been devised on the bases of speech development, developmental needs of children, and/or the logical thinking of programme designers. In reality, though, sequence is only relevant when related to the language knowledges and inadequacies of particular learners, the nature of the material to be read, and the purposes for reading. Reading skills are actually a system of strategies the learner acquires for discovering, evaluating and utilizing meaning. If the strategies are appropriate for the purpose of the reading and the nature of the material on hand, a given reading task will be successful.

Therefore a teacher should help the learner diagnose his language strengths and weaknesses in relation to the material to be read. For example, if the reader is beginning to encounter numerous words with the vowel pattern of *ea* within them, and he is unable to figure them out even with the help of the existing context, the teacher should structure some help. He should be given opportunities, using context familiar to him, to note that the vowel pattern of *ea* is most often pronounced in two ways—ē or ā. He may then go back to the less familiar context and try his new strategy. For those readers who have already generalized the *ea* pattern, there is no need for them to 'be taught'.

The nature of the material to be used must also be carefully explored, for there is no reason for the learner to attempt to acquire a strategy at a given point in time if he will not be able to use it. A complete reading programme cannot be presented in any meaningful way within the framework of any given set of reading materials. Strategies for unlocking ideas should be acquired as a reader utilizes printed materials throughout a school curriculum. The wide variety of patterns of writing requires a variety of strategies for interpreting them. For example, it might be argued that one strategy a mature reader ought to develop is the ability to note cause and effect relationships in printed material. This strategy can be practised in some narrative materials, but the cause-effect writing pattern occurs most often in expository materials, particularly in social studies. Here, then, is the most reasonable time and place to learn how to unlock ideas presented in a cause-effect pattern.

Purpose constantly interacts with both the reader, the writer, and the material to be read. Any piece of material can be read utilizing different strategies for different purposes, and the task is hardly ever clearcut. For example, if the reader is searching for the solution to a problem, he doesn't care much what the writer's purpose was, as long as the information is available. In all probability if the writer's and the reader's purpose happen to coincide, the task will be a trifle easier. However, a very different set of strategies has to be employed when the reader is trying to discover the writer's purpose, particularly if the writing is somewhat subtle.

Conclusion

Looking at *reading* from a psycholinguistic viewpoint, one becomes very much aware of the complexities involved in having two people —the reader and the writer—carry on a meaningful dialogue. It becomes evident that more study is needed of the process, or rather processes, of reading.

McCullough made an important and complex observation when she stated:

> As teachers study the signals to meaning from the point of view of a reader who does not know all that the author knows about his subject, or know all that the teacher knows about interpreting signals, they can begin to assess the value of certain observations under certain conditions, and determine strategies for teaching in all types of literature from preschool to the end of formal instruction. Thought processes must be cultivated and expressed in English. The versatility of English to express the same thought in numerous ways must be experienced in listening, in analysis, and in expressing. Expectation of the directions the author may next take must provide readiness for whatever comes. Children must know that the ecology of literature, like the ecology of earth, is a matter of interrelationships. All of these achievements relate to what the author has presented. The reader's cognitive and effective reactions after that, are something else again, and no small order!

References

McCullough, C. M. (in the press) What should the reading teacher know about language and thinking? in Hodges R. E. and Rudorf E. H. (eds) *Language and Learning to Read* Boston: Houghton Mifflin

Smith, F. (1971) *Understanding Reading* New York: Holt, Rinehart and Winston

Smith, F. and Goodman, K. S. (1971) On the psycholinguistic method of teaching reading in *Elementary School Journal* January 1971, 177

9 The cognitive clarity theory of learning to read

John Downing

Cognition versus perception

Elkonin (1972), the Russian authority on reading, wrote recently:

> ... the perception and discrimination of printed characters is only the external side of the process of reading, behind which lies hidden the more essential and basic behaviour, which the reader produces with the sounds of language. The speed of the movement of the eye does not define the speed of reading. Nor does the so-called 'span of apprehension' determine the speed of reading (i.e. the number of graphic symbols perceived simultaneously). Of considerably greater importance than the speed of eye movements and the span of apprehension is the speed of the underlying more central processes concerned with the behaviour of creating the sound form of the word and connected with it, its comprehension.

The theory to be presented in this paper is concerned with those 'underlying more central processes' which Elkonin regards as the heart of the problem of learning to read. Reading research in the past has been overconcerned with the external aspects of reading—perception, eye movements, visual discrimination, letter-name knowledge etc—at the cost of neglecting the conceptual and reasoning processes behind these surface features.

The cognitive clarity theory

The theory may be stated formally but quite simply and briefly in five steps.

Step one

Writing or printing is a highly abstract form of language which has been of universal concern for only about a century. Prior to that it was restricted to a tiny elite section of the population. Hence, any evolutionary development of a special area of the brain for the reading process, as some theorists of congenital dyslexia contend, is biologically impossible. Therefore, learning to read involves applying general intellectual abilities to the task.

Step two

When people read, it is extraordinarily difficult to see what they are doing. It has taken great ingenuity and much expense for psychologists even to measure the movements of the eyes in reading. What chance has an ordinary child of four or five years of age to catch on to what the grownups are doing when they read? Reading is usually a silent activity, and there are very few outward signs of what the behaviour involves. No wonder that such young children find that 'reading is a mysterious activity, to which they come with only the vaguest of expectancies,' as reported in Reid's (1966) investigation of Scottish five year old beginners.

Step three
For these reasons, children enter the first stage of the learning to read process in a state of confusion about the purpose and nature of the task of acquiring literacy. They do not *know* or *understand* what its purpose is. They do not *know* or *understand* what kinds of activities they must learn. They do not *know* the basic concepts involved in thinking about the tasks of reading and writing. Hence this original condition is one of *cognitive* confusion.

Step four
Under reasonably good conditions, the child works himself out of the initial state of cognitive confusion into increasing cognitive clarity about the purpose and nature of the skills of literacy. This progressive development of cognitive clarity resembles the gradual clearing of the fog of confusion which is the natural state of the beginner. The child increases his cognitive clarity by solving the many problems with which he is bombarded on first being faced with the need to learn to read and write. The first and most important problem is 'What is written language for? What can I use it for?' etc. Then there is a host of conceptual problems e.g. 'What is a word, a sound, a letter, a number, a line, a page?'

Step five
Although the initial stage of literacy acquisition is the most vital one, according to this theory, cognitive clarity continues to develop throughout the later stages of education as new abstract concepts of language are added to the student's understanding.

A fair amount of evidence can be adduced for the cognitive clarity theory. The following researches all show the initial cognitive confusion of the beginner:

1 In Reid's (1966) Edinburgh study mentioned above, intensive interviews with five year old beginners found that they showed a 'general lack of any specific expectancies of what reading was going to be like, of what the activity consisted in, of the purpose and use of it.'

2 Vygotsky's (1962) investigation into 'the tremendous lag between the school child's oral and written language' in Russia concluded that 'it is the abstract quality of written language that is the main stumbling block,' and the child 'has little motivation to learn writing when we begin to teach it. He feels no need for it and has only a vague idea of its usefulness.'

3 The present author (Downing 1970) replicated Reid's (1966) interview study, but with English children, with the following conclusions: 'Young beginners have difficulty in understanding the *purpose* of written language.' Also, 'they have only a vague idea of how people read and they have a special difficulty in understanding *abstract* terms,' (i.e. as are used in describing the parts of language, e.g. letter, word etc).

4 The Downing (1970) study also included experiments in which these five year old children had to categorize auditory stimuli into certain linguistic units. Not one single child used the category 'a word' or 'a sound' according to the adult's concepts of these linguistic units.

5 Meltzer and Herse (1969) asked American first graders and kindergarten children to cut 'a word' off a card which had a sentence printed on it. The results showed the same confusion over this concept.

6 Vernon (1957) reviewed all the evidence on reading disability and concluded: 'Thus the fundamental and basic characteristic of reading disability appears to be cognitive confusion.' Also, 'this confusion resembles that of a young child who is just beginning to read'. Thus the retarded reader is one who 'remains in a state of confusion over the whole process'.

Evidence for the gradual development of cognitive clarity in the normal child can be seen in Reid's (1966) original longitudinal study, but it is demonstrated rather more clearly in the present author's (Downing 1972a) followup of the five year old children in the interviews and experiments mentioned in paragraphs 3 and 4 above. The experiments on the children's categorizations of 'word' and 'sound' were conducted three times—two, six, and nine months after first entering the infants department. The data indicated that these children could be divided into three groups according to their rate of growth in understanding these two linguistic concepts. When the other data from the research were analyzed, it was found that these groups differed systematically in five aspects of the growth of cognitive clarity:

1 understanding the communication purpose of written language
2 conceptualizing the symbolic function of writing

3 understanding the concepts of decoding and encoding
4 learning linguistic concepts
5 developing the corresponding technical terminology for such abstract units of language

In all of these respects, the behaviour of the children in the three successive phases of this study clearly demonstrated how they were groping for solutions to the problems which faced them in trying to understand the purposes and nature of the tasks of literacy. As these problems were solved one by one, so their confusion diminished and cognitive clarity grew.

A model of the literacy acquisition process

Further indirect evidence for this theory may be adduced from the crossnational study of reading completed recently by an international team of scholars in this field (Downing *et al* 1972). In this Comparative Reading Project, as it has been termed, the present author (Downing 1972b) found that the analysis of the data from the fourteen countries (Argentina, Denmark, Finland, France, Germany Great Britain, Hong Kong, India, Israel, Japan, Norway, Sweden, USA, USSR) could be most readily understood in relation to the following model of the literacy acquisition process:

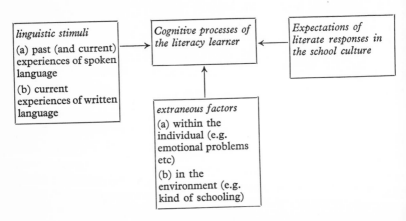

In this model the cognitive processes of the literacy learner have their appropriate position of central importance. It is here that the child's struggle to move from cognitive confusion to cognitive clarity takes place. This struggle to solve the problems involved in understanding how to read is aided or hindered by forces from three directions. It is as if the cognitive processes of the literacy learner are assailed simultaneously by three 'voices'. On the one hand the voice of linguistic stimuli speaks to him in terms of his comparatively long past experience of his own spoken language and his new experiences of the written language which he is being required to learn. On the opposite side are the demands of the voice of the school culture laying down what kinds of literate responses are expected and acceptable. The third voice, though labelled extraneous, is by no means unimportant. It is not one voice but many — a cacophony of demands, both internal and environmental. Somehow or other the learner must work out his own cognitive solution to his problems in literacy acquisition, despite all this clamour.

Applying this model to the data from the fourteen countries in the Comparative Reading Project, it became clear that there are many hazards in the child's educational (Downing 1972c) and linguistic environments (Downing 1972d) which may cumulatively cause the total level of cognitive confusion to be raised above some individuals' threshold of tolerance. These then become the reading disability cases described by Vernon (1957) as *remaining* in a state of cognitive confusion.

The chief hazard is mismatch between the *linguistic stimuli* and *expectations of literate responses* parts of the model. Three kinds of mismatch were found to be of critical importance in increasing the level of cognitive confusion in the beginning reader:

1 Mismatch between the child's past and current experiences of *his own language* (L¹) and the teacher's expectations of literate responses *in her language* (L²).
2 Mismatch between the child's perception of the written language and the language of the literate responses expected by the teacher (L²).
3 Compound mismatches in which both the above occur, usually accompanied by the further mismatch between the child's own language (L¹) and the written language with which he is being presented.

Numerous studies indicate the confusion caused by mismatches of type 1. The most extreme form is where the child's language (L¹) is a foreign language in comparison with the language of literacy (L²). Confusion mounts and many children become retarded or fail completely (cf Macnamarra 1966; Modiano 1968). A less obvious form of mismatch is the case where the child's *dialect* (L¹) differs from that of his teacher (L²), but Österberg's (1961) experiments in Sweden prove conclusively that this too is an important cause of increased difficulty in literacy acquisition.

The serious difficulties caused by mismatches of type 2 are also well established by the evidence of scientific research. The present author's (Downing 1967) experiments in contrasting learning to read

67

in the traditional orthography (TO) of English with learning to read in the simplified or regularized system of i t a (Initial Teaching Alphabet) provide the strongest evidence of the increased cognitive confusion caused by the perceived lack of fit between the TO writing system of English and the structure of the language in which the literate responses are to be made. But this type of mismatch has other more subtle forms. For instance, as Reid (1971) has pointed out, the special styles of written language such as 'said he', 'this is a ...' have no place in the beginning stages of literacy teaching because they are foreign to the style of even the everyday speech of acceptable speakers such as the teacher.

Clearly if both types of mismatch occur, probably involving the additional mismatch between the L^1 of the child and the L^2-based writing system he is supposed to acquire, there will be a case of cognitive 'confusion worse confounded'.

Several seemingly puzzling research results are explained by the cognitive clarity theory:

1 *How can beginning in one alphabet (i t a) produce superior attainments later in another alphabet (TO)?* Initial cognitive confusion is reduced by the simpler code system of i t a. Once cognitive clarity is achieved it is general and can be transferred to other systems of writing such as TO.

2 *How can learning to read in two languages be easier than learning to read in only one?* If the Mexican-American child speaks Spanish, for example, cognitive confusion is reduced by allowing him to develop initial literacy in Spanish. Thereafter, his cognitive clarity can be readily transferred to developing literacy in English.

3 *Why is it that many researches have found such a high correlation between early knowledge of the names of letters of the alphabet (e.g. Gavel 1958 etc), yet experimental teaching of letter-names (e.g. Ohnmacht 1969; Johnson 1970; Samuels 1970 has no effect whatsoever on reading progress?* Knowledge of the letter-names is merely a sympton of cognitive clarity. Teaching children to mimic the symptoms obviously will not help their lack of the underlying cause i.e. cognitive clarity.

4 *Why is it that some reading disability cases are superior in visual discrimination to normal readers?* For example, Serafica and Sigel (1970) report that in their comparison of normal and disabled boy readers:

The boys with reading disability in this study do not seem lacking in an analytic ability. If the initial phase of learning to read requires differentiation of graphic symbols from one another, the nonreaders were better equipped for that task than were the boys who showed no reading problems.

This is one of several studies which reveal that visual discrimination is not a serious problem in learning to read. What is more important and what was probably lacking in these disabled readers, was the very opposite of discrimination i.e. the ability to *categorize* written symbols in a logical relationship to the conceptual system they represent (i.e. an aspect of cognitive clarity).

Hopefully, these examples may show the potential explanatory value of this cognitive clarity theory of learning to read.

References

DOWNING, J. (1967) *Evaluating the Initial Teaching Alphabet* London: Cassell

DOWNING, J. (1970) Children's concepts of language in learning to read in *Educational Research* 12, 106–112

DOWNING, J. (1972a) Children's developing concepts of spoken and written language in *Journal of Reading Behaviour*

DOWNING, J. (1972b) Cognitive universals in literacy in Downing, J. *et al Comparative Reading* New York: Macmillan

DOWNING, J. (1972c) Educational environments in Downing J. *et al Comparative Reading* New York: Macmillan

DOWNING, J. (1972d) Linguistic environments in Downing, J. *et al Comparative Reading* New York: Macmillan

DOWNING, J. *et al* (1972) *Comparative Reading* New York: Macmillan

ELKONIN, D. B. (1972) USSR in Downing, J. *et al Comparative Reading* New York: Macmillan

GAVEL, S. R. (1958) June reading achievement of first-grade children in *Journal of Education, Boston University* E40, 37–43

MACNAMARA, J. (1966) *Bilingualism and Primary Education* Edinburgh: Edinburgh University Press

MELTZER, N. S. and HERSE, R. (1969) The boundaries of written words as seen by first graders in *Journal of Reading Behaviour* 1, 3–14

MODIANO, N. (1968) National or mother language in beginning reading: a comparative study in *Research in the Teaching of English* 2, 32–43

ÖSTERBERG, T. (1961) *Bilingualism and the First School Language: An Educational Problem Illustrated by Results from a Swedish Dialect Area* Umeå, Sweden: Västerbottens Tryckeri AB

REID, J. F. (1966) Learning to think about reading in *Educational Research* 9, 56–62

REID, J. F. (1971) The most important R (Part 2) in *Teachers World* 3190, 18

SERAFICA, F. C. and SIGEL, I. E. (1970) Styles of categorization and reading disability in *Journal of Reading Behaviour* 2, 105-115

VERNON, M.D. (1957) *Backwardness in Reading* London: Cambridge University Press

VYGOTSKY L. S. (1962) *Thought and Language* Cambridge, Massachusetts: MIT Press

Part three Extending and utilizing language skills

10 The development of the skills of literacy

Donald Moyle

Introduction

The study group relating to the development of reading and related skills was planned for teachers in junior and secondary schools and also for those working in the field of higher education. Although the main focus of the programme was on reading, neither beginning reading skills nor remedial reading techniques were included. On the contrary, its subject matter underlined the 'literacy at all levels' theme of the conference by concentrating on those developmental skills which need to be mastered if the fluent infant reader is ever to become an efficient adult reader.

Talks and discussions included an examination of the ways in which the skills of comprehension, study skills and reading for pleasure may be encouraged, as well as an appraisal of certain reading materials, teaching techniques and testing devices which may be used to further these ends. In this paper the main areas dealt with by the various contributors are summarized (with the exception of the paper entitled Improving children's comprehension through appropriate questioning, by Helen Huus, which appears in full in chapter 13).

Reflections on the nature of reading

Over the years British teachers have overindulged their interest and emphasis in the area of beginning reading, despite pleas by many writers to view reading as a skill in a wider context. An examination of books produced in Britain on the subject of reading, and particularly those on diagnosis, reveals that they concentrate almost exclusively upon perceptual abilities and word recognition skills. A significant contrast is to be seen in the work of Strang (1970), where two-thirds of the book is concerned with the diagnosis of needs in the areas of fluency, comprehension, attitudes and study skills.

It would seem, therefore, that there is a constant danger of helping children to master the decoding activities involved in reading and yet omitting those skills and interests which will help them to read for pleasure, study purposes or personal enrichment with the ease and efficiency which could be theirs. In Gardner's (1968) words this amounts simply to 'producing more statistically respectable non-readers'.

Learning efficiency demands that there are times when a specific skill must be practised in isolation from reading as a whole. However, there would seem little excuse for divorcing the learning of reading skills from the uses to which such skills can be put. Fries (1962) has in fact proposed this by his insistence that there should be complete mastery of the decoding process before attention is given to meaning and understanding. Stauffer (1970) takes an almost opposite position, insisting that even the very first sentence a child reads should be meaningful to him. The position adopted by Stauffer is that reading is a thinking process and as such the print is the stimulus for wider mental activity. Stauffer would demand that the extension of decoding skills comes through the material with which the child is working, and the teacher should never prepare the child for material by dealing with word study or word recognition work related to it before the child has read the material.

Morris (1962) takes a more extreme position. Whilst he agrees with Stauffer that the more mechanical aspects of reading must arise from materials which the children enjoy and find meaningful, he suggests that the reaction of the child is paramount. Stauffer wants the child to contemplate the author's meaning, whereas Morris wants the child to respond with his own interpretation, whether or not the author's purpose is fully understood.

We shall be examining some of the issues involved in the development of those skills which make efficient reading possible, and the dangers of compartmentalizing reading into a number of skill areas. In addition, it must not be forgotten that the child needs more than skills. He needs to have experience, to be able to accept, interpret and express ideas and to use the results of his reading creatively. Above all he must be enabled to enjoy reading in the spheres of his interests and literary tastes or he is unlikely to be an efficient reader however many skills we endeavour to teach him. If these things are remembered, reading will not be divorced from the other language arts.

Effective reading

Anthony Pugh, who was concerned with the concept of 'effective reading' in secondary schools and among adults, defined effective reading as 'that level of skill growth which enables the individual to vary and align his reading rate, his approach and the techniques he employs, according to the purpose for which he is reading, and also according to the nature of the material and its level of difficulty'.

The extension of reading skills in the secondary school has always been neglected. It has usually been assumed that children can extend their attainment simply by reading without further guidance or help. The organization of the secondary school, with its extensive use of special subject teachers, yet lack of one individual to keep oversight of reading progress or plan reading lessons to practice skills, leads to a gap in provision and help.

English is considered a subject but reading is not. Most English teachers in past years have seen themselves as purveyors of literary appreciation, of feeling and taste. They were, of course, aware of a body of knowledge in the form of grammar but, unfortunately, children rarely understood the messages offered by linguistics. There is a real danger that linguistics might come to be regarded as a panacea which will swallow the time which could well be used for the development of those skills more likely to lead the child to efficient reading and a deeper understanding of literature.

Teachers of subjects other than English often regard themselves as providers of information and communicators of ideas, rather than instructors in those skills required for reading and thinking within the special subject area. Yet each subject has its own specialized techniques which influence the way in which books within the area should be tackled. Accordingly, the subject teacher should be able to help the child with all matters, from the interpretation of diagrams and maps to the way in which great thinkers within the area have organized their thinking. In this connection two particular points were considered important: first, whether specialist reading teachers and consultants should be employed within schools or whether subject teachers can be persuaded to regard reading teaching at all levels as part of their jobs; and second, which strategies and techniques in reading are appropriate to different materials and different ages.

The reading materials and exercises employed by certain commercial firms who advertise short, expensive courses, which promise rapid increases in reading efficiency, were appraised and experimented with. It was found that such courses often emphasized speed above all other considerations. To illustrate this point the group participated in a practical exercise in which they read two passages and immediately answered comprehension questions on them. In the event, a number of members of the group did manage to improve their quotients, based on the division of words read per minute by the percentage of correct answers achieved. The suggestion was made that such work probably does result in people feeling they have improved their efficiency. Many criticisms were levelled at this type of exercise, including the following:

1 It was unlikely that the same speed would be used in normal situations.
2 The questions could often be answered without reference to the passage.

3 There were wide variations in the levels of the questions, and thus the quotient as worked out for one passage could never really be compared with that from another passage.
4 To read passages of this type does not really help the reader to develop a range of strategies suited to purposes and materials.

It was stressed that there is still a great deal to learn concerning the nature of higher order reading skills and possible methods of acquiring them. Such accomplishments as speed reading form only a minor part of the total range of skills and to overemphasize them might well do more harm than good.

Two models for improving advanced study skills were discussed and examined; SQ3R Method (Robinson 1961) and De Leeuw's Phased Reading Method (1965). The SQ3R Method incorporated the following steps:

1 survey i.e. glance through the material to appreciate the structure
2 question what you need to know from the survey
3 read thoroughly
4 recall i.e. stop from time to time to see if the content has been memorized, and make brief notes
5 revise, with the help of notes; skim through the article to ensure that nothing important was missed and that no wrong impressions were gained

De Leeuw's Phased Reading Method, which is really more suitable for study purposes, incorporates the following stages:

1 examine the table of contents etc
2 decide how much needs to be read and in which order
3 if reading the whole book, glance through the first and last chapters
4 decide what you expect to find of use to you
5 glance through the remaining chapters
6 read the whole book, making brief notes or marking passages
7 after reading each chapter make a brief synopsis
8 make a mental summary of the whole book and check through your notes

This particular method of phased reading is extremely useful, especially in the case of textbooks.

However, much literature is intended to persuade rather than to inform and when reading strategies are employed there is always an inherent danger of neglecting critical reading. In order to avoid this trap, it is a good idea in any reading to consider

1 meaning—what is the information content?

2 tone—how does the author address the reader?
3 intention—what appear to be the author's aims in this piece of writing?

Reference skills
John Sceats discussed reference skills, considering them as one aspect of the way in which children handle their reading materials. The school curriculum in recent years has placed much more emphasis upon searching out information and comparison of ideas. If the child is to do this he must be able to read, yet the general level of attainment in reading is rarely indicative of how successful a child is likely to be in searching for particular items in an efficient manner.

Reference skills cannot exist until children begin to use some sort of index. It would appear that children do not use activities of this type naturally. Therefore teachers must search for interesting and motivating ways of introducing children to the use of various types of index— a task in which we have so far not been notably successful.

Although in the literature on reading, reference skills are often described as important, very little research has been conducted and little has been written on how this area of reading might be dealt with in the classroom. Yet it is essential that reference skills should be taught and practised.

The earliest stages of reference skills probably involve the dictionary, and there seems to be a considerable gulf between a picture dictionary such as might be employed in an infant school and the range of junior dictionaries at present in schools. The picture dictionary is, of course, very limited in that many parts of speech cannot be illustrated. Here are some of the questions we should ask ourselves in relation to the use of dictionaries

1 Do dictionaries help children in the development of language?
2 Do dictionaries help in the development of the skills of literacy?
3 How should dictionaries be used?
4 How are the skills of using them established?
5 How should the words within the dictionary be ordered? (Alphabetic grouping is the most common but they could be grouped in classes, e.g. clothing, transport, etc)

The following concepts about dictionaries also need to be developed.

1 Books must be considered attractive and a dictionary is a book, though of a special kind.
2 A dictionary is a word store and can be consulted about meaning, spelling and, later, pronunciation.
3 The dictionary is a source book for talking and a treasurehouse of interest.

4 Alphabetic order within words is not fully appreciated until the child is approximately eight years of age but its application and usefulness must be understood.

It is quite easy for the teacher to give a definition in speech or even to demonstrate meaning. In book form definitions present more difficulty, especially in the early stages of reading. Dictionaries compiled for children of seven and eight frequently fail to produce acceptable and understandable definitions. All too often many of the words used in the definition have not been defined in the same dictionary and are unhelpful to the child, for example: 'Thunder—the noise that follows a flash of lightning.' In the dictionary from which this example is taken, 'follows', 'flash', 'noise' and 'lightning' are not themselves defined. It would seem essential, therefore, that all words used in definitions, except those of extreme simplicity, should themselves be defined in the same dictionary.

Teachers always commend dictionaries but children either do not use them or use them inefficiently, which can build up bad habits. The child using a dictionary faces a basic problem; he tends to feel that if he can spell a word he does not need to look it up in a dictionary, and if he cannot spell it then he cannot find it in the dictionary.

Dictionaries are descriptive not prescriptive. They present the more common meanings of words, not usually all the meanings nor yet what the words mean in different contexts.

Reading laboratories
Christopher Walker suggested that reading laboratories represent a significant attempt to present a growth structure for the development of reading skills beyond the beginning stages. They do not by any means present the total reading situation nor do they absolve the teacher from planning and teaching. They do, however, give the teacher rather more time to diagnose the needs of children and also to become more involved in the wider work of the classroom.

The advantages and disadvantages of using reading laboratories were set out as follows.

The advantages of laboratories
1 They have a high interest value.
2 Every allowance is made for individual differences in interests, attainments and learning rates.
3 They are compact to store and access.
4 A focus for the improvement of reading skills and a careful ordering of them is presented, and growth is in small steps.
5 They present an acceptable challenge to the majority of children.
6 The system of self-competition is highly motivating.

7   They have been shown to give a considerable boost to comprehension attainment.

Criticisms of laboratories
1   The approach is somewhat clinical and the literature a little flat.
2   The material is too self-contained. (This means that the teacher will need to expand the work and ensure that the skills learned are used in other reading situations.)
3   The only reference skills taught are, in fact, dictionary skills.
4   Individual work can be too limiting. (The teacher must ensure that a balance is maintained between laboratory work, other work and group discussion.)
5   The level of the questions is not high enough at the evaluative and critical levels.
6   The sequence of skills is not always obvious and more work is sometimes needed to ensure mastery of a given stage.

Group directed reading—thinking activities
Christopher Walker borrowed the title for this session from Stauffer (1970), who insists that reading must be thought of in terms of a thinking process. By applying all his thinking powers, the child can extract a good deal more from what he reads and make it more meaningful and personal for him. Before reading a passage or a story, the teacher and the group should decide upon their purposes in reading it, on the basis of their needs and interests.

With adequate guidance and questioning by the teacher, certain activities can be used to facilitate learning in the following areas:

1   increasing powers of observation and reflection
2   reasoning—inferring, demonstrating and making predictions
3   increasing mastery of word recognition
4   developing vocabulary and conceptualization
5   mastering the skills of oral reading

Stauffer suggests that such an activity should proceed by steps. In one instance this can be achieved by using elastic bands to fasten down the pages of a book so that only the pages under consideration can be consulted. To illustrate the point, members of the study group were involved in a practical exercise, in which they first read an original story in sections. They were then asked to comment in terms of what the story was about, what could happen next, how they knew what might happen next, and to point out the clues which led them to that particular conclusion. By engaging in this exercise the group was made well aware that thinking with reading material is far more enjoyable and stimulating than passively accepting the author's communication. Further, retention and insight were brought to a high level as each individual in turn stimulated others with a new idea, prediction or inference.

It was also suggested that such discussion need not always take place on the examination of a single text but could be extended to compare the views of different authors on the same subject or stories written around situations involving similar emotional reactions.

Cloze procedure

In introducing and discussing the cloze procedure, I indicated that it is a technique based on the human tendency to complete an incomplete pattern or sequence. Thus if a word is omitted from a sentence the reader attempts to supply the word to complete the meaning.

Cloze procedure has been used widely in America, as a criterion measure for the validation of readability formulae, but has rarely been used in assessing the difficulty level of books themselves. Recently, this approach to measurability has been used increasingly in Britain.

In estimating readability, extracts are chosen at random from the book and every nth word deleted. Deletion rates would seem to vary; one in ten words seems suitable for children under ten years, whereas the intelligent adult can deal with text where every fifth word is deleted. When the selected words have been deleted the subject attempts to complete the spaces. Results suggest that the reader who can complete more than 40 per cent of the spaces using the author's original words can comprehend the passage fully.

As a measure of readability, and also as a reading test, cloze procedure would appear to be sensitive to more of the elements which make up intelligent reading than any other measure suggested to date. However, it is somewhat affected by intelligence and by differences in language environment. Furthermore, it does not take into consideration interests or motivational factors.

In the Group Directed Reading-Thinking Activities discussed by Christopher Walker, the reading and thinking are both influenced by preconceived purposes. The presentation of a cloze procedure exercise might perhaps allow rather more insight into the author's purposes, his use of language structures and indeed perhaps some of his inadequacies. The presentation to children of passages treated in this way has been found to produce a great deal of discussion which adds to the children's insight into the passage. As an illustration of this point, members of the study group were offered practical experience in the cloze procedure. They were first asked to work individually at their own level with reading matter in which every seventh word had been deleted. Having filled in the spaces, they came together in small groups to discuss their responses, agree on the one which appeared most apt and then compare their findings with the original text used by the author. They were also asked to indicate the kind of mental activity which was necessary to deduce each word.

The result of this exercise was a very long list of levels of comprehension, linguistic knowledge, word recognition, reasoning and inspired guesswork which had been used. This suggests that this activity, which proved so enjoyable for both children and adults, is also most effective in encouraging a deep examination of a short passage. It also appeared that the activity was most appropriate for use with literature and other materials presenting ideas and opinions, but somewhat less so with material which was entirely factual.

Planning the reading programme

In our society, literacy is almost an essential ingredient of human happiness and certainly few people become successful in material terms without it. In school few of the children who cannot read can hope, at the moment, for an education which appears relevant to them, which is enjoyable or helpful to their future. It is thus essential that in setting our aims we view the development of reading not only from both present needs in the junior and secondary school, but also in the light of the needs an adult is likely to have in the world in future years.

At all stages reading must be viewed as something to use and enjoy; an activity which expands the horizons and adds to the fullness of each individual's personality. The communication of skills must not therefore be divorced from using them. Higher order skills certainly need to be taught but they must also be used.

The teacher is becoming increasingly a guide and advisor rather than a purveyor of knowledge. In many areas structured materials have been replaced by a more open-ended situation of stimulation, experience, exploration and discovery. In all this the teacher must have a more detailed knowledge of the skills that have to be mastered and the normal pattern through which children can grow. One could set out all the skills in a number of columns with rows representing the stages of development within each. However, learning is an individual matter, and growth often presents a varied front among children who in general terms appear to be at the same level. It must also be ensured that individual activities are related to the total task, for the relationship between skill areas is as important as the individual skills themselves. Furthermore, whenever an area of skill growth is isolated for special practice, care must be taken that the skill is consolidated in the total reading situation, to ensure generalization and future usage of that skill.

Finally, our aim is to produce a reader—one who will read for himself and profit from and enjoy the activity. This will only be achieved if the teacher can convey his own enthusiasm for reading and if he can ensure the communication of the total range of skills.

F

Above all at every stage the child must gain satisfaction, enjoyment and success in the medium.

References

BROWN, A. L., DOWNING, J. and SCEATS, J. (1971) *Words Children want to Use*: A handbook to Chambers young set dictionaries Edinburgh: Chambers

FRIES, C. C. (1962) *Linguistics and Reading* New York: Holt, Rinehart and Winston

FRY, E. (1963) *Teaching Faster Reading* Cambridge: Cambridge University Press

GARDNER, W. K. (1968) Paper presented to the Fifth Anuual Conference of the United Kingdom Reading Association at Edinburgh (Unpublished)

GILLILAND, J. (1971) The assessment of readability—an overview in Merritt, J. E. (ed.) *Reading and the Curriculum* London: Ward Lock Educational

HEATLIE, S. and RAMSAY, E. (1971) An investigation into the alternative methods of assessing the readability of books used in schools in Merritt, J. E. (ed), *Reading and the Curriculum* London: Ward Lock Educational

HERBER, H. L. (1970) *Teaching Reading in Content Areas* New York: Prentice Hall

HUUS, H. (1961) *Reading for Comprehension in South Penn Study Council: A handbook of Developmental Reading* Danville: Interstate Printers and Publishers

DE LEEUW, E. and M. (1965) *Read Better, Read Faster* Harmondsworth: Penguin

MORRIS, R. (1962) *Success and Failure in Learning to Read* London: Oldbourne

MOYLE, D. (1971) Readability: The Use of Cloze Procedure in Merritt, J. E. (ed), *Reading and the Curriculum* London: Ward Lock Educational

PARKER, D. H. (1963) *Schooling for Individual Excellence* New York: Nelson

ROBINSON, F. P. (1961) *Effective Study* New York: Harper

STAUFFER, R. G. (1970) *Directing Reading Maturity as a Cognitive Process* New York: Harper and Row

STRANG, R. (1970) *The Diagnostic Teaching of Reading* New York: McGraw-Hill

TINKER, M. A. (1965) *Bases for Effective Reading* Minneapolis: University of Minnesota

11 Reading in the secondary school: an unassumed responsibility

A. K. Pugh

Introduction

Reading is probably the most intensively worked field in education, yet reading development in secondary education is almost entirely overlooked. Existing work is largely concerned with an intensive examination of specific areas. In this paper I offer a more extensive view, in the conviction that our approach has generally been too restricted and has failed to identify sufficient of the fundamental problems for any constructive action to take place.

There is a real problem. Even students who have succeeded in our language-based examination systems find themselves handicapped by lack of techniques with which their schools failed to provide them. At the other end of the scale Hoare (1971), drawing evidence from the Crowther Report (1959) and other sources, has reliably estimated that 60 per cent of young people become reading drop-outs, in that they give up reading hardbacked books within two years of leaving school.

Undoubtedly one cause of apathy in schools is the lack of research and theory. Hughes' (1970) useful book *Aids to Reading* appears to contradict this. He begins by saying: 'There is an abundance of literature on the teaching of reading, but the majority of books and articles are primarily concerned with the theory of teaching reading.' Hughes, of course, is falling into the trap of narrowing his definition of 'teaching reading' to 'teaching remedial and initial reading'.

Theory and research related to secondary school reading in this country can be fairly quickly summarized under three headings: surveys of the reading interests of adolescents; theories of reading development; reading testing.

The reading interests of adolescents

By far the most thoroughly investigated field is reading interests. Yarlott and Harpin (1970 and 1971) begin a report of their own findings with a useful summary of the research of other investigators in Britain and New Zealand up to 1969, although they ignore American work in this field. Their own research also ignores children's ephemeral reading. More important faults are that they seem content merely to recommend a change of the books for GCE examinations, 'provided that books are carefully chosen and sensitively presented', and that they evade more fundamental questions.

One important point made in the report is that 'to disregard (the pupils' own tastes) entirely is to risk alienating that good will towards literature which manifestly exists in a majority of abler pupils, and to risk incurring open hostility to the teaching of English'. Yet, if the line between liking and antagonism is so fine among abler pupils choosing to study literature, it is hardly surprising that my own research with samples of thirteen and fourteen year olds from all streams of secondary schools revealed that few of them liked the reading books given out at school. On the other hand I discovered, as did Alderson (1968), that teenagers do a surprisingly large amount of voluntary reading.

The main findings of my own research (Pugh 1969 and 1971), based on samples of 80 and 123 children, were as follows:

1   Children of thirteen and fourteen do much more reading of their own accord than is generally realized.
2   A large number of the children, in free expression answers, showed a positive attitude to reading.
3   Public and school libraries and the advice of friends were the main influences on children's selection of their private reading; the influence of parents and teachers was small.
4   In both surveys the number of children who always or usually liked the reading books given out at school was smaller than those who liked them sometimes or never.

I concluded that the following three hypotheses warrant further investigation:

1   Teachers use books which are too difficult for their children.
2   Teachers are unaware both of the extent and the kind of reading done by secondary school children in their free time.
3   Children's distaste for school books creates, as well as illustrates, a general dislike of school.

The third hypothesis has the widest implications. In this connection, Neville and Pugh (1971), reporting on work undertaken in a junior school, note that an emphasis on the importance of reading not only brought about remarkable gains in reading performance and interest, but also created a more positive attitude to school among the children and an increase in their parents' interest in school.

Theories of reading development
Another area of research concerns theories of reading development in the secondary school. Although Gray and Rogers (1956) could say fifteen years ago that 'For more than three decades keen interest has been expressed in the characteristics of mature readers', remarkably

little interest has been shown in the characteristics of adolescent readers. Roberts and Lunzer (1968) have provided a model of reading development, but their chapter is heavily weighted towards initial and adult reading, and largely omits the secondary school stage. It is significant that they had to construct their own model because, as they say, 'In spite of the voluminous literature that faces anyone who approaches the topic of reading, we have been unable to discover a satisfactory analysis of the process as a whole.'

Roberts and Lunzer's view is that 'reading is a linguistic process', and a valuable paper on the intermediate skills presented at the UKRA conference two years ago by Merritt (1970) approaches the reading of younger secondary school children from a psycholinguistic point of view. The practical implications of this view are well spelt out by Merritt.

Reading testing
Reading testing is the third area of existing research activity. However the tests published by the NFER, the only tests quoted by Bate (1961) as being in even relatively common use, test a limited range of reading abilities, and could well encourage schools to regard comprehension as the only feature of reading worthy of attention. In any event, the tests cover only the first four years of secondary school. It is interesting to note that the only other British test which could be used, Black's (1962) *Comprehension Test for College of Education Students*, also emphasizes only this one limited aspect of reading ability.

There is an urgent need for batteries of tests which provide profiles of reading attainment in the secondary school. Such tests could prove instrumental in helping teachers to identify areas of concern, by drawing attention to the skills and abilities required in adolescent readers. It is encouraging to know that the NFER has recognized the problem and is slowly undertaking anglicization and English standardization of Gates and MacGinitie's revision (1965) of Gates's well known *Reading Survey* test series (1939–1958). There are five tests, for children from five to fifteen, in which speed, accuracy, vocabulary and comprehension are all measured. Unfortunately these tests, like those of Bate, refer only to pupils over fifteen.

Secondary schools' lack of concern with reading
I should now like to turn to some factors outside the classroom which discourage secondary schools from becoming concerned with reading.

Surveys undertaken by the DES
One main reason for the lack of concern in secondary schools about reading is undoubtedly the complacency of the DES over reading

standards, as expressed in *Progress in Reading* (DES 1966) and re-iterated, despite the Black Papers (Cox and Dyson 1969a and 1969b) in *Reports on Education* (DES 1970). The subject is contentious and I do not wish to imply that the Black Paper contributors were right. On the other hand, neither would I agree with the DES when it blandly asserts that: 'There is substantial evidence, however, from both national and local samples, that reading standards in schools have risen considerably since 1948.' 'Local samples' means children surveyed by Morris (1966), but the main field research on which her report was based, was carried out between 1955 and 1957. While her report is extremely valuable, the use made of it by the DES here does it a disservice. The 'national samples' used for *Progress in Reading* are more difficult to criticize because data is not available. Daniels (1969) however, at the time of the Black Paper controversy, drew attention to the test used in the surveys, pointing out that it could probably best be described as a test of vocabulary and comprehension. Thus it reinforces the limited models of secondary school reading previously mentioned.

Arguments over reading standards have included Burt, in the Black Papers, bemoaning a decline in educational standards, while the DES expressed itself as satisfied with progress made. Meanwhile, evidence of infant reading standards in the West Riding (Pickles *et al* 1970) shows the validity of norms devised by Burt over fifty years ago.

The provision of books
While the DES influence is important, the body most directly affecting a school is its LEA, and recently a great deal of concern has been expressed regarding inadequate book and equipment allocations by LEAS. *The Times Educational Supplement* (1971) speaks of 'the great school books scandal', while the Educational Publishers Council (1970) states: 'A particular situation has developed in the provision of books and equipment for use in the classroom which can, without any exaggeration, be said to have reached crisis proportion.' Their point is not overstated when one realizes that not only does book expenditure represent only one per cent of total educational expenditure, but that during the last decade it was actually falling in real terms.

LEAs are also frequently deficient in their library provision. The Library Association (1970) has stated that: 'It is considered essential that schools of 800 pupils and above should have the services of at least one full-time chartered librarian.' The request sounds modest. Yet one has to realize, that in November 1970, only 123 chartered librarians were working in schools together with a further 37 non-chartered members (of the Library Association).

The contrast between the actual state of affairs and the picture painted in the DES pamphlet *The School Library* (1967), where it is implied that most secondary school libraries approximate to the model it describes in that they are well housed and have a librarian, is startling.

Organization of the curriculum

The last, and perhaps most important, extraneous cause of difficulty is the way in which the curriculum in secondary schools is organized into separate subject areas. Factors which have contributed to our subject orientation include historical accident, the demands of examining bodies, the real or supposed inability of teachers to teach a range of subjects to adolescents, and the feeling that good specialist teachers should be shared out fairly evenly among the pupils.

Some of the effects of a subject-based curriculum are to encourage the teaching of information at the expense of developing those skills needed to learn a subject; to compartmentalize a child's learning and thus to perpetuate the system; to encourage, as Barnes (1969) has pointed out, the use by teachers of jargon which is often beyond the pupils' level of linguistic attainment; and to cause the English teacher to be regarded as the only teacher whose job it is to develop language skills. His response is frequently to find a corpus of information to convey, be it literature or linguistics, and thereby evade a responsibility for which he feels ill-equipped by his own higher education.

Parker (1963) and Herber (1970) have supplied their own answers to the problem. The methods they recommend differ as much as their underlying philosophies. Parker believed that there was a need for a complete reorientation in the attitudes of teachers—'retooling teachers' he called it. He described a teacher's role in education as guidance; his role in training as direction.

Herber has rejected the role that Parker foresaw for the teacher, probably because in practice the approaches of subject teachers changed very little. He has devised an approach to teaching reading in content areas which avoids upsetting the subject-based curriculum concept of secondary education. His solution is to have reading teachers specializing in the reading problems of various content areas working alongside the subject specialists. Herber's approach seems to me to be a harmful compromise with an unsatisfactory system. The artificial division into content teachers and skill teachers would cause both administrative and learning problems.

Remedying the situation

A major cause of difficulty is that (*pace* Herber) secondary school teachers (although they should do so) do not regard the development of those language skills which are essential for the learning of their own subject as part of their jobs. Paradoxically, it is quite usual for teachers in England to be called upon to teach English in addition to their other subjects, as would seem to be recognized by the retention of a compulsory English course in colleges of education.

Other barriers to the successful development of reading in the classroom include faults in the choice and presentation of books, undesirable attitudes to books, and a distaste for, or unawareness of, the children's own cultural interests. The main problem, however, is a lack of overall aim in reading development which is largely a result of the fragmentary way in which reading is taught.

In any school one can find examples of books in most subjects which, while often excellent in content, are given to children for whom they are totally unsuitable. As we have no system of grading books, and as knowledge of readability in this country is very recent, the selection of appropriate books is dependent upon a combination of the teacher's experience and the child's reaction (see Heatlie and Ramsay 1971). However, not all teachers buy books as intelligently as they might do (*Bookseller* 1970 and Pugh 1971), and, moreover, many of the books they use were selected by their predecessors. Few children are consulted by their teachers when books are chosen, and once the books have been bought it is too late. As a result, one finds many children stumbling through books which are far too difficult, and thereby developing an aversion to reading, while failing entirely to develop fluency and other skills required in adult reading.

The next problem is the manner in which books are presented. Clearly this must vary from subject to subject; no one could expect a child to read a Latin primer in the same way that he would read a light novel. Teachers in all subjects need to state more explicitly the uses to which they expect books to be put, and to suggest strategies the children could employ in using the books. The kinds of questions asked in checking on children's reading need to be more carefully examined. As the questions to be asked largely dictate the strategy the child will adopt, they can be used to encourage purposeful reading.

Some common classroom practices require thorough rethinking, as their practical usefulness may be far outweighed by their educational uselessness. Activities that come to mind include reading around the class, memorizing passages, using class sets of books, especially in English literature, and having a chapter set for homework.

Flower (1969) has drawn attention to the harmful attitudes to books one still finds. He mentions the undue respect given to books as a result of their scarcity value in earlier days. This respect still remains in far too many schools, partly because the books still have scarcity value in schools. Teachers have a special duty to show how books can be used as tools, and to emphasize that books are to be used, not worshipped. Flower also points out that reading is often not regarded as serious work, especially in homes where there is no tradition of reading.

Perhaps the most important barrier is the unwillingness of teachers to take an interest in the cultural activities of their children. Often this is a result of the teachers having different educational and social backgrounds from their children. It seems also to demonstrate a fear of being shown to be ignorant in an area with which the children are more familiar than the teacher. However, progress can often be remarkable when teachers do work from what the children know and like in reading. As mentioned earlier, with reference to surveys of reading interests, there is a large discrepancy between children's attitudes to private reading and to school reading. Children do read a great deal and indeed reading of all kinds appears to fulfil a real need for adolescents. The teacher should not throw out the comics and other ephemeral literature which some of his pupils enjoy; rather should he show interest in them and work from them. He will then stand a better chance of taking the children from where they are to where he thinks they should be.

Conclusions

I have indicated that the main problem regarding reading standards in secondary schools is the lack of an overall aim. Clearly the overall aim must be to produce efficient adult readers. That schools fail to do so cannot be disputed. Certain ways in which schools might improve their practices have been suggested but, in the last instance, it must be the teachers themselves who decide the means to be employed. As Morris (1966) concluded from a large amount of observation, evidence and experience: 'Each school's success or failure in promoting good reading standards and/or progress depended mainly on the quality of its head or staff in that order.'

References

ALDERSON, C. (1968) *Magazines teenagers read* London: Pergamon

BARNES, D. *et al* (1969) *Language, the Learner and the School* Harmondsworth: Penguin

BATE, S. M. (1961) *Secondary Reading Tests 1–3* London: Ginn (for NFER)

BLACK, E. L. (1962) *Comprehension Test for College of Education Students* Slough: NFER

BOOKSELLER (1970) How school teachers choose their children's books in *Bookseller*, no. 3385 7th November, 2290

COX, C. B. and DYSON, A. E. (eds) (1969a) *Fight for Education* Hull: Critical Quarterly Society

COX, C. B. and DYSON, A. E. (eds) (1969b) *The Crisis in Education* Hull: Critical Quarterly Society

DANIELS, J. C. (1969) Educational standards in JACKSON, B. and McALHONE, B. (eds.) *Verdict on the facts* Cambridge: ACE

DEPARTMENT OF EDUCATION AND SCIENCE (1966) *Progress in Reading 1948–64* London: HMSO

DEPARTMENT OF EDUCATION AND SCIENCE (1967) *The School Library* London: HMSO

DEPARTMENT OF EDUCATION AND SCIENCE (1970) *Reports on Education* no. 64 London: HMSO

EDUCATIONAL PUBLISHERS COUNCIL (1970) *Crisis in Educational Spending* (mimeo) London: Publishers' Association

FLOWER, F. D. (1969) *Reading to Learn* London: BBC

GATES, A. I. (1939–1958) *Gates Reading Survey* New York: Bureau of Publications Columbia University

GRAY, W. S. and ROGERS, B. (1956) *Maturity in Reading* Chicago: University of Chicago

HEATLIE, S. and RAMSAY, E. (1971). An investigation into alternative methods of assessing the readability of books used in schools in Merritt, J. E. (ed.) *Reading and the Curriculum,* London: Ward Lock Educational

HERBER, H. L. (1970) *Teaching Reading in Content Areas* New Jersey: Prentice Hall

HOARE, R. J. (1971) Book wormlings in *The Guardian,* 10th March

HUGHES, J. M. (1970) *Aids to Reading* London: Evans

LIBRARY ASSOCIATION (1970) *School Library Resource Centres* London: Library Association

MERRITT, J. (1970) The intermediate skills in *Reading Skills: Theory and Practice* London: Ward Lock Educational

MINISTRY OF EDUCATION. (1959) *15 to 18* (The Crowther Report) London: HMSO

MORRIS, J. M. (1966) *Standards and Progress in Reading* Slough: NFER

NEVILLE, M. H. and PUGH, A. K. (1971) *Junior School Reading: A Structured Environment* (Reading video no. 4) Leeds: Trinity and All Saints Colleges

PARKER, D. H. (1963) *Schooling for Individual Excellence* New York: Nelson

PICKLES, O. G., CASTLE, A. B., and HOUGHTON, W. C. (1970) *Infant Reading Standards* (mimeo) Shipley: West Riding School Health Service

PUGH, A. K. (1969) Some neglected aspects of reading in the secondary school in *Reading, 3* no. 3, 3–10

PUGH, A. K. (1971) Secondary school reading; obstacles to profit and delight in *Reading 5* no. 1, 6–13

ROBERTS, G. R. and LUNZER, E. A. (1968) Reading and learning to read in Lunzer, E. A. and Morris, J. F. (eds) *Development in Human Learning* London: Staples

TIMES EDUCATIONAL SUPPLEMENT (1971) The great school books scandal in *Times Educational Supplement* 5th March

YARLOTT, G. and HARPIN, W. S. (1970) 1,000 responses to English literature (1) in *Educational Research 13,* no. 1, 3–11

YARLOTT, G. and HARPIN, W. S. (1971) 1,000 responses to English Literature (2) in *Educational Research 13,* no. 2, 87–91

12 Reading for different purposes

Helen K. Smith

Authorities in reading are in general agreement that reading involves more than the recognition and pronunciation of words. They see it as a complex act in which the reader is required to use higher mental functions—organizing, selecting, and relating ideas; judging; reasoning; and problem-solving. In addition, the competent reader reacts thoughtfully or emotionally to the ideas read and utilizes these ideas to create insights and ways of thinking. A reader's purpose is basic to ideas gained, retained, or used.

An examination of the lists of purposes which experts have discussed, reveals at least two major kinds: first, the life purposes or motives which the writer has called *primary purposes* and second, desired behaviours or instructional objectives related to comprehension, here called *secondary purposes* (Smith 1967). The primary purposes are really the ultimate ones for which people read. They are the broad, general, long-range purposes for which a reader selects and reads particular selections or books. The writer has classified the long-range or primary purposes into the following eight major classifications: enjoyment, intellectual demands, utilitarian purposes or meeting the practical demands for living, socioeconomic needs or demands, vocational or avocational interests, personal needs or demands, problem-solving, and inspirational, spiritual, or religious needs (Smith 1967).

Secondary purposes include such comprehension behaviours as reading for the general impression or general idea; details; sequence (time, space, ideas), directions; comparison; cause and effect relationships; generalizations and conclusions; anticipation of ideas or prediction of outcomes; characterization; description; mood; tone; sensory imagery; fact and opinion; fact and fiction. This paper will emphasize secondary purposes. Although research has not shown a breakdown of comprehension into the foregoing skills, practitioners have found similar lists useful guides when they conduct instruction in reading. There may be other skills. The foregoing appear to be interrelated with and dependent upon each other. Reading teachers must not lose sight of the long-range purposes for reading. They can become so involved in the teaching of skills that they may forget the real reasons for learning to read. Skills are indeed very important, but a reading programme does not end when all pupils can pronounce the words in their textbooks.

In 1909 McMurray in his book *How to Study and Teaching How to Study*, showed a great deal of insight when he wrote that there was 'no dividing line between good study-purposes and good life-purposes. The first must continually merge into the second; and the interest aroused by the former, with its consequent energy, gives assurance of interested and energetic pursuance of the latter'.

Authorities have stated many times that purpose is an integral part of mature reading. Mature readers have a purpose for reading and read in harmony with their purpose. The idea of reading in accordance with one's purpose is not new. Francis Bacon wrote in his essay, *Of Studies*: 'Some books are to be tasted, others to be swallowed, and some few to be chewed and digested; that is some books are to be read only in parts; others to be read curiously; and some few to be read wholly, and with diligence and attention.' Although Bacon did not use the word *purpose*, he advocated in the early 1600s that different approaches should be used for different kinds of reading.

Most reading specialists recognize two kinds of reading adjustments for different purposes: first, the procedures used in reading, and second, the rate used in reading. Good readers are able to make the necessary adjustments because there is reason to do so. They may use many kinds of comprehension skills and techniques, depending in each case upon their purpose as well as the difficulty and complexity of the content.

Although experts have frequently stated that approaches to different kinds of reading should vary, they have given relatively few definite suggestions as to the way these adjustments should be made. Gray (1937) explained how the processes may vary with the different purposes for reading when he stated:

> The purpose of one's reading determines to some degree the processes involved in comprehension and interpretation. For example, analysis, selection, and judgment are very prominent when one is reading to discover important points and supporting details or to find passages related to a given problem; association and organization are essential when reading to grasp the author's organization or to supplement or validate previous experiences; critical evaluation is important when appraising the worth, relevancy, or consistency of statements, and when weighing the validity of the evidence presented; association, organization, and retention are prominent in reading to reproduce or to make specific use of the facts apprehended; and emotional responses to the events and situations presented are prominent when one is reading to develop appreciation or literacy taste.

The reader with a purpose reads more effectively than the reader with no purpose. He does not necessarily read an entire selection for the same purpose and at the same rate. He may use different rates of reading for the same purpose. For example, one can read to get the general idea of a selection at a very rapid rate or at a moderate or at a slow rate. Readers may read for several purposes during a single setting and may change their purpose within the setting.

If the reader does not have a clear purpose in mind, confusion may result. Spache (1963) wrote:

Without express prereading instructions, the reader does not know what type of facts or relationships to attempt to retain. Without directions, he is likely to retain neither main ideas, nor details, nor relationships since he knows not what he is seeking. In fact, most ineffectual or superficial reading is due to lack of purpose in the mind of the reader.

Aimless studying results when students have not formed the habit of reading for specific purposes. Time can be wasted if the reader has not learned to adjust his reading rate to his purpose. For example, if a person reads habitually in a study attitude, he may find he is spending a disproportionately large amount of time in reading simple or light material.

In spite of the frequent suggestions concerning purposeful reading, there is considerable evidence that many students and adults do not adjust their reading to their purpose. Shores (1961) found that the sixth grade subjects in his study reported using the same techniques for the two purposes he investigated—main ideas and ideas in sequence. Approximately 90 per cent of the subjects in the study by Sister M. Herculane (1961) were aware of the need to determine the purpose and speed; however, they did not use this knowledge in actual performance. Smith (1967) found that in a twelfth grade population, good readers used a greater variety of approaches than poor readers when they read for two different purposes, details and general impressions. It appeared that the good readers in this study had learned on their own to make adjustments in their reading, as they could not describe any instruction they had ever received in purposeful reading.

Since many students do not adjust their technique or rate to their purpose, they should be taught how to read for different purposes and to adjust their reading to their purposes as well as to the content and the difficulty of the selection. Instruction in purposeful reading should begin in the lower elementary, or primary, school and continue as the students advance in school.

There is a dearth of research concerning methods and instructional materials to be used in the teaching of purposeful reading at any educational level. When Smith (1967) observed how few adjustments were made when twelfth grade pupils read for different purposes, and realized how little they really knew about reading techniques that could be used, she proposed to determine the effectiveness of direct, planned instruction in reading for different purposes for ninth grade students who did not show on tests which were designed for the study that they adjusted their reading to different purposes. The instruction in the study was conducted for one academic year by teachers of English who were untrained in reading procedures. The results of this study revealed that purposeful reading could be taught to ninth grade students, as at the end of the experiment the students were able to identify the most appropriate purpose for which selections should be read, and to read for each purpose significantly better than control students did. It was encouraging that teachers untrained in reading could, with the assistance of a reading consultant and materials especially prepared for this project, successfully teach purposeful reading within the established curriculum (Smith 1966).

How can teachers teach or promote purposeful reading? In the first place, pupils should be fully aware of the purposes of materials they have been asked to read. They should know what they are expected to obtain from their reading. They should be helped to see the direction of their learning. Meaningful assignments, discussions, 'setting the stage' for the content to be read, and direct statements by the teacher concerning their expectations would direct pupils in their reading. Assignments and directions must be specific. Telling pupils to 'read the next ten pages' will not help them focus on the main aspects of their reading.

Second, since the ultimate aims of purposeful reading instruction in school are the self-direction and independence of the reader, pupils need to learn how to set their own purposes. For some pupils this will be a gradual process. Teachers will need to continue setting purposes for such pupils and guiding them in setting their own goals. This can be done in several ways. For example, the teacher could begin by stating the purpose or by directing the pupils to read a statement of purpose if it is given in their textbooks. Sometimes a suggested purpose will be stated in the teachers' manual but not pupils' texts. Teachers can guide students by suggesting that the pupils ask themselves questions to which they would like to find answers. Teachers might suggest one question such as 'Where will the space station be?' After this, pupils might ask such questions as 'What will it look like?'; 'How big will it be?'; 'How will people reach the space station?'; 'What will be in the space station?'

Other ways teachers can help their pupils set purposes include asking what kind of story this might be and what the title suggests; having pupils read the first paragraph to see what the setting of the story is or to determine what might happen; reading a chapter overview in science or in social studies and determining what should be learned; or performing scientific experiments and determining what information additional reading might provide. After previewing materials, students can ask themselves such questions as 'What is my purpose?'; 'What do I expect to get from this selection?'; 'How can I best arrive at my goal?'; 'What do I know about the topic already?' Such questions as these help the reader form appropriate mental sets for their reading.

The third suggestion for instruction in purposeful reading is that pupils should be given a wide variety of purposes for reading, both in their reading periods and in their content area subjects. Instruction should include opportunities for all types of thinking related to purposes. Purposeful reading instruction cannot be relegated to one period called reading. The same purpose might be approached differently in two or more content subjects, such as cause and effect relationships in science and in social studies. Each purpose should be introduced by itself and later combined with other purposes. No one purpose should be overemphasized to the neglect of others. For example, reading for details or facts has often been emphasized so much that other purposes have been neglected or omitted.

Fourth, the kinds of questions asked should be in harmony with the purposes for which students have been asked to read. Pupils can become adept in thinking in many ways if they are asked to read for a variety of purposes and if the questions are appropriate for these purposes. If pupils are asked to read for general impressions, they should not be held responsible for detailed information. If they are asked to read to compare two characters, the questions should be centred around that purpose.

There should be both prereading questions which act as a guide and post-reading evaluation of comprehension. When the questions are appropriate for the purpose, the student is asked to exhibit his understanding of the kinds of ideas for which he was instructed to read. If questions asked by teachers do not relate to the stated purposes, pupils lose faith in directions and instruction given them and become confused about their real goals.

At all levels *why* questions should not be neglected for the *who* and the *what* questions. Open-ended questions will help students formulate answers based on their own thinking.

Pupils should also have opportunities to formulate questions related to different purposes. Perhaps deeper comprehension results when students ask questions than when the teacher does.

Fifth, students should be taught *how* to read for the different purposes. It is not uncommon to find the following directions for pupils in reading textbooks or workbooks: 'Read for the main thought' or 'Check the title most appropriate for the selection you have just read.' Seldom are pupils told *how* to derive the main thought or how to accomplish any of the other purposes. This situation is probably due to the fact that there is not much research or expert opinion to guide this kind of instruction. People differ in the procedures they use in their reading; yet some guidance is needed if students are to read effectively.

An attempt was made in the research undertaken by Smith (1966) to suggest procedures that might be used for different purposes. This research should be continued in order to provide even more definitive suggestions for pupils. Briefly, some of the suggested procedures used for the eleven purposes taught included the following: identifying key words (considered here as the words which carried the meaning of the selection); recognizing the importance of signal words, such as 'first', 'second', 'next', and 'finally' when reading for sequence, or 'like', 'as', and 'in a similar way' for the purpose of comparison; determining the topic or summary sentence; diagramming some of the materials read. For example, when reading for comparisons students wrote the topic sentence at the top of the page, formed two columns and wrote at the top of each the objects being compared, and listed in the two columns briefly how they were alike or different. To understand implied meanings the students studied the writing techniques of the writers, such as effective repetition, word choice, description, symbols, and dialogue. They attempted to identify authors' biases, inconsistencies, emotive statements etc. They prepared titles for selections; they followed the sequential development of ideas in selections concerning science, social studies, and literature. They made generalizations and conclusions based upon evidence; they determined what the author's purpose probably was and compared it with their own purpose in reading; sometimes these were not the same. After students practised reading for each purpose in the specially-prepared materials, they were helped to use these skills in the regular curricular material. This transfer of the use of the skills to textbook materials was one of the most valuable parts of the experiment as students saw the relevance of the skills they were practising.

If purposeful reading is an integral part of proficient reading, as many experts maintain, and since most students have not demonstrated in research studies that they know how to make adjustments for different kinds of reading, it becomes apparent that teachers at all levels need to provide opportunities for a variety of kinds of purposeful reading situations and to give suggestions for reading for these different purposes. As teachers observe their own reading and that of others, they will undoubtedly add to the suggestions given in this paper. The development of a flexible approach to reading for different purposes will help students become more independent and more mature readers.

References

GRAY, W. S. (1937) The nature and organization of basic instruction in reading in *The Teaching of Reading: A Second Report* Thirty-Sixth yearbook of the National Society for the Study of Education, Part I Bloomington, Illinois: Public School Publishing Company.

HERCULANE, SISTER M., OSF (1961) A survey of the flexibility of reading rates and techniques according to purpose in *Journal of Developmental Reading* IV, 207–10

MCMURRAY, F. M. (1909) *How to Study and Teaching How to Study* Boston: Houghton Mifflin

SHORES, J. (1961) Are fast readers the best readers? – A second report in *Elementary English* XXXVIII, 236–45

SMITH, H. K. (1966) Instruction of high school students in reading for different purposes in Unpublished Cooperative Research Project no. 1714, University of Chicago

SMITH, H. K. (1967) The response of good and poor readers when asked to read for different purposes in *Reading Research Quarterly* III, 53–83

SPACHE, G. (1963) *Towards Better Reading* Champaign, Illinois: Garrard Publishing Company

G

13 Improving children's comprehension through appropriate questioning

Helen Huus

Introduction

There was a time in the teaching of reading when it was believed that if children read well orally, they could understand what they were reading. Consequently, the research in reading concentrated on eye movements and other 'mechanics of reading' to the exclusion of meaning. But children who learned to 'bark at print,' as the Australian Dr Fred Schonell put it, would do just that—call words, even perhaps with proper cadence and phrasing.

Gray defined four levels of meaning or comprehension, starting with perception, which requires word attack or decoding skills; *comprehension*, which includes the meaning skills; *reaction*, which utilizes critical reading skills; and *integration*, which is the reader's application of his learning to himself. Other reading authorities define reading and meaning differently, but a common thread running throughout most of these definitions and models is the decoding beginning, followed by skills that allow the reader to reconstruct and utilize what the author may have wanted to communicate.

The decoding level

In order to get meaning from reading, children must be able to 'decode' the symbols, for these have no meaning of their own: words merely stand for something else that everyone has agreed upon, just as a trade mark is a symbol for a concept or company.

One of the difficulties in teaching the skills necessary for the decoding process is that often the samples used by teachers with children are known words, and the reader thus has many clues to their pronunciation and meaning. When complete unknowns are met, the reader is at a loss as to how to proceed. The dictionary may be of little help, for sometimes the reader does not know when he has pronounced the word correctly when using the phonetic respellings.

The ability to pronounce words is the first skill necessary to comprehension, for unless the print is translated into words, the reader can go no further. And this is exactly the difficulty that many pupils have.

The meaning levels

One of the most flexible and easily available ways to teach comprehension skills is to use questions and exercises that point up these various skills. The questions can be structured to apply to different levels of comprehension so that a teacher knows which levels he is reaching in the daily lessons. While these questions will require successively higher thought processes, even young children are capable of utilizing all levels with material appropriate to their maturity and reading ability. Actually, a reader swings back and forth among levels as he reads, checking and relating as he moves along.

Literal or fact comprehension

Literal comprehension is the lowest level and requires the reader to be able to tell *what the book says*—to repeat or paraphrase the content included in what he has been reading. This kind of parroting has sometimes in school been accepted as superior work, but it only requires the student to retain the material from the book in his memory long enough to be able to give it back, either in the words of the book or in his own words, depending on the teacher. The *who, what, when* kinds of questions usually bring forth answers dependent upon literal comprehension.

The skills needed for this level of comprehension include the following:

1 *Understanding the vocabulary.* Unless the reader has a rich background of word meanings or labels for concepts, he will be unable to gain even the literal meaning. The 'bloomers' children often make are traced back to their misinterpretation of the meaning of a word.

2 *Recognizing the structure.* Once the individual meanings are grasped, words must be understood in the context in which they occur; this necessitates understanding sentences, paragraphs, stories, and the sequence of stories or episodes in a longer work. Knowing the relationships denoted by various connectives such as 'and', 'but', 'for', 'because', 'nevertheless', 'moreover', 'however', 'furthermore', 'consequently', 'meanwhile', and 'next' is essential if the flow of thought from paragraph to paragraph is to be understood and the reader is to visualize forward movement in the selection. Knowing the referents of pronouns like 'it' and 'which' is another necessary understanding if readers are to grasp ideas correctly.

Structure relates to the organization of the selection, the framework around which the author weaves his ideas, and the order in which he presents them to form a logical whole. Teachers should try to ask questions that will require pupils to answer by using *larger* portions of the text rather than asking many *minute* questions over details. Some of these larger kinds of questions are: What are three events that led up to the seizing of the fort? What results occurred following the capture of the fort? What were five main ideas you obtained from reading this selection?

Knowing main ideas and the details that support them is basic to outlining, and outlining is *one* of the most useful, if not *the* most useful, study skill that a student can possess, whether in elementary or graduate school. Starting the foundation early is important, and once pupils know what is 'main' and what is 'supportive', it is a short step to writing an outline in proper form.

3 *Making a summary* If pupils understand the structure (the main ideas and details in whatever organization these are given), making a summary is easy, for it only requires these ideas to be put into briefer terms, combining several ideas into one, and eliminating details that are not important.

4 *Following directions* Another skill of literal comprehension is following directions. This is important in performing a chemistry experiment, a cut-and-paste exercise for young children, or reading a blueprint, a recipe, or homework assignment for others. When an exercise requires interpretation, the comprehension necessarily goes beyond the literal, but often pupils only need to read and understand literally to be able to accomplish many of their school exercises and assignments.

Interpretation

The second level of comprehension—interpretation—requires the reader to work out ideas not stated, to read between the lines, to fill in the gaps in order to gain the meaning intended by the author—*what the book really means*. The various skills necessary to interpret meaning have been differently defined by reading authorities; seven aspects will be included here.

1 *Sensing the author's purpose* Few authors have told why they wrote a particular work. It may have been to entertain, to convince, to impart information, to experiment with a certain form of composition, to propagandize, to editorialize, to explain, to advertise etc. Unless the purpose is stated directly, in which case only literal comprehension is needed, the reader must infer purpose from what an author may have implied or from the content of the selection itself.

Students learn to make such inferences by finding biographical material about the author that may shed light on his purpose, by inferring purpose from statements he has made, by analyzing the style of his writing, and by reading his other works to find out what views he holds.

2 *Finding causes, reasons, or agents* To find causes, reasons, or agents necessitates connecting unrelated events (or related ones), comparing similar happenings, tracing sequence to find connections, and asking *how* and *why* questions.

3 *Determining the mood or feeling tone of a selection* Hints on mood or tone are found in the level of language used, from the very informal to the ultra formal, and in the style of writing: sentence structure, vocabulary, figures of speech, and cadence or rhythm.

4 *Analyzing characters and their motives* Clues to characters are provided through descriptions about them, their actions, the conversations they have, the events in which they participate, what others say or do not say about them, and through the illustrations. Finding such clues in the story, then comparing the characters with real life characters the reader knows, is one way to anticipate future actions of the character and to evaluate his qualities. When characters are the same age as the pupils, the parallels are often easy to locate. Pupils could make a list of character traits, citing the part in the story that gave them the information or the clue.

Some questions teachers could ask to bring out characterization include: How do you think the main character felt? How do you think the other characters felt about him? How would the selection be different if it were rewritten from a different point of view? How did the character change throughout the story? Why would you like (or not like) to have this character for a friend?

5 *Noting relationships not stated specifically* Selections provide many clues to concepts that are not stated in so many words — ideas about time, character, space, geographical location, setting, dress, tools, and so on, as well as relationships between and among ideas presented in the text, such as that between picture and text, topic and level of language (to denote era or place), tone and vocabulary (tongue-in-cheek or ultra formal), and country and vocabulary (*mesa, tortilla,* and *serape,* for example).

6 *Drawing conclusions and making generalizations* Conclusions are drawn from a series of inductively reasoned ideas, which lead to a statement that is true of the samples. A generalization is made from several conclusions on the same point and is in a larger dimension than one conclusion. A generalization generally holds, which is one reason for its label, and is a truth as stated from the specifics of the conclusions.

Geography and other sciences, social studies and mathematics are easy subjects for finding conclusions and generalizations, and though the terms are often stated in the same breath, they are not synonyms; readers need to learn their differences and how to arrive at each. A simple illustration from social studies will suffice. Actually, this example was constructed by a group of teachers who were trying to simplify the idea for students of age twelve and thirteen. It stated:

There is a battleship called the *New York*, another the *Missouri*, and another the *Iowa*. What conclusion can you draw from these statements? *That some battleships are named after states.*

An aircraft carrier is called the *Lexington*, another the *St Louis*, and another the *Los Angeles*. What conclusion can be drawn? *That some aircraft carriers are named after cities.*

A submarine is called the *Nautilus*, another the *Skate*, another the *Sea Horse*. What conclusion can be drawn from this? *That some submarines are named after sea animals.*

What generalization could be made from these three conclusions? *That there is a pattern for naming ships of the US Navy; that similar ships are named for similar things.*

7 *Speculating between events and beyond data* Figuring out events between chapters of a book or eras in history, or predicting what will happen next in a story are ways this aspect of interpretation can be taught. Students enjoy predicting, and such speculating is useful in reading, for it sets a readiness for what is coming, keeps the reader checking to see if his forecasting is correct, and indicates that he has grasped the mood and significance of the selection. One interesting way to utilize prediction is to obtain some of the space fiction of the 1950s by Arthur Clarke, Isaac Asimov, or Robert Heinlein and let the pupils compare it with the realities of today; or get old news magazines and let students read the predictions given by the commentators, then compare these with the actual events as reported later. Such items as population trends, inflation, scientific advancement, election results and the like make interesting reading when the predictions and the results can be compared.

Evaluation
At the third level of comprehension is evaluating the quality— *how good the book is.* For stories, this entails judging the merit of theme, plot, characters, style and ethic, or the author's purpose, the accuracy, recency, or clarity of science and social studies material. The reader asks first, 'How good is this?', then 'Good for what?', and then 'Is this what I need now?'

Evaluation or critical reading requires judging both good and bad qualities in comparison with a standard which is used as the base. Criteria for judging need to be determined as a class discusses different stories, comparing one against the other and deciding which is best and why. Questions to elicit such information include: What makes this a good story? How consistently real are the characters?

Is the plot logically developed and plausible? How is the style related to the idea and the era? How satisfying is the ending?

Critical questions need to be determined for various types of writing —factual accounts, essays, drama, editorials, and others. Recently, much has been written on critical reading; so material is available.

Reaction

At the fourth level of comprehension is reaction, both emotional and intellectual—*how the book makes one feel.* Elizabeth Peabody, an early American teacher, once said: 'There is no greater illusion than the common idea of the method of learning to read, by pronouncing pages of matter, which is not moving the mind or heart of the reader.'

Reaction may take the form of amusement, laughter, or a subtle, less obvious appreciation; it may evoke tears, storming, and ranting and raving; it may stimulate letters to the editor; it may set forth a barrage of rebuttal. Writing that makes a difference to the reader may have very tangible results—from reading *Consumer's Guide* to teachers' manuals. In fact, some writing is meant only to be useful in its end product; just reading it is insufficient to gain the full import or impact.

Intellectual reaction may also be clothed in appreciation for the style of writing, the beautiful expression, the unique idea, the approach, the pattern, the figures of speech, and so on. Or it may take a critical turn and evaluate.

As a result of the emotional and intellectual reactions, the reader may be led to form opinions on what he will believe from one writer and with whom he will agree or disagree. While the factors in opinion-formation are complex, it is certain that what a person reads does influence his ideas, else why go to school at all?

Integration

At the fifth and highest level of understanding is the reader's ability to integrate his reading into his own background, to assimilate the ideas and put them together with his previous ideas, thus making the reading an integral part of his personality from that time on i.e. *the lasting effect the book has.* The evidence of such assimilation is found in the behaviour of the person, in his performing an act, in his making of explanations, in his recognition of allusions, in his purchasing a product, in his making a blueprint or a dress, in hanging a garage door or playing a game, in arriving at his proper destination or making a chair. The tangible results of reading are evident everywhere; the illiterate finds many avenues closed to him in jobs, recreation and aesthetic enjoyment.

A reader has a chance to expand his interests for himself, if he but has the books. His changed behaviour because of reading may show in other areas as well—in his mental health, his moral conduct, his social poise, his health and safety, in his conversation, and in a more outgoing personality because of the confidence the knowledge of his reading has given him.

One never knows what opportunities may arise for using something one has read, because until the opportunity arises, the thought may never have occurred. With the knowledge comes the recognition of a chance to use the knowledge; thus reading enhances personal living and provides satisfaction. All of this contributes to the reader's background, in conjunction with his environment, his family and other personal contacts, his religious training, and his community experiences. The sum total makes the individual; reading contributes its share but it could make an even greater impact than it often does if a wide range of materials and adequate time to read could be made available.

The teacher's challenge here is to ask the kinds of questions that will relate the material to the students in the classroom; that is not to place themselves imaginatively in the Greek and Roman era, for example, but to see how Greek and Roman civilization impinges on their lives today.

The reader who asks 'What does this mean to me?' is asking the important question. Students today who are seeking relevance are actually admitting that alone they can see no connection but require a teacher's help in relating their reading to contemporary needs.

This is what education in school is about—it must be relevant to out of school activities. As Francis Bacon said: 'Reading maketh the full man; and reading does affect the nature of man's personality and of his behaviour.

Summary
Comprehension is based on the reader having an adequate decoding system. Comprehension includes what the book says (the literal), what the book really means (interpretive), how good the book is (evaluative), how the book makes him feel (reactive), and finally, what the book means to him (integrative). When the reader takes a book for his own he makes it fit and puts it on. So what started out as printed tracks on a page ends up as a moving force for humanity, and contributes to the ultimate meaning an individual may find in his life. This is the goal that teachers are trying to reach; and in so doing they also enhance and enrich their own lives.

14 The subskills of comprehension

Constance M. McCullough

One of the most endearing stories of the Christmas season is that of the little juggler who, penniless, took refuge in a monastery. He alone of all the people there had nothing to offer the Virgin. There in the chapel he watched the monks as they offered their gifts. Then, to their horror, he stood before the statue of the Virgin and gave his only treasure—his skill at juggling. At the end of his juggling act he knelt, and the statue, moved by the quality of his mind and heart, reached out and touched him in blessing.

This story has something to say to the teacher of reading, who is in many senses a juggler too. But this paper will confine itself to the juggling that creates in the child the ability to evoke the author's conception and intent, the juggling that impresses the child with the idea that reading is a search for understanding.

The metamorphosis of a teacher

The teacher can easily become confused by the many tasks a reading programme presents, and the many trends in educational practice which beckon and beguile. He may be enticed from attention to the heart of the reading programme, which is the search for under-standing and the evocation of the author's conception and intent. He begins to think that a different organization will solve all of his problems. Or he becomes convinced that a new material provides the entire answer. Yet all the time there is a job to be done, and that job demands insight.

Over the years the teacher learns that every type of organization has shortcomings and every material has limitations for which the teacher must compensate. So instead of being motivated solely by the prospect of a new organization or new material, he learns to be motivated also by increasing delight in the living act of reading, in the growing power of the child to engage in it, and in the discoveries both child and teacher make about language, thought and reality.

Relativity in decoding

Perhaps the greatest lesson the teacher needs to convey to the child is the relativity which pervades both language and life. Even the decoding of a word is an opportunity to sell this principle. An exchange of two letters is the only difference between the word 'quiet' and the word 'quite'. A person reading *g-o-i-n-g* for the first time could choose to read it as a word of one syllable: /g oi ng/. But the appearance of this word in a sentence like 'I am going to school' leads the experienced English speaker to expect a progressive form of a verb.

The different spellings of 'heir' and 'air' signal the reader to expect someone to open a window when the sentence is 'The air is stuffy' and to effect avoidance if 'the heir is stuffy.'

When a word is spelled *t-e-a-r*, the reader must look to the context to determine whether it is a tear to be shed or a tear that shreds.

If the word is used as a verb instead of a noun, as in 'Don't tear your shirt', the reader learns to turn his thinking from the salt water to the rip.

In these examples the reader is helped by attention to the order of letters within the word (quiet, quite), the variant spellings of the same sounds (heir, air), alternative ways of decoding the same form (going, tear), and the role of the word in the sentence (going, tear).

When the child misreads the word *f-r-i-e-d* as 'friend', relativity may come to his rescue. The context may suggest that the role of the word rules out a noun, as in: 'He ——ed the shrimp in butter.' Or the case may be that the words associated with the word 'fried' are not ordinarily associated with the idea of *friend*, as in: 'He ate ——shrimp.' One sometimes hates one's friends but one seldom eats them.

In the sentence: 'He liked—— shrimp better than boiled', the child who may tolerate the oddity of *friend* shrimp as a combination, may finally gag on the contrast between *friend* and *boiled*.

Notice that in this last example:

1 The child must be used to reading for meaning. If something doesn't make sense, he returns to it to see what is wrong.

2 The child must also be accustomed to signals to contrast: liked —— better than.

3 He must furthermore be skilled in thinking about the contrasts in his experience, and in remembering a contrastive idea to match the one which presents itself to him: 'Liked fried better than what?'

4 He must also know when something is missing from the author's structure, and supply it for himself: 'He liked fried shrimp better than *he liked* boiled *shrimp*' It may be helpful to a reader to think of this arrangement of words: 'He liked fried shrimp better than (he liked) boiled (shrimp).

Relativity in word meaning

These behaviours are necessary to decode the word form and to determine the word meaning. For example, teachers are familiar with

exercises which require the reader to choose the proper meaning for a word of multiple meanings, for example:
'Choose the meaning appropriate to 'band' in the sentence 'The band played several marches.'

1 Something which ties things together
2 A group of musicians
3 A range of wave lengths

The reader must understand the meaning of the word before he can be sure of the meaning of the sentence; yet his conjecture as to the meaning of the sentence helps him converge upon the proper meaning of the word.

The child chooses an answer, and whether he is right or wrong, he has a reason for his choice which should be discussed. Here are some possibilities:

1 Did he know all the things that 'band' could mean, or did he just pick a number?
2 Did he know how to decode the word form, or did he misread the word as, say, 'hand'? Did he then flounder among the unsuitable choices?
3 Did he read 'band' as 'hand' and decide, regardless of the sense of the sentence, that a hand can tie things together?
4 Was the reader helped by the fact that the sentence states that something acted upon something else? Did he sense, even if not analytically, that a range of wave lengths doesn't play marches; that one might expect a sentence starting with a range of wave lengths to tell where it is or what it is, or what is done in relation to it? In other words, was the reader able to eliminate the third meaning because of his knowledge of several meanings of 'band' and the sentence structures commonly expected in relation to those meanings?

Relativity in larger units of composition
In units of composition larger than a single sentence relativity is more complicated. Take as an example the following sentences which might initiate a paragraph: 'Mars is the fourth planet from the sun. It travels in an elliptical path through space around that small star.'

Knowing the book or chapter from which these sentences are taken would help the reader with the meanings of some of the words. For instance, Mars is the name of a chocolate bar in the United States, as well as a god of war and a planet in our solar system. If the book is on astronomy, the chocolate bar can be ruled out. The god of war is eliminated because he is not a planet.

In order to understand these sentences and their relationships to each other, the reader must know what a *planet* is and is not, what a *sun* is and is not, what is meant by *space and path*, what is meant by *elliptical*, and what is meant by *small* in relation to the concept of a *star* (a big house is smaller than a small star). He must know that *the* sun is a particular sun.

He is in danger of misinterpreting the sentence unless he chooses a special meaning of 'from' or realizes that the author has shortened a longer expression: 'Mars is the planet which is fourth in order from the sun.

If the reader knows that a planet cannot be a sun and a sun is a star, then he gathers that 'it' in the second sentence refers to Mars rather than to the sun.

He knows that a path through space is not a path made of substance but is a course or direction.

The good reader knows that the first sentence tells what something is, and the second tells what it does. The form noun-linking verb-noun is a common form for a statement which names or classifies. 'Fourth from the sun' describes the order or position of the concept Mars. The second sentence describes where Mars travels, by what course it travels, and the relationship in which that course is taken.

Relativity in expectation
How can the reader anticipate what the author is going to do next? He can expect something only if he can remember what the author has expressed and the order in which he has expressed it. If the author has told what something is and one thing that it does, what else might he say? If he sticks to his subject after two sentences dealing with Mars, what else might he say?

Here the reader's awareness of all the kinds of things which can be known about a concept helps him to guess. What other qualities, behaviours, does it have? What are the relationships between these qualities or behaviours and the rest of the world? What theories, principles, laws, generalizations, are possible or known in relation to the concept? How can these theories be applied? What illustrations can be offered as proof of their truth? What language is associated with the concept? The reader doesn't sit there thinking all of these things, but he does draw upon his knowledge of them in establishing his expectations.

Actually so far the author of the two sentences has presented only one main idea: that Mars is the fourth planet from the sun. The second sentence simply expands the meaning of planet.

One expectation could be that the next sentence will continue to deal with the concept planet. Another could be that it will add individual characteristics of Mars, such as its colour, which make it easily distinguishable in the night sky.

If, however, the next sentence deals with the position of Venus, the paragraph can conceivably end with a statement that the earth has these two planets as its nearest travelling companions. In that case, the reader must adjust to the idea that the purpose of the paragraph was not to feature Mars but to place the earth within a system.

Where will the next paragraph go, and the next after that? The author is the architect; the reader studies the architecture and anticipates it. Divergent thinking about possible directions the author may take is a valuable experience for a group of children.

Relativity in the reading programme

If one purpose of education is to make children become readers, current reading programmes may be considered successful to varying degrees. Many children read, enjoy reading, and read widely. But if the purpose of education is to make the most of children's potential, if it is to make children better readers than their parents or their teachers, then the success of current programmes is more in doubt.

The subskills of comprehension, about which little enough is known, must be explored by teachers and pupils alike, not only in reading on a casual basis, but directly in intensive individual and group study. As the teacher himself studies the demands that the written language makes upon the reader, he will have more to juggle in his development of subskills of comprehension. The logical barriers between vocabulary and comprehension, reading and grammar, reading and writing, form and meaning, reading and thinking, language and life, will fall away. By crossing these rigid boundaries, the teacher and pupils together will see the miracle of the living language, a network of interactions which make comprehension possible. Together they will evolve a realization of the dynamic quality of their own roles in relation to that print. Even from prereading years, the child should be trained to be more than an inchworm.

What has all of this to do with the Christmas story of the little juggler? Teaching is more than the fulfilment of rituals. It is more than going through the approved motions and expecting a miracle. The true teacher evokes the miracle through his own study and art and skill, and faith in the human potential. Because both the teacher and the child are at work at the frontiers of understanding—neither of them an ultimate authority but both reflecting a phenomenal human invention—they develop and enjoy a mutually motivating and enlightening relationship.

Bibliography

DEIGHTON, L. C. (1967) The flow of thought through an English sentence in *Vistas in Reading* Newark, Delaware: International Reading Association, 322–326

GOODMAN, K. S. (1968) *The Psycholinguistic Nature of the Reading Process* Detroit, Michigan: Wayne State University Press

HANNA, P. *et al* (1971) *Spelling; Structure and Strategies* Boston, Massachusetts: Houghton, Mifflin

HODGES, R. E. and RUDORF, E. H. *Language and Learning to Read* Boston, Massachusetts: Houghton, Mifflin

McCULLOUGH, C. M. (1967) Linguistics psychology, and the teaching of reading in *Elementary English* 44, 353–362

SMITH, F. (1971) *Understanding Reading* New York: Holt, Rinehart and Winston

STRANG, R. M. (1970) *Learning to Read—Insights for Educators* Toronto: Ontario Institute for Studies in Education

TINKER, M. A. and McCULLOUGH, C. M. (1968) *Teaching Elementary Reading* (chapters 3 and 13) New York: Appleton, Century, Crofts

15 Reading comprehension: reading or comprehension?

Miriam Balmuth

Introduction

Until a short while ago, the major question in the field of reading was which was the best method to use for beginning reading instruction. Although this question has not been fully answered, for some reason (perhaps exhaustion from enormous expenditure in pursuit of it!) we have become more relaxed about it. The general feeling seems to be that even if one clear-cut 'best method' is not completely at hand, we can put together some quite adequate instructional procedures for beginning reading. We are also rather relaxed about our goals in beginning reading. For the most part, they include the acquisition of a sight recognition vocabulary and the ability to use phonic and context clues in independent word attack.

At this time, particularly from the point of view of the classroom teacher, we are all freer to seek out new questions, turning perhaps to the next major problem (one that is vital and relatively uncharted) — the comprehension of written material. For no matter what method was used for beginning reading instruction, and no matter how long or short a period of time was considered sufficient for the achievement of adequate word attack skills and a wide sight recognition vocabulary, for every reader, there is a point at which attention must be given to his understanding of reading matter: how to evaluate it and how to extend it.

Evaluating reading comprehension

This area is still relatively unfamiliar. Reading comprehension is an abstract process which takes place without any visible signs. In fact, it may seem to be occurring when the reader gazes at the text — even moves his eyes, lips, head — and yet it may not be taking place at all.

I am reminded of a story told by a colleague who was the father of a four month old son. Since the father was a reading specialist, he was often asked by acquaintances whether his son could read yet to which the father always replied: 'Of course he can — silently.'

It is this silence that makes reading comprehension so difficult to measure. The most frequent method used to evaluate reading comprehension is to question the reader. However, constructing questions to determine whether a selection has been comprehended is extremely difficult, since many ramifications and implications are present in selections of any level of depth. Also, even though test questions may be pertinent and carefully constructed, they are usually developed in an objective format. This means that they are limited in the amount of comprehension information that can be elicited; also correct answers may be the result of guessing.

Orally presented questions, such as those asked during the course of a discussion about a selection, may be more open-ended and permit more exploration of what the reader understood, but they are highly subjective and are themselves limited by the teacher's ability to elicit and evaluate responses objectively.

Similarly, even where methods other than questions are used to evaluate reading comprehension, such as the cloze technique or asking the reader for spontaneous recall of the contents of a selection, there are definite limitations in our ability to encompass all possible aspects of a full comprehension.

Factors involved in reading comprehension
We are left, then, with the problem of a process which we know exists and with which we must deal seriously, but which we can only measure imperfectly, or for that matter, cannot even isolate. For another characteristic of reading comprehension is its tendency to be greatly affected by many factors which are themselves complex and difficult to sort out. In any attempt at clarifying and understanding reading comprehension, these other factors must first be identified and their impact noted.

Let us try to do this by thinking of a teacher setting out to determine the reading comprehension ability of a group of children. In the great majority of situations, he will ask the children to read one or more selections and then to answer questions about each selection. If the questions are answered correctly, it will be assumed that the children have good comprehension of what they have read. If the children answer incorrectly, it will be assumed that they have poor comprehension of what they have read. In many instances, particularly when the selections are part of a standardized silent reading achievement test, the evaluation of the children's comprehension of the given selections will be extended and considered an evaluation of their general reading comprehension ability rather than just of their comprehension of the given selections.

Let us think of what generally occurs in such a situation and consider the circumstances which may have resulted in a child's not answering the questions correctly. The following are among those that might be listed (in no particular order of importance, since any of these circumstances may have been in operation for any given child):

1 The questions were ambiguous, poorly worded, or different in format from those he had been given in the past.
2 His visual acuity was too poor for him to see the material clearly.
3 A number of words in the selection were not in the child's sight recognition vocabulary, and his word attack skills were insufficient to enable him to decode them.
4 The style of writing was different from the styles used in the reading material to which he was accustomed.
5 His reading pace was so slow that he found it difficult to keep the entire selection in mind as he read.
6 It was close to lunchtime and he was hungry (or tired or emotionally upset or ill) and he could not keep his mind on what he was reading.
7 The room was noisy (or hot or cold or stuffy) and he could not keep his mind on what he was reading.
8 The subject dealt with in the selection was so unfamiliar to him that he did not have enough background knowledge to understand many of the implications of the material.
9 The subject matter was so uninteresting or perhaps even repellent to him that he did not concentrate enough to follow the text.
10 Although he could decode all the words in the text, he did not know the meanings of many of them and so could not follow the meaning of the entire selection.
11 Although he could decode and understand the individual words in the text, he had not had enough experience in reading connected texts to know how to function with a selection of the given length.
12 His intellectual capacity, as measured by intelligence tests, was too limited to deal with the abstract processing required.

The list includes factors that are very common and not at all confined to young children. Any of them may be operating at any time that anyone reads anything. In addition, more than one of these factors is frequently present during the reading of a single selection.

The question now arises of what happens when none of these negative factors is present. Does comprehension of reading material automatically follow as an end product of decoding under ideal circumstances? Or is there indeed a specific skill or process that exists, and if so, what is its nature?

Past efforts to determine the nature of reading comprehension
In seeking an answer to this question, one might look to the literature in the field of reading. Over the years, there have been many efforts to give suggestions and set up curricula concerned with reading comprehension. But the classroom teacher who is concerned with planning a reading programme which will develop children's skill in reading

H

comprehension is faced with a morass of terms, lists of skills, and categories of conceptual levels which may overlap or vary considerably from author to author. What makes the task of setting up a realistic programme most difficult for a teacher is the lack of any clearly conceived theoretical framework for the skills and activities that are suggested. Since our understanding of the nature of reading comprehension is vague and cluttered, our instructional methods are not rooted in any clearly defined goals.

One of the reasons for the relaxation concerning beginning reading which was mentioned earlier in this paper may be that a series of efforts to compare different theories and approaches in various combinations has been strongly made and widely disseminated. Even if no one final answer was found, much greater insight into the factors involved in beginning reading resulted. We are now better equipped to examine various approaches, to gain a fairly clear idea of what each attempts to do, and to determine how each compares with others.

No such work has been done on reading comprehension; perhaps because such an approach is much more difficult in this area. Diverse models have been presented at various times. Cleland, in 1969, compiled a simple listing of seven such models. Simons, in 1971, compiled a different list of seven models. However, these models have not been compared in any organized investigation. In fact, the implications of each individual model have barely been explored.

One striking feature (and probably one that is responsible for much of our difficulty) was noted in almost all the writings about reading comprehension: in hardly any of the myriad discussions of reading comprehension in books and articles written, from Huey in 1908 to the present, is there any statement made concerning reading comprehension which would not be equally applicable to comprehension of oral language or, in many instances, to the most general kind of thinking. So much effort seems to have been expended in considering the language and thinking aspects of reading comprehension that the simple fact that written language is characteristically different from spoken language has usually been overlooked, and these characteristic differences have rarely been taken into account when reading comprehension as a whole has been considered. An examination of any of the lengthy and repetitive lists of skills designed for teaching reading comprehension will reveal this congruence of thought about reading comprehension and spoken language comprehension.

Characteristics of reading comprehension
Now that some of the difficulties and confusions regarding reading comprehension have been touched upon, let us proceed to examine how it functions, and then compare it with spoken language comprehension.

Before doing this, however, it would be helpful to consider two concepts which are perhaps not familiar and which may prove to be valuable. The first one is that of 'redundancy' which, when applied to communication, refers to the repetition of the same idea in a given body of information. The greater the redundancy, the easier it is to understand what is being communicated. Thus in spoken language, a nod accompanying the spoken word 'yes', or the statement, in either written or spoken language, 'Yes, and I always will', are both examples of redundancy.

The second concept involves two terms: 'attention' and 'concentration'. Attention refers to the state in which one is freely open to experiences or stimuli, but does not attempt to focus on them in order to reorganize them in the light of one's interests or needs. Concentration refers to the conscious focusing on experiences or stimuli in order to reorganize the incoming information. Thus, when a symphony is being played, one may be aware that it is playing, may even hum along, but not follow the themes or decide which instruments are being used. Similarly in reading we have all experienced the phenomenon of reading either silently or aloud with appropriate phrasing and even with eloquent expression, but with no conscious idea of the meaning of what we were reading, since we were paying attention, not concentrating.

Now let us consider the task confronting any reader who is faced with a reading selection that he has never seen before. In such a situation, he must focus on the flat, longitudinally-presented material before him and decode it in the same rigid sequence in which it has been set down. As the decoded information unwinds, the reader must concentrate intensely in order to organize the information he receives into a mental structure that is meaningful to him in the light of the information and concepts he has accumulated during his lifetime. Then, continuously concentrating intensely, he must continuously reorganize the structure he has built while he continuously receives new information as he goes on reading. For a beginning reader who is still struggling with decoding, this must indeed be strenuous.

Comparison between written and spoken language comprehension

Obviously the processes involved in comprehending written and spoken language are very similar. Spoken language must also be decoded in the sequence in which it is presented and spoken language also requires continuous reorganization for its comprehension. However, the reading comprehension task must be accomplished without any of the clues of pitch, tone, or phrasing which exist in spoken language communication and to which the beginning reader has become accustomed in his prereading communications. Face to face spoken communication, which occurs most frequently, offers the additional advantages of ideas communicated by facial expressions and bodily gestures. The redundancy of such nonverbal information is not only helpful in itself, but for the beginning reader, their unaccustomed absence must make the unadorned words before him seem very stark. Parenthetically, since the concept of redundancy applies to written as well as to nonwritten information, the practice of having a good deal of repetition in beginning reading books is not only helpful for the establishment of a sight recognition vocabulary (which was the aim in providing it) but it is also helpful for providing a verbal redundancy which beginning readers can learn to use for reading comprehension at an early stage in their development.

Another factor which may operate in spoken language, which aids in its comprehension, and which is not present in written language, is the simultaneous presence of the speaker and the person spoken to. It enables the speaker to receive various clues concerning the effectiveness of his communication and can modify what he says in a way that the author of a book cannot. The written material remains static, and the reader can receive no clarification beyond that which has been set down.

One further difference between the kinds of language communication, and one which is at least as important as those already mentioned, is the type of language used in each. Far too often we hear the statement: 'Reading is talk written down.' From this it might be inferred that one needs only to decode the words and make some sort of superficial transfer of the comprehension process to reading and the task will be essentially the same. In fact, from a purely verbal point of view and excluding the nonverbal factors mentioned above, reading is very rarely 'talk written down.' A true transfer from speech to writing is indeed so difficult that one of the most taxing of literary tasks is to write plausible dialogue. For not only does each of us have a different vocabulary of individual words that we use for speaking and for writing, but the kinds of sentences we use in each situation are different. For example, much talk is in the form of phrases, rather than full sentences. The subject matter is often very different from the fictional or informative type that we find in written material. Finally, most talk takes the form of conversation, with more than one participant, rather than the one-sided kind of communication inherent in written material.

From this discussion, all the advantages appear to be on the side of spoken language. Fortunately, however, there are a number of very real advantages to be found in the written format. First and foremost there is the advantage for which written language was invented in the first place i.e. it characteristically stays in one place and can be read and reread in a way that ephemeral spoken language cannot. This stability supplies a form of redundancy which can be extremely useful as an aid to comprehension, since it provides infinite opportunity to ascertain and review the contents of the text.

Another unique feature of reading comprehension is the use of various kinds of punctuation, type, and format to convey information. These nonverbal, purely visual clues supply not only some of the same sort of information that is given by the phrasing, tone, and pitch of spoken language, but in certain instances provide information that is not conveyed orally. Thus, over and above the use of full stops, commas, question marks, and other punctuation which can duplicate the nonverbal information of speech, written language may utilize italics, paragraphs, capitalization of proper nouns, boldface type, question marks or exclamation points within parentheses, and other clues which do not have counterparts in oral form.

A similar comparison may be made that highlights the even greater number of differences between reading comprehension and the comprehension of information which is communicated in nonverbal formats.

Conclusion

The answer then to the question posed in the title of this paper—'Reading comprehension: reading or comprehension?' is that neither the term 'reading' alone nor the term 'comprehension' alone conveys sufficiently the nature of the process that is involved. Because of the type of reorganization of information that is required, comprehension does not automatically follow as an end product of the attentiveness required by decoding, even under ideal circumstances, and so is not simply 'reading'. But this reorganization must occur under the specific conditions imposed by the characteristics of a written format, which makes the process different from the kinds of comprehension that result from a reorganization of information obtained through other formats. It should not then be thought of as simply 'comprehension'.

So we conclude that since we are dealing with a unique process, one which requires a special kind of intense concentration on a completely visual, rigidly sequential, two-dimensional graphic language, we ought to refer to it in a specific way to help keep these characteristics in mind. The term 'reading comprehension' seems adequate for this purpose.

Implications for teachers

Much more remains to be discovered about reading comprehension, particularly instruction in so-called comprehension skills, so at this time it seems wisest to put most of our energy into those aspects about which we now have some conception. We can then set up certain guidelines when planning instructional programmes.

First of all, since we are aware of the newness of the task for our beginning readers, let us provide ample opportunity for silent reading of even the simplest sentences, in order to accustom the children to this new form of communication in stages of increasing difficulty. Such opportunity with appropriate material, should continue throughout the school years.

Secondly, since we know how lack of competence in decoding words may hamper reading comprehension, let us do two things: provide material for reading comprehension practice that does not present decoding difficulties for the individual reader, and provide opportunity for the acquisition of decoding skills with the oral reading that is necessary for ascertaining the current level of decoding competence.

Thirdly, since we know that there are visual clues unique to written matter which convey very specific information, we should provide opportunity for the children to become familiar with each of these clues and its function.

Fourth, since we are aware of the intense kind of concentration that is required for reading comprehension during silent reading periods we should provide an atmosphere as free as possible from the distracting internal and external factors that were noted earlier.

Fifth, since we are aware that there is wide variation in the styles that exist in written matter and that familiarity with them helps reading comprehension, let us try to encourage and facilitate the reading of as wide a variety of reading matter as possible. Reading aloud to children from a range of sources might be an additional aid in developing this type of familiarity.

Sixth, and last, since we are aware that much is still unknown about reading comprehension, let us remain alert to ideas and new findings that will emerge, hopefully in the near future, and enable us to be even more effective in our work.

References

CLELAND, D. L. (1969) Do we apply what we know about comprehension? (Pro-Challenger) in Banton Smith, N. (ed.). *Current Issues in Reading* Newark, Delaware: International Reading Association

HUEY, E. B. (1908) *The Psychology and Pedagogy of Reading* New York: Macmillan

SIMONS, H. D. (1971) Reading comprehension: the need for a new perspective in *Reading Research Quarterly*, 6, 3, 338–363

16 Research and practice in improving listening

Dorothy Kendall Bracken

Introduction

During the past seventy years educators have spent a great deal of time and effort on improving reading skills—not so with listening skills. In fact, not until after 1940 did researchers do much about investigating listening as an essential part of the language arts matrix —equally as important as reading, speaking and writing. All this time it was estimated that pupils spend one-half to two-thirds of their school day in listening; and adults probably listen three times as much as they read!

In the 1950s tests of listening ability were devised, such as the *Listening Comprehension Test* (Brown and Carlsen 1955) for high school students, and the Reading Capacity Test (Durrell and Sullivan 1945) a test based on listening, for elementary school children. (The 1969 revised edition is called the *Listening-Reading Tests*). Also, during the 1950s Nichols and Stevens (1957) wrote one of the first books devoted to listening *Are You Listening?* These two educators declared: 'Incredible as it may seem when we think about it, this book, to our knowledge, is the first close analysis ever made of the oldest, the most used, and the most important element of interpersonal communication —listening.' It was during this decade, too that David Russell produced *Listening Aids Through the Grades: One Hundred and Ninety Listening Activities*.

Research studies reporting the relation of listening skills to reading skills

Perhaps the major contributions of the 1950s and the 1960s were the reports from research projects and doctoral dissertations. Various phases of listening were chosen for investigation: Don Brown investigated 'auding as the primary language ability'; Ware Marsden chose 'A study for the value of training in listening achievement in reading'; Walter F. Stomer reported 'an investigation into some of the relations between reading, listening, and intelligence'; and Edward Pratt wrote on 'The experimental evaluation of a program for the improvement of listening'.

In the winter 1970 issue of the *Reading Research Quarterly*, Sam Duker's article, 'Listening bibliography', contained the following annotation: 'Gives brief annotations of 1,332 references concerning listening.' It is obvious that there is no lack of interest in improving listening skills or carrying on research related to listening and all of its complex facets.

From the research by Kelty (1953), Lewis (1951), Lubershane (1962), and Hollingsworth (1967), there has emerged a significant idea: when we improve certain skills in listening, those same skills improve in reading.

Kelty was interested in the effect that training in listening for certain purposes had upon the ability of fourth graders *to read for those same purposes*. The purposes she selected were:

1 deciding upon the main idea of a selection
2 deciding upon the supporting details given in a selection
3 drawing a conclusion.

The experimental group was given thirty fifteen-minute lessons in listening for thirty days. The control group received no instruction in listening. Kelty concluded that practice in listening for certain purposes favourably affects the ability of fourth-grade pupils to read for those same purposes.

Lewis carried on a study with elementary grade pupils in order to determine the effect of training in listening to get the general significance of a passage, to note details presented on a topic by a passage, and to predict the outcomes from a passage. Three hundred and fifty-seven intermediate pupils in twelve classrooms were used in a programme of training in listening, consisting of thirty lessons of approximately fifteen minutes each. One lesson was given each day for six weeks, the teachers reading the selections to the pupils. Each lesson included a listening exercise for each of the three purposes stated above. Lewis concluded that training in listening for the three purposes seemed to have a significant effect upon the ability of intermediate grade pupils to read for those same purposes.

Lubershane chose to study the problem of whether instruction in listening improves reading ability. His study included fifth graders, thirty-five pupils in the experimental group and thirty-seven in the control. No listening exercises were given to the control group. The Metropolitan Reading Test was administered before and after training. The experimental group was given auditory training exercises designed to improve written responses to oral commands. He concluded with a statement that auditory training may prove of value in reading programmes, although no definite statistical proof of the value of these exercises in improving reading ability was found. The generally greater growth in reading ability in the experimental group suggested strongly that the auditory exercises had a positive effect on reading growth.

In summarizing several research reports in which the effects of listening have a direct relation to progress in reading, Hollingsworth (1967) concluded: 'Many of these research reports show that *through improvement of listening abilities reading can be improved*. Listening *does* have a positive effect on reading achievement.'

Would it not then seem appropriate to teach skills first through listening and secondly by reading? Have we been remiss in not using a listening-reading method in the improvement of reading instruction?

Orr *et al* (1965) propose that educators use compressed speech (see last section of this paper) as a research tool to explain the knowledge of the relationship of listening and reading.

The study of interaction between reading and listening, as a communication phenomenon, can now begin to be studied through the use of compressed speech as a research tool. For example, let's suppose that we take a group of average students and give them intensive training in rapid reading: does it do anything to their listening comprehension? Before we couldn't ask that question, now we can. Or turn the problem around; a group of students, give them intensive training in listening comprehension, as a function of listening rate: does that change the characteristics of their reading behaviour? Again, this is a question we couldn't ask before and I think it's a fascinating question. Such studies may enable us to attack this whole problem of central processing and the similarity, if not the identity, of the listening comprehension process and the reading comprehension process.

Difficulty of the listening skills
Perhaps educators are just now beginning to recognize the difficulty of the listening act. Friedman (Cramer 1969) says:

If we accept that both the stimulus parameters and the task requirements determine some of the listening behaviours, then we may ask what is listening proficiency? Listening behaviours consist of rejecting as well as processing certain portions of the speech. I'll venture a private definition and say that selecting appropriate portions and/or aspects of the stimulus is one activity that is necessary. You must attend to the right things in that stimulus. It is necessary for the listener to filter out the portions that he doesn't want, and select the ones that he does. Then he must select appropriate listening behaviours for the task requirements. He has, in some way, to connect the internal work that he is going to do with stimulus, to the parts of the stimulus that he has accepted. Then of course, what he does, he must do with accuracy and with required speed.

Others (Cramer 1969) have tried to define the

... tasks that confront the listener, who is essentially reading by listening. Possibly we can compare reading by listening to obtaining information from the print-page-display. The person who processes the print-page-display . . . has considerable control over the amount of information that he can retrieve. . . . He can vary the rate at which he processes the display. He can take advantage of the redundancy in the display. He can look ahead . . . his reading rate is continuously varying in accordance with the momentary demands placed upon him as he processes . . . it is a spacial display. On the other hand, the person who reads by listening is not able to do this. The listener has direct access only to the information specified by the acoustical energy that is present at a given instant. He does, of course, have some access to remembered listening experiences . . . but . . . the listener cannot vary the rate at which he processes . . . he cannot listen ahead and he cannot listen back. . . .

Again Orr (Cramer 1969) in explaining the psychological nature of listening commented:

What the individual is doing when he is comprehending a message, whether it is a listening message or a reading message, is associating the concepts that are coming in through the sensors to a pre-existent cognitive structure. . . . There are obvious differences in reading and listening, but I would like to propose that these are similar processes in respect to cognitive integration. . . . The activity we are talking about is the mental effort associated with attempting to place incoming concepts in the context of one's existing cognitive structure.

Sterritt, Martin, and Rudnick (1969) contrast the difficulty of listening and hearing:

Vision and hearing differ from each other in a number of ways, one of which is that vision gives us a great deal of information about precisely how things are laid out from left to right, up and down etc—how things are arranged in *space*. Hearing, on the other hand, gives us only a crude picture of spatial arrangements, but is organized instead as a sequence of events strung out in *time*. Therefore, when we talk about auditory-visual integration, we are usually also referring to *temporal-spatial* integration, the ability to integrate information that is arranged as a string of events in *time with information given as an arrangement in space*.

Lundsteen (1969) says:

When the mode of reception of the verbal data with which to think critically is purely auditory, there are more difficulties than when reception is by reading. Reading imposes a helpful constraint of a relatively permanent medium.

Basic and cognitive listening skills

If we assume that the listener has no auditory defect, we can consider oral input as being one of two types: fundamentally basic or characteristically cognitive. The basic, or primary, requirements of auditory acquisition are: discriminating, focusing (or attending), tracking, remembering, sequencing. The operation of the higher processes of cognitive listening skills is based on these skills.

First, discriminating. Teachers are perhaps more familiar with the basic listening skill of discriminating than with the others. They give practice in auditory discrimination in relation to the teaching of reading. Every teacher needs to screen each individual in his class for auditory discrimination skills at the beginning of each school year if he is to know who can profit most from help in phonetic analysis as a word attack skill. Perhaps the teacher uses an auditory discrimination test, such as the subtest in the Gates-McKillop Diagnostic Reading Test (1962) or the Wepman Auditory Discrimination Test (1958). A test which the teacher can use at the secondary level can be found in a new listening skills programme, *The Listening Progress Laboratory* (Bracken, Bridges and Kinder 1970). These auditory discrimination tests, plus the tests (for elementary pupils) in the *Listening Skills Program* (Bracken, Hayes and Bridges 1969) will help the teacher to identify those pupils who need practice in this basic skill.

Second, focusing, or attending. The efficient listener has the ability to focus or attend. He focuses on the speaker's ideas and attends only to the speaker. He is skilful in 'tuning in' the spoken word and 'tuning out' extraneous sounds.

Third, tracking. Can the listener effectively receive a message when there are competing messages? While some listeners may be able to discriminate and 'tune out' environmental noises, they may not be able to hear two-voiced messages and successfully track, or follow, one of them. How skilful is a listener using a telephone when he must listen to the voice at the other end of the line while someone is speaking beside him? Tracking, used in this sense, is a difficult basic skill.

Fourth, remembering. Many educators consider listening the most *difficult* of all the language arts. As noted, one of the reasons for this is the demand for interpreting temporal order. Output by a speaker and the resultant input by the listener is time-oriented; the success of the listener depends not only on discriminating, focusing and tracking, but also on auditory memory, and sequencing. Remembering and sequencing are more difficult in listening than in reading, for there are no visual 'props', no replay, no rereading, no comparisons. In reporting on the results of the PACE Project in Alameda County, Wilkin (1969) writes: 'Words and sentences are made up of a series of sounds presented in a temporal order, and this order is a major dimension of language.'

In contrast to the basic skills of listening, there are *cognitive listening skills*. Some classroom teachers give students help in the cognitive listening skills by structuring many normal classroom listening situations. One opportunity for such an activity is when the teacher reads stories and poems to the class. By setting a purpose for the pupils, she can help them improve their listening for directions, for the main idea, for details, for cause and effect, for fact and opinion, or for any of the enjoyable purposes of creative listening. One of the most important of all cognitive listening skills is critical listening. In the *New England Reading Association Journal*, Devine (1969) summarized the results of several studies in critical listening:

> Certain implications may be drawn from the studies described here. First, it seems clear that critical listening can be taught to pupils in grades five to nine. (*Huck and others have proved that critical thinking can be taught at all levels, including primary.*) Second the data indicates that it can be taught with equal effectiveness to pupils who score low on standardized intelligence tests and to those who score high. Finally, teachers working with the materials note that many of the skills in critical listening are so closely related to skills in critical reading, that they can be taught together, thus effecting some economy in teaching time and effort.

Practice exercises, either commercially produced or made by the teacher, can also be used to increase proficiency in the various basic and cognitive listening skills. If recordings for practice are purchased, the suggestions in the teacher's guide usually offer many additional ideas for extended activities in listening throughout the day. Likewise, language texts and curriculum guides offer invaluable suggestions to the teacher.

Compressed speech

During the past few years, researchers have given attention to compressed speech, sometimes known as 'speed speech'. Compressed speech is speech in which the recording of words per minute is increased without changing the pitch or tone of the speaking voice. Distortion-free speech at increased rates of from ten to fifty per cent can now be offered to the listener.

Since one of the crucial problems facing educators today is to find better ways of communicating information rapidly and reliably, speeded speech training is desirable for all students. The knowledge explosion has forced the use of new and better ways of saving valuable time without sacrificing proficiency in comprehension and retention.

Implications for practical classroom use of compressed, or speeded speech, have been suggested by Orr, Friedman, and Williams (1965). These include:

1 the improvement of *normal* speed presentations
2 encouragement of long range retention of material because of the close attention demanded while listening to compressed speech
3 an excellent means of reviewing previously presented material.

Another very practical application of speeded speech is its use in building readiness or giving an overview to material to be listened to and studied in greater detail at a later time. Such an activity might be likened to the s in the sq3r formula, which suggests that *in reading* the first step in a good study procedure is to survey or overview the material. With these psychological and practical implications, opportunities to practise and master the skill of listening effectively to speeded speech are long overdue in the classroom.

The idea of compressed speech is not new. In the 1940s educators, psychologists, and researchers began serious consideration of the desirability and practicality of training listeners to receive oral messages when speech was produced faster than 130 to 170 words per minute (the approximate range of normal speaking rates). At that time, the problem was to produce speech which was faster than 170 words per minute without distortion. In the 1950s ways were discovered to accomplish this goal.

Invented by Mark Springer, the Mark II, manufactured by Automation GmbH in Heidelberg, West Germany, is a speech rate-deviation device distributed in the United States by Infotronic Systems. Speech may be compressed or expanded by first recording the speaker on a normal tape recorder operating at 15 inches per second. The tape is then threaded through the Mark II, and the Mark II's output is connected to both the input of any ordinary tape recorder and an amplifier-speaker combination for listening. (This may be a part of the tape recorder being used). A simple turn of a knob and the original tape is running through the Mark II. Another knob calibrated in percentage of original time changes the tape's linear speed over a wide range and with it the reproduction speed of the recording.

What is the ultimate *aim* of speech compression? Most experts in the field agree that it would be desirable to produce a speech compression device at a price which will make it possible to equip entire classrooms as well as study carrels with individual units for each student. This would permit the student to set his own pace and learn at his maximum speed capability, while allowing him to slow down for sections which he finds difficult, and to speed up for material which he finds easy.

Faulke (1969) has said:

Ideally, we would like to think of a system in which the listener had direct control: that is, in which he could adjust presentation rate in accordance with his continuously changing demands. Unfortunately, at the present time, this is not really practical because such compression equipment would be too expensive, but this may not ultimately be the case.

In 1968 at the National Reading Conference, a symposium was held on the topic 'rate controlled speech and listening comprehension'. It was there that Cramer (1969) spoke of hearing some compressed samples from Grant Fairbank's device at the University of Illinois and of his reaction to it:

I was particularly impressed with the rapidity with which I could come to understand speech at rapid rates. When I first heard a passage at two and a half times the normal rate, it was like viewing a passage on a reading machine that was going a little faster than I could read: you can see things going by, sort of, and you can get a little bit here and a little bit there, but you really can't make sense of it. But all of a sudden, by the time I had listened to compressed speech only two or three times, it was perfectly clear; I could understand everything. It didn't take much time to learn to understand the distortions that take place when you drop out bits of speech.

And, now, reports on two training programmes. Parker (1970) has reported on an experiment using 429 junior college students who were divided into three levels of aptitudes: high, average, and low.

Six groups heard listening selections that differed from group to group in rate of compression and/or mode of presentation. Two groups heard the selections at normal speaking rate, two at one-third compression, and two at one-half compression. For each speaking rate, there were two modes of presentation—an aural-only mode and an audio-ocular mode that included simultaneous presentation of the printed page to match the aural messages.

The simultaneous presentation of the printed page resulted in significantly better comprehension for all aptitude levels hearing compressed speech, but was not significantly superior for the high and low aptitude levels hearing the selections at the normal speaking rate. There was no significant decline in comprehension for each of the aptitude levels when normal speech was compressed one-third. One-third compression was significantly better than one-half compression for each aptitude level utilizing the aural-only mode, but there was no significant difference in comprehension scores at the same degrees of comprehension when the audio-ocular mode was utilized. One exception was the low aptitude group.

A second report deals with thirty-two male college students.

The purpose of the study was to determine whether training with the use of distortion-free, time-compressed speech could increase human capacity to receive spoken language without significant loss of comprehension. Male college students... received systematic practice in listening to progressively increased rates of speech from 325 to 475 words per minute. Results indicated that increases up to double normal rate produced no significant loss in comprehension for experimental students; statistically significant differences between the performance of the experimental and control groups at higher rates indicated comprehension of rapid speech to be a trainable phenomenon. The data also suggested that listening to speeded speech may have a beneficial effect on reading skill.

Summary
This paper has made the full swing from the relation of listening to reading, an explanation of the difficulty of listening, classification of both basic and cognitive listening skills, consideration of compressed speech, and finally back to not only the beneficial effects of special training for improved listening, but also the gains in reading to be expected as the result of teaching listening skills.

References
BRACKEN, D. K., HAYS, J. D., and BRIDGES, C. J. (1969) *Listening Skills Program—Intermediate Level Teacher's Guide* Tulsa, Oklahoma: International Teaching Tapes

BRACKEN, D. K., BRIDGES, C. J. and KINDER, R. (1970) *The Listening Progress Laboratory* Palo Alto, California: Educational Development Corporation

BROWN, J. I. and CARLSEN, R. G. (1955) *Listening Comprehension Test* New York: Harcourt, Brace and World

CRAMER, L. *et al* (1969) Symposium on rate controlled speech and listening comprehension in *National Reading Conference Yearbook*

DEVINE, T. (1969) *New England Reading Association Journal* Winter, 4

DURRELL, D. and SULLIVAN, H. (1945) *Durrell-Sullivan Reading Capacity Test and Achievement Test* Columbus, Ohio: World Book

FAULKE, E. (1969) Symposium on rate controlled speech and listening comprehension in *National Reading Conference Yearbook*

GATES, A. I. and MCKILLOP, A. S. (1962) *Gates-McKillop Diagnostic Reading Tests* New York: Teachers College Press, Columbia University

HOLLINGSWORTH, P. M. (1967) Can training in listening improve reading? in Durr, W. K. (ed.) *Reading Instruction: Dimensions and Issues* Boston: Houghton Mifflin

KELTY, A. (1953) *An experimental study to determine the effects of listening for certain purposes upon achievement of reading for those purposes* Unpublished doctoral dissertation, Colorado State College of Education

LEWIS, M. S. (1951) *The effect of training in listening for certain purposes upon reading for those same purposes* Unpublished doctoral dissertation, Colorado State College of Education

LUBERSHANE, M. (1962) Can training in listening improve reading ability? in *Chicago School Journal* 43, 277–281

LUNDSTEEN, S. (1969) Critical listening and thinking in *Journal of Research and Development in Education* 3, Autumn

NICHOLS, R. G. and STEVENS, L. A. (1957) *Are you listening?* New York: McGraw-Hill

ORR, D., FRIEDMAN, H. and WILLIAMS, J. (1965) Trainability of listening comprehension of speeded discourse in *Journal of Educational Psychology* 56, 148–156

PARKER, C. C. (1970) Effect of rate of comprehension and mode of presentation on the comprehension of a recorded communication to junior college students of varying aptitudes Paper read at American Speech Association Conference

STERRITT, G. M., MARTIN, V. E. and RUDNICK, M. (1969) Sequential pattern perception in reading in Spache, G. D. (ed.) *Reading Disability and Perception* 1968 Proceedings volume 13, part 3 Newark, Delaware: International Reading Association

WEPMAN, J. M. (1959) *Auditory Discrimination Test* Chicago: University of Chicago

WILKIN, B. R. (1969) Auditory perception—implications for language development in *Journal of Research and Development in Education* 3

17 Selecting literature for children

Helen Huus

Introduction

Literature for children is part of the ongoing stream of literature in general, and as such is a respected and respectable study in itself. For this reason, the wording of the title was chosen deliberately— 'literature' rather than 'books,' and 'for children' rather than 'children's literature'. The differences are subtle, but real.

A dictionary (Thorndike and Barnhart, 1957) defines 'literature' as 'writings of a period or country, especially those kept alive by their beauty of style or thought', Literature has no topics or subjects of its own; it encompasses such trivial creatures as fleas and fireflies and such glorious splendours as found in Arabian Nights or the court of Kubla Khan. While some critics would limit literature to imaginative writing, others include writing of whatever _genre_ and topic that meet the standards of literary merit. Otherwise, books like Robert Louis Stevenson's _Travels with a Donkey_ and its American counterpart John Steinebeck's _Travels with Charley_, Rachel Carson's _The Sea Around us_, and St Exupéry's _Night Flight_ would be eliminated.

Literature is a 'way of knowing'; it strikes a responsive chord in the reader that allows him to see himself in relation to his world with a clarity hitherto unknown. William Stafford (1968), one of the eminent contemporary American poets, describes what he calls 'the limber art of reading literature' this way:

> You start anywhere, with anything in a literary work and lend yourself to what comes next, and next, and then . . . You cannot rule out any kind of material, any word, any syllable, any topic or hint that the writer has put into the work, or any nuance that has found its way there. The significance of anything you encounter depends—it all depends.
>
> You accept what you find. You enter any work with the impulse to be a willing follower. The first requisite is openness. If you interfere beforehand, if you ignore signals because you have adopted an early course of interpretation of your own, you have already lost your way.

As the reader lets the author lead him through a work, what he obtains from the writing on the page depends in part upon associations that

I

are stimulated and the experiences he can recall that enlighten the meaning. When descriptions are so clear and vivid that he is caught up in the action, for a time he *is* the hero or heroine. How to select books that provide such experiences for children is the problem.

Literature for children

But where does one begin? What is a book for children? Is it one written exclusively for them? If so, what of *Alice* and *Wind in the Willows* and *Winnie the Pooh* and *Charlotte's Webb* and *The Hobbit*? These form what I call the big five and they are of universal interest, and appeal to all ages.

Is a book for children one they choose to read? If so, *The Yearling, My Friend Flicka, Rascal, Kon-Tiki, Robinson Crusoe,* and *Gulliver's Travels* would qualify, yet originally these were not written for children.

Is it a book dealing with children? If so, Kay Thompson's *Eloise*, the story of a child who lived and romped in New York's elegant Plaza Hotel, should be included, yet it is hardly fare for children. Neither is the *Space Child's Mother Goose*, by Frederick Winsor and Marian Parry, with its sophisticated take-offs of the originals. The same can be said for *The Chas Adams' Mother Goose*, which is peopled with the ghoulish creatures that haunt his cartoons in the *New Yorker* magazine.

Literature for children includes those books of literary quality that children can hear or read for pleasure and profit. Most of these books fall into the categories of short story, novel (or longer books), biography, fable, myth and poetry.

Certainly literature should stretch a child's imagination, should acquaint him with the characters and concepts that form the body of allusions an educated person is expected to recognize and understand, should make him sensitive to human problems and their solutions, and should allow him to glory in the language in which these ideas are couched. Literature should extend and expand his horizon so that through books he can experience a wide range of emotions and actions that might otherwise remain unknown. But all the while, he is enjoying the experience and perhaps learning lasting lessons.

Selecting books

The process of selecting literature for children consists of three stages or steps, the first of which is much easier than the other two. The initial step entails determining the topics or aspects on which to judge the quality of the work as literature. Unfortunately, much of what is written under the guise of 'criteria for judging' simply lists or describes the topics to be considered. While knowing these topics is a first step, it alone is insufficient for making sound judgements. In a lively article entitled 'Coming to terms with criticism', Paul Heins (1970) lists ten areas for discussion, but does point out that each influences the other.

The second step consists of setting the base line, of creating a yardstick or standard against which to compare various works in order to determine how closely they approximate to the standard or ideal. Since individuals vary in their levels of ability and taste, differences in what constitutes the standard are likely to occur. The problem of determining an acceptable standard is not an easy task, even when an individual is working alone.

The third and final step is the actual process of making the comparison and arriving at a judgement. The work being evaluated is then placed on a kind of 'continuum of quality' in comparison with others of its type and topic. This is the most complicated of all, for the appropriate balance, mix, or weighting of the topics as each affects the total needs to be determined. The end result cannot be a mere accumulation, but rather a *gestalt*, where the total is greater than the sum of its parts.

This somewhat methodical procedure is rejected by critics who tend to prefer a free-wheeling plan and leave the judging completely in the hands of experts considered competent to make decisions. Perhaps a middle of the road approach is more realistic. Analysis of a work may pinpoint or corroborate a vague feeling of a book's inadequacy by convincing the reader that the work lacks certain elements; likewise, great enthusiasm for a book can be supported when examples are cited that indicate its fine qualities.

Criteria for selection

Before putting this three-step process to work the topics or aspects to be considered must be chosen. I suggest these five, listed in rank order:

1 literary merit
2 artistic format
3 originality
4 purpose
5 appeal to children.

My justification for the order is this. Starting with the first, each book needs to survive each successive screening until it ultimately reaches the child. A book that is literary passes the first hurdle and is then judged on its artistic merit. When the scrutiny has proved successful, the book is then evaluated on originality, then on purpose, and finally on appeal to children. In my opinion a book for adults would be judged in the same manner, though purpose and appeal might be different in kind as well as degree.

Literary merit

The quality of a book as literature hinges on the author's treatment of the elements that make up a story or poem or essay or other type of writing. Literature of substance has a theme, an overarching idea that encompasses the total work. Themes deal with universal truths, with common aspirations and ideals that reveal the humanity of the characters. Themes may treat serious, crucial aspects of civilization and character formation, or they may deal with ridiculous or fanciful trivia meant solely to entertain. A simple fairy tale like *Cinderalla* has the theme of kindness rewarded (or is it that it pays to have a fairy godmother?).

The setting of a story may be historical or contemporary, realistic or fanciful, or it may move back and forth between the two. Katherine Millhous's *Through These Arches* tells the story of Independence Hall in Philadelphia, shifting from 'then' to 'now' by means of different type faces, and Lucy Boston's *Green Knowe* stories move, almost imperceptibly at times, between the real and the fanciful.

Plot *is* the story, the solution of the problem, the step by step method or the series of incidents that lead to the climax and the resolution of the conflict. In longer books, each chapter may contain a subplot which also contributes to the plan of the book as a whole. The easy Henry Huggins books by Beverly Cleary do this, as does the exciting *Caddie Woodlawn*. Some books contain the sophisticated story within a story pattern, for example *The Golden Fleece* by Padriac Colum or the easy reading book by Else Minarik, *Little Bear's Visit*, which utilizes this pattern in a very simple way: Little Bear goes to visit his grandfather who tells him a story which is then presented in the book. Some books, like *Hans Brinker and the Silver Skates*, contain more than one plot—the winning of the skates, the father's recovery of his health and money, and the tourist's view of Holland.

Characters in books for children include real people, fanciful creatures, animals acting like themselves or like people, and inanimate objects personified, like the Little House, Little Toot, and of course, Winnie the Pooh. Readers become acquainted with story characters from descriptions of how they look, what they think and say and do, what others say about them, and illustrations.

Style is the writer's mixture of ideas, vocabulary, syntax, figures of speech, point of view, and timing—his flair for the dramatic. It assumes great importance in distinguishing literature from prosaic writing but style is merely the vehicle for conveying thoughts and thus a means to an end, not an end in itself.

Point of view refers to the storyteller and his vantage point. Some storytellers intrude into the story, as does Edmund Ormondroyd in *Time at the Top*. Some stories are told in the first person; one from a mouse-eye view in *Ben and Me*; another from a mother's view in *An Anteater Named Arthur* by Bernard Waber. A few use the second person, though usually books for children are told in the third person.

All these factors contribute to literary merit, but the total impact comes from their interrelationships. The emotional reactions of the reader reflect the vividness of his experience, yet isolating one crucial, causal factor is almost impossible.

Artistic format

Books are more than words; they are covers and binding and paper and type and illustrations. Together, these give the book a certain 'feel' and 'look'. Artistic bookmaking is a craft in itself; when illustrations are added, the product that results presents the reader with an aesthetic as well as literary experience—not found, I fear, in reading most paperbacks.

Illustrations are evaluated on artistic principles of colour, line and shape, balance and movement, on the congruity of medium and colour to content, on the way in which illustrations complement and extend the text, and on the overall design of the book as a whole.

Originality

Originality consists of a fresh or new approach; the novel way an object or idea is treated, the ability of author and illustrator to dream up a different approach or to revive a previous idea, to create an innovation that may change the direction of books in general. Colour printing, for example, was one such innovation; so was Genevieve Foster's 'world of' books, where she presents what she calls a 'slice of history', showing what was happening all over the world during the lifetime of the central character. Shirley Glubok created a new art book for children when she used stunning photographs of art objects organized around a central theme such as *The Art of the Eskimo* or *The Art of Ancient Egypt*. Originality gives a book its flair, and often the essence of the uniqueness is so simple that one wonders why it has not been used before.

Purpose

Supplementing the other factors is purpose. Books appropriate for one occasion may not be suitable for another. Purpose is related to the age and ability of the reader, the activity concerned, the difficulty of the material, the depth of penetration desired, motivation, time available, and other factors. The famous story of the child who returned his book with the comment that it 'told him more about penguins than he wanted to know' is an example.

Appeal to children

The final criterion for judging books is the appeal to children. Appeal is based upon factors of personality and reading ability, general or peculiar interests, environment, availability, promotion, current events, or fashionable trends. A distinction must be made between the instant appeal of books relevant to the reader's already-developed interests, and books which can be made appealing to him with proper introduction and guidance. When children do not even know something exists, how *can* they be interested?

Another aspect related to appeal is the ethic of the book. Children are immature and hence lack the experience and judgment to recognize some of the subtle innuendoes that may influence them without their being aware of it. Perhaps depriving them of certain books smacks of censorship; if so, I plead guilty. If adults do not know what is good for children, then who does?

Standards for comparison

Setting standards against which to compare books is anything but easy. There is no set standard, such as the brass rod in the Bureau of Standards in Washington, DC, which is the official yardstick, or Greenwich Mean Time, which is the standard for the entire world. Standards for children's books tend to be on a sliding scale, greatly dependent upon the individual making the judgment.

Experience with the best

To acquire a standard, the reader needs to be exposed to works of accepted excellence. The classics, the award books, the work of known authors who have proved their worth are materials on which to begin. Books which children can understand but cannot yet read should be read aloud to them. In fact, I have said repeatedly that each teacher including secondary and college teachers of literature, ought to read aloud to every class every day—well, *almost* every day! Students are thus given an opportunity to extend their vocabularies, to hear cadenced prose or rhythmic poetry, to absorb the atmosphere of a story without being bound by difficulties of coping with print. Once this acquaintance with good books has been started, standards gradually emerge as topics are discussed and comparisons made.

Development of levels

For each of the critical topics a scale of values could be established, perhaps on five levels, with a specific description of quality at each level. Constructing this scale would be a major task, yet in making such qualitative distinctions, pupils and teachers would be held to the task of justifying their comments and judgments. Yet even a descriptive scale represents a mere accumulation and omits the important *gestalt*; therefore, some items on the scale must necessarily point to the interrelationships.

Evaluation of quality

What remains at the third step is to measure the unknown work against the scale or standard to determine its 'fit' and its strengths and weaknesses. This matching requires thought, weighing aspects of the book against others like it and against the arbitrary standard. The taste of the reader or critic, the quality level he accepts, and his intellectual ability to note fine differences, to see relationships where none apparently exist, to balance parts and then make a decision all enter into his evaluation. Time may prove him right or wrong.

The reader or critic, having taken his stand, then willingly justifies his decision and awaits the attacks that may occur. If he consistently selects books that are agreed to be excellent and which children read eagerly, his reputation as an authority is established. If, in addition, his comments reflect his own background and are spiced with wit and humour, he also becomes well read.

Conclusion

This may sound very restrictive; it is not meant to. In the long run, each critic goes through these stages almost unconsciously, and then makes his judgment without apparent recourse to any specific method. Once he has arrived at this state, assuming the level of his taste and discrimination prove successful, he no longer needs to utilize these steps, just as an experienced teacher may no longer refer to a guide or a seasoned cook to a recipe.

The road to glory is not easy. Fortunately for teachers, Zena Sutherland, Virginia Kirkus, Helen Painter, Virginia Haviland, and the Children's Book Council in the United States, and Naomi Lewis, Margery Fisher, John Rowe Townsend, Roger Lancelyn Green, and the National Book League in England help sort out book production and point the way to books of quality. It is up to the parents and teachers and librarians to connect the books with the children. This is the challenge in today's changing world of books.

References

HEINS, P. (1970) Coming to terms with criticism *The Horn Book Magazine* in XLVI August, 1970 p. 374

STAFFORD, W. (1968) Critic, fact, fiction in Huus, H. (ed.), *Evaluating Books for Children and Young People* Perspectives No. 10, p. 2 Newark, Delaware: International Reading Association

THORNDIKE, E. L. and BARNHART, C. (1957) *Thorndike-Barnhart High School Dictionary* Chicago: Scott Foresman

18 International activities to promote children's reading and children's literature (with special reference to central Europe)

Richard Bamberger

The movement to improve children's literature

In central Europe, endeavours in the field of children's literature rested mainly on theoretical discussions which became so fierce that we speak of the *Jugendschriftbewegung*, the English equivalent of which would be 'activities in the field of children's literature'. This movement, which was born at the end of the last century, represented an attempt to persuade writers, publishers and parents that poor or mediocre literature for children is a crime against the child and against the art of writing. This struggle, which lasted for over fifty years, gave a sound basis for the golden age of children's literature which sprang up after the second world war. The five most important trends in the movement 'Activities in the Field of Children's Literature' in central Europe are as follows.

The trend against poor and mediocre children's literature

The task of criticizing children's literature lay almost exclusively in the hands of teachers. Subcommittees of the teachers' associations regularly published recommended lists of what they considered to be good books for children. The first publication of this sort appeared in Switzerland in 1862. Lists were printed regularly from 1870 onwards. It was in reaction to literary criticisms based on moral, patriotic and religious viewpoints (e.g. Engelbert Fischer *Die Großmacht der Jugendliteratur* 1877–1886), that Wolgast wrote his now famous book. Fierce debates resulted, as some Catholic representatives of children's literature regarded Wolgast's remarks against moralizing religious tracts, as an attack on the Catholic religion. Similarly, other comments were seen as a betrayal of German nationalism. However, the misunderstanding of Wolgast's intentions did cause the general public to become aware of the problems relating to children's literature. It took more than three decades for the aesthetic point of view to win the upper hand, and inexpensive editions of tales, originally written by great authors for adults, to be edited for classroom reading. *Billige Reihen* (Cheap Series) were founded. Their finest successor is the *Schweizerische Jugendschriftenwerk* (Swiss collection for the young) which now consists of more than a thousand little 32-page booklets.

The struggle for the rights of the child
This trend was a reaction against the over emphasis of the aesthetic point of view, which had resulted in the selection of children's books being restricted almost exclusively to literature written by great writers for adults. The champions of this psychological trend were Berthold Otto and Ernst Linde who, as early as 1905, advocated that simplified editions of books for children should be written in the simple, everyday language of the child. At the same time, librarians began to express the need for excitement in literature, which led to many new adventure stories and new series of books for girls.

The trend to promote a new type of literary education
This movement, which emphasized the literary development of children and aimed at encouraging good taste and creating permanent reading habits, found its guide in the writings of Wolgast and his successors. Its work was carried on primarily by the Hamburg periodical, the *Jugendschriftenwarte*. Wilhelm Fronemann, author of *Das Erbe Wolgast* (Wolgast's heritage, 1927), attempted to combine the aesthetic, the psychological and the didactic points of view in promoting personal reading interests and developing life-time reading habits.

In addition, between the first and second world wars the public libraries in north and central Europe began to lay more stress on library work with children. Teachers and librarians began to meet and exchange views on a new type of literary education.

The trend to convert the theories into practical achievements
This trend found its application in the production of children's literature, and in school and public library work. The stimulus to the production of books for children was exemplified mainly by the consideration of books for translation from various countries.

After the first world war it was mostly English and Scandinavian books which were translated by other European countries, especially the German-speaking ones. These translations of the world's best books convinced critics and authors that children's books could also be great literature. During the 1920s and 1930s, a small number of the best books from other countries were translated and many of them are still reprinted.

After the second world war, American books headed the list of translations in Europe, but from 1955 onwards books from many other countries were also translated more frequently. As a result of this attempt to bring the best books from all over the world to young readers, a world literature for children was created.

In the smaller countries like Holland and Scandinavia, about 50 per cent of the production of children's books consisted of translations; whereas in the German-speaking countries about 25 per cent of the children's books were translations. However, the 50 per cent of the Scandinavian production does not amount to even half the number of titles translated into German. Translations raise the level of the children's reading in any given country by a considerable amount. For example, an examination of a list of highly recommended children's books in German revealed that 40–50 per cent are translations. Secondly, translations seem to provide a challenge to the original writers in the respective countries. This trend towards a world literature for children may also be seen as an effort to promote international understanding.

The books that appear in translation are usually of the highest quality and present themes on common human values—dreams, joys and hopes. A few modern examples which have been translated all over the world are Karl Bruckner's *The Day of the Bomb,* Aimée Sommerfelt's *Veien til Agra* (*The Road to Agra*), Astrid Lindgren's books, Russell Hoban's *Bedtime for Frances,* Fatio/Duvoisin's *Happy Lion,* Maurice Druon's *Tistou les pouces verts* (*Tistou with the Green Thumbs*), and Erich Kästner's *Der kleine Mann* (*The Little Man*).

The trend towards systematic research
This trend was based on individual achievements in the field since the end of the nineteenth century and it developed systematically in various institutes founded after the second world war.

The International Youth Library in Munich, founded by Jella Lepman, set up one of the largest collections of international books for children.

The International Institute for Children's and Juvenile Literature in Vienna, a documentation and information centre for children's literature and reading research, has set itself the task of coordinating not only the efforts of different countries but also the work of all associations and institutions concerned with children's reading. *Bookbird* is published quarterly by the Institute. In 1971, at the Institute's initiative, an International Press Service was founded to promote cooperation between the specialist journals. It is issued monthly and aims to ensure faster dissemination of news on children's literature.

The *International Forschungsgesellschaft zur Jugendliteratur* (International Research Society for Children's Literature) was founded at the Johann Wolfgang von Goethe University in Frankfurt not quite a year ago. It hopes to find a way to ensure coordination of work and cooperation of effort among researchers in many countries.

In addition to these international ventures, there is also an ever-growing number of national institutions concerned with children's literature, for example the *Svenska Barnboksinstitutet* (Swedish Institute for Children's Books); the *Centro Didattico Nazionale* with its periodical *Schedario* in Florence, Italy; the Johanna-Spyri Institute in Switzerland; the Institute for Juvenile Literature in East

Berlin; the *Bureau Boek en Jeugd* in Holland; and the *Conseil de Littérature de Jeunesse* in Belgium with its periodical *Littérature de Jeunesse*.

Other countries also channel their activities in children's literature through specialized periodicals. Among them are the Scandinavian and English journals for school librarians (e.g. *School Librarian*; *Børn og Bøger*; *Skolbiblioteket*), *Jugend und Buch* in Austria, *Zlaty Maj* in Czechoslovakia and *Detskaya literatura* in the USSR.

All these institutes and periodicals have the common aim of intensifying research in the field of children's literature, an area still very much neglected in the universities of Europe. Here again, as in so many aspects of children's literature in Europe, a north-south decline is evident. Interest in children's literature decreases, as does its quality, as we move from the north to the south of Europe.

Practical work in the promotion of children's books
Almost everything done in the way of practical work in Europe is also undertaken in the United Kingdom; and frequently it is more successful. One example is the work with parents in preschool institutions, kindergartens and parent-teacher associations. In Austria, a 112-page year book for parents on various educational questions, particularly the importance of children's books, is published in an edition of over 200,000. In central and southern Europe the chief stress is on buying books. In contrast, in England, the Scandinavian countries and the Communist countries in Europe, library work with children's books has been developed, whereas in central and southern Europe such work is practically nonexistent.

In order to stimulate private book buying after the second world war, various junior book clubs were founded in Europe. The Austrian Children's Book Club, a nonprofit-making organization, today has 830,000 members. It aims to make good books available to children at a reduced rate. Each member can buy four books of his choice each year, from a list of about 250 books, at 25 per cent discount. The rebate is granted jointly by publishers and the book trade. Each member also receives a yearbook, one third of which is given over to exciting complete stories; one third comprises specialized contributions planned as aids to school work; and one third contains extracts from Book Club books, intended as stimulation to further reading. The Yearbooks are used as 'second readers' in schools and provide teachers with opportunities to discuss the books which children read on their own. The Yearbooks play an important role in stimulating children to read more and better books. With the advent of these Yearbooks, children's books became a decisive force in Austrian reading instruction.

A special activity which has been most favourably received in Austrian schools in particular, is the campaign called 'Lure into reading'. Valuable and exciting juvenile books have been selected and boxes made up, each containing thirty copies of the same book. These boxes, intended for class reading, are loaned to class after class and to school after school. A special method of introducing these books has been developed, designed to catch the children's imagination and make them feel that it is a great privilege to be allowed to read them. The method has proved its value in every case, particularly with adolescents who are in many ways the most difficult age group to approach and interest.

The teacher takes about fifteen minutes to tell the beginning of the story. He then reads aloud from the book for another quarter of an hour. The pupils are thus given a chance to enter into the action, feel the atmosphere of the book and become acquainted with some of the characters. If the teacher finishes reading at a particularly exciting point in the story, his announcement that the children may use the rest of the lesson to read the story for themselves is enthusiastically received. At the end of the lesson the pupils are allowed to take the books home and are told that the class will discuss them in a week's time. By the end of the week, virtually all pupils have read the book and are able to participate animatedly in the discussion, which the teacher leads unobtrusively.

Reports by many teachers show that even the most reluctant and slow readers can be won over by this method and will in fact read a complete book within a few days. Another advantage is that the children, with the reading experience fresh in their minds, conduct a positive and meaningful discussion with very little help from the teacher. The campaign has thus proved highly successful in introducing all children to good juvenile literature.

Book clubs in other countries are usually connected with publishing houses. However, efforts are often made to go beyond the framework of merely promoting book sales. Reading competitions in which those children who have read the most books and are most familiar with good children's literature are presented with awards, have proved successful. The focal point of the efforts to win young readers varies from country to country. In the eastern block, in particular in the Soviet Union, the task is shared evenly between school, library and pioneer clubs. In the Scandinavian countries, schools and libraries take the lead. In central Europe, the most successful promotion of children's books takes place in the schools. Cooperation between work in the field of reading and in the field of children's literature has been quite successful in Austria.

The discovery that many children do not read books because they cannot read sufficiently well, led to campaigns like 'Intensive therapy in reading' and 'Reading diagnosis and reading therapy' sponsored by the Austrian Children's Book Club, which hopes to improve reading achievement by introducing a wide variety of reading material.

International cooperation in the future

One of the most important aspects of children's literature work in Europe, and throughout the world today, is international cooperation among all the interested institutions and parties. The International Board on Books for Young People was able to move beyond the frontiers of the German-speaking countries and to spread throughout Europe and the world, as was the international periodical *Bookbird*, which originally developed as a cooperative project of IBBY and the Vienna Institute. Much of the real work in this area took place at international congresses which brought together people working for children's literature in various countries. Common interests were discovered, and many new ideas which stimulated work in the individual countries arose from the discussions. It was the spirit of these meetings that contributed greatly to the development of a golden age of illustrated story books in Europe. The most beautiful children's books from throughout the world are now translated into other languages.

We are currently faced with another challenge on the international level which is closer cooperation between those who try to guide children towards books and those who teach reading. Good readers and good libraries ought to be the goals of the promoters of children's books and of children's reading. When this cooperation is fully realized, especially when more of the best children's books from all over the world are translated into many languages, the teaching of reading and the improvement of reading ability will be greatly helped.

Part four Reading difficulties

19 Children with reading difficulties

Peter D. Pumfrey

Introduction

This study group was intended for remedial teachers, teachers in special schools and class teachers in primary or secondary schools who were dealing with children with reading difficulties. Within the context of the conference's general theme of 'Literacy at all levels', our study group was specifically concerned with a consideration of 'promising practices' in diagnosis, intervention, assessment of change and in-service training as four important aspects of the services provided both for the child with reading difficulties and for the child's teacher.

In order to present an integrated account of the study group's work, I have allocated the contributions, on the basis of their major emphasis, to one of the four categories mentioned previously (see Table 1). Each speaker submitted a summary of his/her topic to me in order to help compile this report. I have drawn extensively on these summaries, quoting them verbatim whenever possible, and I would like to acknowledge the contributors' invaluable help and accept responsibility for any distortions that may have occurred.

The diagnosis of reading difficulties

The Concise Oxford Dictionary defines diagnosis as 'identification of disease by means of patient's symptoms'. Drever (1964) extends this to the 'determination of the nature of an abnormality, disorder or disease'. The use of the concept of 'diagnosis' in the context of the investigation of children's reading difficulties is controversial. This is due in part to disagreement as to whether the medical model implicit in the term is applicable to education. It is feasible that interindividual differences in reading skills or subskills are normally distributed. Thus we might reasonably expect a wide range of attainments in and attitudes towards these skills at any age level. Teachers are expected to respect the individuality of the child whilst at the same time ensuring that each child conforms to certain patterns of behaviour, for example, learns to read. Often those children falling at the lower end of the

Classification or contributions according to their major emphasis

Category	Contributor	Title of contribution
1 Diagnosis	Bracken, D. Kendall	The concept of the learning centre and its relation to reading failure.
	Tansley, A. E.	The diagnosis and treatment of acute difficulties in learning to read.
	Skeffington, M.	Comments on A. E. Tansley's contribution.
2 Intervention		
i preschool programmes	Quigley, H. Widlake, P.	The Peabody Language Development Kit and its use in England. The effects of preschool language programmes.
ii machines and programmes	Cunningham, C. Clift, P. C.	Teaching machines and remedial reading. Reading skills in the remedial teaching of reading.
iii phonic approaches	Bleasdale, E. Niven, C.	Reading by Rainbow: the use of a simple colour code. Phonic Workshop – an idea under development.
iv structured language experience approach	Westwood, P.	Remediation of reading difficulties through the language experience approach.
3 Assessment of change	Bookbinder, G. E. Monroe, M. Pumfrey, P. D.	What do remedial teachers remedy? Evaluating reading instruction. Children's attitudes to reading.
4 In-service training	Morison, A. J. M.	Reading Centres in Manchester: how are they distinctive?

hypothesized normal distributions are categorized as children with reading difficulties. To some extent the difficulties in reading that such children experience are generated by adults' wish for a conformity that is possibly at variance with the nature of human beings. In contrast, relatively little is heard of those children at the upper end of the normal distribution who are extremely competent readers.

This should not be taken to indicate a belief that the improvement of standards of reading skills generally and the amelioration of reading difficulties in particular cannot be achieved. The complexity of the reading process makes it possible for a wide range of poor reading habits and attitudes to be learned by the child. In some cases a child's reading difficulties may be directly attributable to an abnormality, disorder or disease of, for example, vision of hearing, which can be identified and then possibly treated so as to enable the child to overcome his reading difficulty. However, in the majority of cases of reading difficulty, highly specific causes cannot be identified. It is possible to calculate the correlation coefficients between a variety of reading difficulties and a host of physical, social, educational, emotional and motivational variables. Because a highly significant correlation is found between, say, poor auditory-visual integration and failure in reading, it cannot be assumed that the poor integration *causes* the reading difficulty. Teachers and researchers are well aware that for almost every child with a specific handicap who has reading difficulties, there are others with the specific handicap who has reading competently. This points to our incomplete understanding of and control over the development of the ability to read, and consequently of our ability to diagnose difficulties adequately.

Diagnosis of reading difficulties is not an esoteric exercise carried out solely by highly trained experts. It can be carried out at many levels (Wilson 1967). The class teacher is constantly engaged in the informal diagnosis of children's reading difficulties and in making modifications to the experiences that the child encounters so as to facilitate the progressive acquisition of higher competencies (Gagné 1969). Should this informal approach fail, the teacher may initiate a more formal examination of a child's difficulties still within the classroom. If the child continues to experience difficulties, referral may be made to someone with more specialized knowledge and expertise.

At any level, the diagnosis of reading difficulties is perhaps most usually and most profitably seen as a process of hypothesis generation followed by an intervention, the result of which leads to a further modification of the hypothesis and thus of the intervention. More prosaically, 'Johnny can't synthesize phonically regular words; why? Perhaps it is because . . ., so I will arrange for him to . . . and see if it helps. If it doesn't, I'll have to think again.'

All teachers concerned with helping children with reading difficulties to learn need to be aware of the principles of educational diagnosis. A comprehensive discussion of the topic can be found in Bond and Tinker (1967) and Sheldon (1970). The following list is adapted from their work.

Principles underlying the diagnosis of reading difficulties

1 Diagnosis is an integral part of effective difficulties.
2 Diagnosis is intended to facilitate the child's acquisition of specified skills or attitudes.
3 Diagnosis is a continuous process in education.
4 Diagnosis is centred on the particular individual's reading difficulty.
5 Diagnosis of reading difficulties often requires more than an assessment of reading skills because reading difficulties may be symptomatic of a wide range of causative factors.
6 Diagnosis of reading difficulties implies that the teacher is aware of the importance of the other language arts of listening, speaking and writing.
7 Diagnosis should involve the use of standardized test procedures, but the teacher needs to be aware of the limitations of currently available instruments in this field.
8 As our knowledge of the reading process is incomplete, any decision made in diagnosing a difficulty should be based on a pattern of scores.
9 The heart of diagnosis is the intelligent interpretation of a series of observations coupled with the ability to relate the interpretation to a plan for remedial teaching.
10 Only by developing and refining diagnostic procedures can our understanding of the reading process by furthered and our ability to prevent and ameliorate reading difficulties advanced.

The work of the highly trained specialist in the diagnosis and treatment of reading difficulties in the usa is typified by the Reading Clinic at Southern Methodist University, Texas. Under the direction of Dorothy Kendall Bracken, the clinic offers to parents in the vicinity a complete diagnostic and remedial service at all age levels on an individual basis for a fee. It is clinic policy that only children of average and above general mental ability are accepted for treatment. Individual diagnosis and individual instruction is a fundamental point of departure. The clinic contains carpeted, sound-proofed, air-conditioned classrooms in which the teachers have an extensive range of materials, machines and books. Dr Bracken informed us that the results obtained in terms of children's progress indicated that, though our diagnostic procedures may be imperfect, they are an important basis on which an individualized programme of remedial reading can be planned with considerable confidence.

K

In Birmingham, A. E. Tansley emphasizes the importance of the integration of various sensory modalities in the reading process. Currently he is working on ways of facilitating this integration as an essential aspect of all children's cognitive development (Tansley 1967), although his work is mainly with children attending special schools and presenting severe reading difficulties in addition to other problems. Tansley believes that it has now been reasonably well established that many children who show reading difficulties in school have suffered from some injury to, or functional impairment of, the central nervous system during the pre-, peri- and post-natal periods. A register of children 'at risk' would have important implications for the early assessment and treatment of children with motor, sensory, perceptual and language problems.

There is also a need, in Tansley's view, for some way of screening children soon after they are admitted to school. In Birmingham a screening test is now being used for children entering the final year of infant school. This screening investigates perceptual, motor and language areas of development. It has been designed to give indications for a prescriptive approach to the educational treatment of learning difficulties.

Remedial programmes for children suffering from reading difficulties must be developed systematically so that children receive treatment for motor problems arising from neurological abnormality or acute environmental deprivation at the preschool age. Tansley has devised, and is further developing, systematic programmes for sensory stimulation and the development of cross-modality function; perceptual training programmes in both auditory and visual fields together with programmes for language development. Tansley feels that such materials are likely to hasten reading readiness.

At the next stage, when the teaching of formal reading begins, the method used with each child must be related to the individual's abilities and disabilities. Tansley has developed a series of diagnostic tests of the various sensory functions and their cross-modal integration that enable the teacher to decide which particular approach to the teaching of reading, or the preparation for it, is appropriate for a given child. Work on these lines is now a common feature in some Birmingham schools.

Margaret Skeffington's critical comment on the tenuous links between remedial activities based on three-dimensional space and reading, which is effectively two-dimensional, accentuated the theoretical and practical difficulties that must be overcome if our understanding of the relationship between representation in its various modes and transfer of training is to advance.

The approaches of these two contributors exemplify the applications of the principles of diagnosis listed earlier, stressing the importance of matching the child's individual abilities and interests to appropriate learning experiences. The growing interest in measures of intra-individual differences in tests such as the Illinois Test of Psycholinguistic Abilities (Kirk *et al* 1968), the Reynell Language Development Scale (Reynell 1969) and many others currently available (Bond and Tinker 1967) indicates the close relationship between the analysis of processes related to reading and the specification of individual strengths and weaknesses in which appropriate remedial activities can then be developed and their efficacy tested (Cashdan 1970).

Intervention
Many children have reading difficulties. It is largely the responsibility of the teacher in his everyday work to investigate these difficulties and, on the basis of his knowledge of the skills and attitudes necessary for competent reading coupled with the nature of the individual child's difficulty, to arrange a series of experiences for the child that will enable the difficulty to be overcome.

In one sense, there is a tendency for the organization of our schools to generate reading difficulties, because of the goals that teachers try to impose on children. In some ways this parallels the insidious influence of the professional persuaders of advertising who generate in us a 'need' for objects or activities that yesterday may have seemed largely irrelevant to the lives that we were leading.

Without taking the argument any further, most teachers and parents would accept that the aim of 'Literacy at all levels' is laudable. Whether reading will in future retain its current importance in view of the influence of radio and television is more a matter of controversy than vital policy in our educational system.

Because of teachers' concern with providing the maximum help for the maximum number of children, flexible systems that are seen to help groups of children with reading difficulties in common, are always of interest. Whilst no teacher expects to find a panacea to all children's reading difficulties in any given method, there is always the hope that current practices might be improved by hearing of the approaches used successfully by other teachers.

The seven contributors to this aspect of the study group's work have been grouped for the purposes of this summary into the four areas (see Table 1):

1 preschool programmes
2 machines and programmes
3 phonic approaches
4 structured language experience approach

Preschool language programmes

Helen Quigley who is involved in the Preschool Project currently being carried out by the NFER gave the following edited comments: It is a received doctrine that an adequate linguistic background is a prerequisite for reading success. This is one of the implicit criteria used in assessing reading readiness (Morris 1959), and would therefore appear to be an area in which nursery schooling should be helpful to the less privileged child.

However, American and British studies to date suggest that whereas traditional nursery schools cater well for the emotional and social development of children, and facilitate adaption to the infant school, they are not so successful in stimulating cognitive development (O'Sullivan 1958; Harrold and Temple 1960). As a result, the early advantages are soon lost (Douglas and Ross 1964).

A first systematic attempt to provide the requisite language experiences for underprivileged children and to evaluate the results has been made in both the Social Science Research Council sponsored Educational Priority Area Action-Research Project and in the NFER Preschool Project by using the Peabody Language Development Kit (Dunn and Smith 1965). Both Projects are using level P which aims to provide a systematic programme covering vocabulary enrichment, syntactical competence and cognitive development for children with mental ages of from three to five years. All the necessary materials are provided together with full and detailed instructions for teaching the 180 sequenced lessons. Kits are also available for use with children up to ten years of age.

Although based on the same theoretical model as the Illinois Test of Psycholinguistic Abilities (Kirk *et al* 1968), Dunn and Smith's aim is overall linguistic and cognitive development rather than the strengthening of specific psycholinguistic processes. They aim to sharpen children's auditory, visual and tactual acuity; to promote convergent, divergent and associative thinking and to develop skills of vocal and motor output.

The level P Kit emphasizes more strongly than the other levels the teaching of syntax patterns and simple grammar in the belief that cognitive development is facilitated by the mastery of the structure of language. A core vocabulary of common words including the names of animals, clothes, toys, foods, colours and parts of the body, is taught first. This vocabulary is then used as a basis for learning syntactic patterns employing a variety of tenses, pronouns, adjectives etc. Finally, these structures are extended to cover such cognitive skills as concept formation, associative thinking, and fantasy development among others. The percentage composition of the activites is approximately:

input skills 26 per cent
linguistic skills 32 per cent

cognitive skills 21 per cent
activities and drama 21 per cent

The more advanced kits place less emphasis on linguistic skills and more on cognitive development, emphasizing problem-solving, concept formation and logical thinking.

Reactions of teachers to the kit have ranged from complete rejection to uncritical acceptance (Quigley 1971). A large part of the rejection seems to be antiAmerican in origin, together with highly trained teachers' natural dislike of being dictated to. There is no doubt that highly structured situations are alien to the English nursery tradition. However, the Nursery Nurse Examination Board trained assistants in nurseries and the National Association for Mental Health trained assistants in training centres have welcomed the direction contained in the kit's manual.

After a trial run of the kit for a year in some nursery schools in Slough, it was decided that whereas the systematic approach was helpful in promoting psycholinguistic and cognitive development, alterations in the cultural and informational content of the programme were necessary to adapt it to the different pattern of linguistics and informational deficit found in underprivileged children in this country.

A small survey was made to ascertain the relevant English patterns and the programme was rewritten for use in the NFER project. Thus the more blatant Americanisms have been deleted and both the format and methods made more acceptable to English teachers. The results obtained so far with the revised version of the Peabody Language Development Kit are promising.

Paul Widlake has also been using the Peabody Kit in Birmingham. Here is an edited summary of his work. As one part of a research design conducted in four geographical areas by the Educational Priority Area Action-Research Project, the Birmingham EPA Project set up an experiment in twelve preschools. Children in Experimental Group 1 were given the Peabody Programme of activities. Those in Educational Group 2 went through a Number Programme, the major aim being to offset the Hawthorne effect to be anticipated when an interested adult works with small groups of children using *any* materials. There were two main control groups but two other groups were also assessed in addition. The design of the experiment was as in Table 2.

Two hundred and eighty children were pretested on the Reynell Developmental Language Scales (Reynell 1969) and on the English Picture Vocabulary Test (Brimer and Dunn 1962). These tests were included in the battery of criterion tests at the end of the experiment.

A preliminary survey indicated that the habit-forming 'drills' in language structures which the Peabody Language Development Kit incorporates, may have received unnecessary emphasis. Children in

Table 2
Design of the Birmingham EPA Project experiment using the Peabody Language Development Kit

	Treatments		
	Experimental Treatment 1 (Use of Peabody Programme)	Experimental Treatment 2 (Use of a Number Programme)	Control
Nurseries	2	2	2
Playgroups	2	2	2 & 1 Middle class group & 1 group with no preschool experience

the Birmingham EPA preschool range command a wide spectrum of syntactical patterns, though they often choose not to display them.

The whole preschool experiment is to be the subject of a separate volume in the EPA reports. A preliminary report of some of the findings of the Birmingham experiment can be found in Widlake (1971). The following three findings are particularly interesting:

1 There was an initial difference of fifteen points on the English Picture Vocabulary Test (Brimer and Dunn 1962) scores of the twelve EPA preschools and that of a 'middle class' preschool, which was used as a control. Even after a year's language intervention programme in the EPA preschools, this gap remained substantial; the EPA standard had still not reached the starting point of the middle class preschool.

Conclusion It is certainly possible to bring about a substantial improvement in the language performance of preschool children in an EPA but it would be unrealistic to assume that all social class effects could be eliminated. However, in this context, 'middle class' may refer more to parental attitudes towards education than to other attributes of social class; and there are good prospects of modifying unfavourable parental attitudes, as the excellent LEA nurseries demonstrate.

2 The playgroups who had worked through the Peabody Programme

were significantly better than the control groups, one of which had lower mean scores on the criterion tests at the end of the experiment than at the start.

Conclusion A structural intervention programme could help play-groups to bring their standards of language work nearer to those of nursery schools.

3 All the nurseries showed improvement on all language measures and there were no overall significant differences between those using the Peabody material and those following a traditional nursery regime. There were, however, *some* differences in favour of Experimental Group 1.

Conclusion Traditional nursery procedures are effective in producing language gains, but would be yet more effective if there were more child-adult verbal intercourse, and if the adults were more aware of the processes by which language improvement could be effected.

There are certain points of agreement between the work of the two investigators and some important points of disagreement. It is possible that the modification of the Peabody Kit carried out by Quigley is an important variable in this respect. There are also important differences between the populations with whom the experiments were tried. As both workers will need to explain the differences between their respective findings, we await a fuller presentation and discussion of their results with considerable interest.

Machines and programmes in the remedial teaching of reading
The effectiveness of a teacher helping a child with reading difficulties in many cases depends upon the teacher's ability to assess the child's current level of functioning in the relevant skills, to decide the type of experiences that the child should be helped to encounter, to provide the materials and facilities that maximize the probability of the hypothesized desirable encounters and to evaluate the effects of these upon the particular skill. In some circumstances, these desirable experiences might well involve a complete absence from the child's environment of any materials concerned with formal reading. How far can machines help in the processes?

The touch-tutor is a teaching machine that can, for example, present a number of visual stimuli (e.g. three pictures side by side) and a word or picture above them. The child touches one of the the three pictures that he thinks should be paired with the printed word (or picture) in the panel above. If he is correct, the word is 'spoken' by the machine and the next frame is presented. If the child is incorrect, the frame remains stationary and the child must choose again. The essence of this machine is auditory-visual integration of stimuli.

Using this machine, Clifford Cunningham analysed the contribution that machines can make to the resources of the teacher concerned with the remedial teaching of reading. Whilst the machine may enable a prescribed set of experiences to be presented to a child, and the characteristics of the child's response to the presentation to be recorded and analyzed (if the machine is sufficiently sophisticated), the quality of the material presented is most important. It is all too easy to be beguiled by flashing lights, buzzers and buttons and persuasive sales literature into purchasing, at not inconsiderable expense, a machine for which there is a relatively restricted number of programmes of value to the teacher concerned with children with reading difficulties. This lack of adequate programmes is understandable because there is no one method for teaching reading to children that is equally suitable for all children. A teaching machine is as valuable as the quality of the programmes that it presents, and in many cases buying the machine may be no more than the acquisition of a rather expensive novelty.

However, the *Yearbook of Educational and Instructional Technology* incorporating *Programmes in Print* compiled by Cavanagh and Jones (1969), contains useful information on a variety of available programmes and machines. Additionally, the Schools Council Research Project in Compensatory Education has produced a helpful booklet on applications of the new media to disadvantaged children (Chazan and Downes 1971). Any teacher considering the purchase of machines and materials likely to help children with reading difficulties would be well advised to consult both of these publications.

The contributions of machines and programmes to help children with reading difficulties are, at present, limited. Nonetheless as the flexibility of machines and the validity of programmes increases, they will make a growing contribution to our ability to help children and also to understand more about the process of learning.

One relatively inexpensive teaching machine that has been used with some success in teaching reading to children with reading difficulties is the Bell and Howell Language Master (White 1967). This machine is in essence a tape player and recorder that allows the simultaneous presentation of moving visual material with auditory output from the machine. A 16"x 3" cardboard strip with a piece of recording tape at its base and room for a variety of pictures and/or words to be written above the tape, can be fed into the machine so that the card moves in a right to left direction. At the same time, the recording on the tape is read out to the child. Thus, for example, the visual and oral presentation of equivalent stimuli may be achieved (a picture of an apple with the auditory stimulus 'apple'). Though limited in its functions, the machine has the advantage that materials for it are readily prepared, though they will only comprise a 'programme' in the technical sense if a considerable amount of time is devoted to its preparation and revision (Lysaught and Williams 1963).

The use of the Language Master in the remedial teaching of reading has been experimented with for some time by Philip Clift, an experienced remedial teacher. On the basis of work by Birch and Belmont (1964, 1965), poor readers appeared to experience significantly more difficulty than good readers in integrating what is seen with associated sounds. Clift sees this as indicating a weakness in these children in learning how to learn. He couples this with the findings of Gibson *et al* (1962) which suggest that the basic unit of language relevant to skilled reading is the grapheme-phoneme cluster in which each letter bears a specific relationship to other letters. Learning to read is substantially gaining familiarity with groups of letters which have an invariant sound association when placed in juxtaposition with other letters or letter clusters. Thus the frequency of grapheme-phoneme coincidence is critical, not merely the frequency of exposure to seen or uttered units alone.

Clift suggests that learning to read may be regarded as the acquisition of learning sets in ascending order of complexity, each succeeding one of which may be antagonistic to earlier ones. Harlow (1949) has shown that antagonistic sets could exist together without conflict in his subjects, changeover from the operation of one set to another occurring on a one-trial basis in certain circumstances.

Children are usually taught the mechanics of reading in British primary schools in three broad overlapping stages. The first of these is the acquisition of a 'sight' vocabulary on a 'look and say' basis; the second an understanding of simple word building based on single letter sound combinations; and the third the identification of certain letter groups and the association of sounds with them in the decoding of complex words.

Clift has examined a way in which the Language Master may be used in connection with this third stage with children who find auditory-visual cross-modal associations difficult to learn, and whose abilities are such that the antagonistic sets which must have been acquired between stages 2 and 3 and within stage 3, require an extended learning period (Clift 1969).

Phonic approaches
Teachers of reading have frequently found that the ambiguities inherent in the relationships between letters and/or combinations of letters and their sounds in traditional orthography present a major stumbling block to some pupils. Great ingenuity has been shown by teachers in devising a multitude of schemes that attempt to make the system more consistent. Useful summaries of some of these can be found in Moyle (1971) and in Southgate and Roberts (1970).

Included here are brief descriptions of two schemes at different stages of development. The first is already produced commercially; the second is still being developed.

Reading by Rainbow is a scheme devised by E. and W. Bleasdale.

Initially it was intended to provide a basic phonic training for five year old children entering the infant school. It has subsequently proved to be of considerable value to seven year old children who have not made adequate progress by other methods.

In the scheme, a four-colour code has been used so that each word can be sounded correctly. Black letters have their usual phonetic sound. Red is used for the long vowel sounds such as a in 'cake'. Blue is used for the d to distinguish it from its reversal b and also for the o sound as in 'too'. Yellow is used for those letters that are not sounded, for example a in 'boat'. There is one symbol only for each sound, yet nothing has been added or subtracted from the traditional orthography. Spelling and letter shapes remain unaltered.

The scheme does not cover the whole language. The authors decided against increasing the colours used as they believed that to do so would increase the number of rules to be learned by the children and detract from the effectiveness of the scheme.

The scheme is simple and the results currently being achieved in a wide range of primary schools indicate that it is meeting a need that is recognized by many teachers. The senior author has written an account of the approach in the UKRA Journal (Bleasdale 1969).

The second scheme, called the Phonic Workshop, is currently being developed by the Bolton Remedial Education Service. Cyril Niven well known for the numerous children's schoolbooks he has written, gives the following account.

The Phonic Workshop is being developed to promote word attack skills for children of normal ability whose progress in reading is held up for want of satisfactory word attack.

If a child continues to be dependent on a sight vocabulary, then he will:

1   have insufficient practice with words that he finds difficult
2   tend to guess wildly from context and illustrations
3   make many mistakes and become discouraged
4   fail to derive enjoyment from his reading.

The Workshop is based on a study of early readers and lists of key words. These indicated that if the child is familiar with consonant blends and can be given a visual clue that imparts information as to when a sound needs to be omitted or changed, then he will be in a position to attempt the majority of the unfamiliar words that he is likely to encounter at this stage in his reading.

The prompting is provided by a diacritical mark—an underlining to indicate 'nonsounding', and one colour signal (red) to represent the use of a letter name. These two cues reduce most of the words exemplified to regularity.

Before the child begins to use the Workshop, it is assumed that certain subskills have been mastered. Thus the child must know the letter sounds and be able to read regular three-letter words. This is taken as the starting point to ensure that the child will meet with a high degree of success, thereby encouraging a more positive attitude towards reading.

The Workshop consists of eighty-two cards following a commonly used gradation of difficulty, working through three-letter words, double consonant blends, consonant digraphs, vowel digraphs, 'long' vowels, vowel plus *r* and various other groups. Discrimination and matching tasks are provided and at later stages, passages incorporating the phonic features that have been recently taught, are presented.

In order to ensure that transfer of training has taken place, stories are introduced after each major section of the workshop (cards 30 and 60) in which the signalling devices are not used. These cards give an opportunity for the identification of any weaknesses that require further help.

The language experience approach and the remediation of reading difficulties

The language experience approach is *one* of the methods which members of the Special Education Course at Manchester College of Education are encouraged to use with many of the nonreaders with whom they work. (A pamphlet dealing with the approach can be obtained from Peter Westwood, Special Education Department, Manchester College of Education, Long Millgate, Manchester 3, provided that a stamped addressed foolscap envelope is enclosed with any inquiry.)

The central thesis of the language experience approach (Stauffer 1969, 1970) is contained in the words of Allen (1961): 'What I think about I can talk about. What I can say I can write or someone can write for me. What I write I can read.'

In order to make any progress in reading, many children with reading difficulties require a highly structured and specific programme of remedial work. With such a need to be met there is a definite danger of providing a very narrow remedial scheme using perhaps visual-auditory-kinaesthetic techniques, flashcards, phonic workbooks, reading programmes or any of a multitude of activities relevant to the child's specific need. Whilst any of these activities may be theoretically sound, they can all be intrinsically boring. The problem facing the teacher is how to cover the necessary skills of word recognition, phonics and comprehension through an approach which is interesting and meaningful to the child. It is claimed by enthusiasts that the *structured* use of the language experience approach allows a teacher to achieve this goal.

The language experience approach uses material produced by the child as a medium through which to teach basic reading skills. Oral language rather than the printed page is the starting point. It is a flexible approach which can be adapted to include any *specific* remedial techniques needed by the child as revealed in the results of diagnostic testing or informal observation of his work. It is particularly appropriate to the older child who is a nonreader. As the approach develops with the child's developing skills, the method is in effect a process of *diagnostic teaching* in which diagnosis and the required action are closely linked.

In the modification of the method suggested by Westwood, the following principles of method are emphasized:

1 The means by which language experience material may be obtained from the child with particular emphasis on recording units of experience. The experience recorded in a variety of ways must be *one seen by the child* as significant.

2 There should be teacher control of the quality and quantity of written material. Whilst an entirely colloquial restricted code expression is acceptable, the teacher may, if he is assisting in recording the phrase, help the child to modify the language in the direction of a more conventional model. For example, Westwood does not believe that it is either necessary or desirable to accept absolutely any child-produced expression describing an experience as the *sole* basis for writing a comment on the experience that the child has recorded in pictorial or other form.

3 The teacher must be aware of the importance of a basic sight vocabulary and ensure that the child's recordings give adequate attention to this. In practice, it seems likely that the very structure of the children's linguistic patterns will broadly be working to the same end as the teacher, but this cannot be left to chance.

4 The initial written recording may be:
   i   by the teacher of the child's statement
   ii a copy by the child of the teacher's recording of the child's statement
   iii by the child with teacher's help
   iv by the child with peer-group help
   v   by the child alone
   vi or by any combination of the above
   It is up to the teacher to ensure that overlearning takes place using any specific remedial approach that is suitable.

5 A record of words acquired in terms of sight vocabulary and spelling vocabulary must be kept by the child. An alphabetically-indexed word box is useful in this respect, and provides a cumulative record of words known and words on which further work is needed.

6 Phonics can be introduced as required to either a group of children or to an individual.

7   Attention should be given to persistent errors and supplementary games and apparatus used to provide experiences that enable the child to discriminate his errors.

The assessment of change in reading attainment and attitude

All teachers who are concerned with helping to improve the reading skills and attitudes of children with reading difficulties must face the problems associated with the measurement of the changes that they help their pupils achieve. A recently published book by Farr (1970) can be recommended to anyone wishing to know more about this topic.

According to G. E. Bookbinder, the use of certain popular reading tests with outdated norms frequently results in teachers grossly over-estimating their pupil's reading progress. Work in Salford indicated that at the lower end of the scale, the Schonell Graded Reading Vocabulary Test and the Burt (Rearranged) Word Reading Test are respectively up to a year and eighteen months below equivalent norms of recently standardized tests (Bookbinder 1970). Bookbinder has produced some revised norms for both the Schonell and Burt Tests. Although he has considerable reservations about the accuracy of his revision, he suggests that they represent present day norms more realistically than those frequently used in teaching and research. Bookbinder's point is supported to some extent by data obtained by Young working in Barnsley in the standardization of his own reading test (Young 1969).

Marion Monroe drew attention also to the uses and misuses of tests in the remedial teaching of reading. Tests are needed to offset the subjective nature of teacher's judgments. These need not be standardized but may be of an informal nature to test certain skills, for example the teacher may tally the number of words read correctly out of a list of, say, fifty words that appear frequently in the books used by the children. Or she may ask each child to read an unfamiliar passage aloud while she checks the errors in oral reading. Such unstandardized informal tests serve the useful function of identifying children who require help in certain reading skills. If used after the child has been helped, they can give a rough but useful indication of the benefit that the child has received.

Standardized tests of reading achievement are being used increasingly in the evaluation of educational outcomes. These tests help the teacher to compare each child's reading achievement not only with the members of his own class, but with city and national norms. It seems likely that in the not too distant future, LEAs will establish a regular testing programme in reading (and other areas) that will enable them quickly to be aware of standards in schools to a much greater extent than at present. Indeed, the National Computing Centre is currently engaged in exploring this field with a number of authorities. In the

USA a number of organizations already provide a comprehensive testing service for schools.

In the assessment of change in reading, attention must not be restricted solely to the proficiency of a child's skills. It is equally important that the child's attitude towards reading (and towards the situation in which his reading instruction occurs) should be taken into account. Indeed, if we had instruments that were sufficiently reliable, valid and able to register small changes in children's attitudes towards reading, it could be argued that tests of attainment might be discarded. Ensuring that children have a positive attitude towards the language arts has been the keynote of a number of important contributions towards helping children with reading difficulties achieve competence, e.g. Ablewhite (1967) and Warner (1963). However, some experts doubt whether children's attitudes towards a particular subject such as reading or towards the language arts are sufficiently stable during the first six years of formal education to be measured reliably. Even allowing that they might be, the instruments currently available have many weaknesses (Pumfrey and Dixon 1970). However, the use of the Georgiades' scale (Georgiades 1967) offers some hope, and the application of the semantic differential and the repertory grid approaches may enable both the development of children's attitudes towards reading and the effects of various interventions, in the case of children with reading difficulties, to be assessed. Clearly, a combination of competence in the skills coupled with a favourable attitude towards the activity, is desirable. At present our tests of attainment are generally superior to our tests of attitudes. Current work suggests that this gap can be narrowed.

In-service training
From time to time, officers of an LEA become concerned about the standards of reading in schools. Typically, certain schools tending to cluster in the less salubrious parts of our industrial conurbations are found to have an extremely high incidence of backwardness in reading. In order to remedy this situation, a variety of interventions are inaugurated. At one time it was fashionable for LEAs to set up Remedial Education Services, whose staff either visited schools on a peripatetic basis to work with small groups of children requiring help with reading, or withdrew children from schools and gave appropriate help at a remedial centre or clinic.

This practice has serious limitations. Whilst some short-term gains in the reading attainment of children receiving this type of help are frequently found, in the long term these gains disappear (Chazan 1967). Thus currently teachers in remedial services are reviewing their practices (Pumfrey 1970).

A. J. M. Morison, Senior Educational Psychologist responsible for the Schools Psychological Service and Remedial Education Service in

Manchester, has been concerned in altering the emphasis of the remedial service from the traditional mould.

What appears to distinguish Manchester's reading centres from other centres in the country are the following four points. The first and major one is the year-round programme of short in-service courses in the teaching of reading for primary school teachers including their headteachers, and also for teachers in secondary school including some heads of departments. These courses are on modern approaches and techniques in the teaching of reading with the emphasis on helping teachers to help children with reading difficulties in the classroom situation. The responsibility for helping these children is placed firmly on the class teacher and the school rather than on a group of peripatetic 'experts' who, in any case, would never be numerous enough to cope with the problem by themselves. The aim of the courses is to increase the teacher's expertise and involvement in relieving the problem of backwardness in reading throughout the city and not only in the particularly difficult areas, though naturally enough the initial emphasis is on teachers from schools in such areas.

Secondly, schools are permitted to recruit an additional part-time temporary teacher to allow release of a full-time member of staff to attend a course in school time. These day release courses last four mornings per week for four consecutive weeks.

Thirdly, the staff of the reading centres offer an advisory service to teachers on a long-term basis as a sequel to the day-release course. This is achieved by remedial staff visiting the schools and by the schools' staff visiting the reading centres.

Fourthly, whilst recognizing the likely effects of a 'reading drive' (Southgate 1965), a systematic attempt is being made to evaluate certain aspects of the work both by the service itself and by research students from the University of Manchester. Although it is too early to estimate comprehensively the effects of the in-service courses, some preliminary evidence is encouraging (Brannen 1971).

In the words of Bookbinder, under whose aegis the Salford Remedial Education Service is developing into a Remedial Advisory Service, 'The responsibility for the teaching of reading remains with the class teacher—*but he is not left to stew in his own juice.*'

References

ABLEWHITE, R. C. (1967) *The Slow Reader* London: Heinemann

ALLEN, R. VAN and HALRORSEN, G. (1961) *The Language Experience Approach to Reading Instruction* in *Reading*, no. 27, New York: Ginn

BIRCH, H. G. and BELMONT, L. (1964) Auditory-visual integration in normal and retarded readers in *American Journal of Orthopsychiatry* 34, 825–61

BIRCH, H. G. and BELMONT, L. (1965) Auditory-visual integration, intelligence and reading ability in school children in *Perceptual Motor Skills* 20, 295–305

BLEASDALE, E. (1969) Reading by Rainbow in *Reading* 3, 3, 28–31

BOND, G. L., and TINKER, M. A. (1967) *Reading difficulties: their diagnosis and correction* New York: Appleton, Century, Crofts

BOOKBINDER, G. E. (1970) Variations in reading test norms in *Educational Research* 12, 2, 99–105

BRANNEN, B. (1971) *The evaluation of an in-service course for teachers in the teaching of reading* Unpublished dissertation, Department of Education, University of Manchester

BRIMER, M. A. and DUNN, L. M. (1962) *English Picture Vocabulary Tests* Bristol: Educational Evaluation Enterprises

CASHDAN, A. (1970) Backward readers—research into auditory-visual integration in Gardner, K. (ed) *Reading Skills: Theory and Practice* London: Ward Lock Educational

CAVANAGH, P. and JONES, C. (1969) *Yearbook of Educational and Instructional Technology 1969/70, incorporating Programmes in Print* London: Cornmarket Press

CHAZAN, M. (1967) The effects of remedial teaching in reading: A review of research in *Remedial Education* 2, 1, 4–12

CHAZAN, M. and DOWNES, G. (eds) (1971) *Compensatory education and the new media* Occasional Publication no. 3 University College of Swansea, Department of Education

CLIFT, P. S. (1969) *Word Study* London: Bell and Howell

DOUGLAS, J. W. B. and ROSS, J. M. (1964) Subsequent progress of nursery school children in *Educational Research* 7, 2, 83–94

DREVER, J. (1964) *A dictionary of psychology* Harmondsworth: Penguin

DUNN, L. M. and SMITH, J. O. (eds) (1965) *Peabody Language Development Kit* Circle Pines, Minnesota: American Guidance Service

FARR, R. (ed) (1970) *Measurement and Evaluation of Reading* New York: Harcourt, Brace and World

GAGNE, R. M. *The Conditions of Learning* New York: Holt, Rinehart and Winston

GEORGIADES, N. J. (1967) A report of a pilot study on the development of an instrument to investigate the attitude of children to reading in Downing, J. and Brown, A. L. (eds) *The Second International Reading Symposium* London: Cassell

GIBSON, E. J., PICK, A., OSSER, H. and HAMMOND, M. (1962) The role of the grapheme-phoneme correspondence in the perception of words in *American Journal of Psychology* 75, 554–570

HARLOW, H. F. (1949) The formation of learning sets in *Psychological Review* 56, 51–65

HARROLD, M. V. and TEMPLE, M. H. (1960) *A study of children in the admission classes of four infant schools, making a comparison between those who have attended a nursery school and those admitted direct from home* Unpublished thesis, Child Development Centre, Institute of Education, University of London

KIRK, S. A., MCCARTHY, J. and KIRK, W. D. (1968) *Illinois Test of Psycholinguistic Abilities (Revised Edition)* Illinois: University of Illinois Press

LYSAUGHT, J. P. and WILLIAMS, C. M. (1963) *A guide to programmed instruction* New York: Wiley

MORRIS, J. M. (1959) *Reading in the Primary School* London: Newnes (for NFER)

MOYLE, D. and L. M. (1971) *Modern Innovations in the Teaching of Reading* London: University of London Press

O'SULLIVAN, D. (1958) *A comparative study of two groups of children in the infant school: (1) nursery children (2) non-nursery children* Unpublished thesis, Child Development Centre, Institute of Education, University of London

PUMFREY, P. D. (1970) Change in remedial education in *Remedial Education* 5, 1, 24–25

PUMFREY, P. D. and DIXON, E. (1970) Junior children's attitudes to reading: comments on three measuring instruments in *Reading* 4, 2, 19–26

QUIGLEY, H. (1970) Nursery teachers' reactions to the Peabody Language Development Kit in *British Journal of Educational Psychology* 41, 2, 155–162

REYNELL, J. (1969) *Reynell Developmental Language Scales Manual* NFER: Slough

SHELDON, W. D. (1970) Specific principles essential to classroom diagnosis in Farr, R. (ed) *Measurement and Evaluation of Reading* New York: Harcourt, Brace and World

SOUTHGATE, V. (1965) Approaching i t a results with caution in *Educational Research* 7, 2, 83–96

SOUTHGATE, V. and ROBERTS, G. (1970) *Reading—Which Approach?* London: University of London Press

STAUFFER, R. G. (1969) *Teaching Reading as a Thinking Process* New York: Harper and Row

STAUFFER, R. G. (1970) *The Language Experience Approach* New York: Harper and Row

TANSLEY, A. E. (1967) *Reading and Remedial Reading* London: Routledge and Kegan Paul

WARNER, S. A. (1963) *Teacher* New York: Secker and Warburg

WHITE, A. (1967) An approach to reading in *Remedial Education* 2, 2, 53–55

WILDLAKE, P. (1971) Language and learning in the pre-school in *Remedial Education* 6, 2, 14–18

L

WILSON, R. M. (1967) *Diagnostic and Remedial Reading* Columbus: Merrill

YOUNG, D. (1969) *Group Reading Test* London: University of London Press

20 The language difficulties of deaf children and hearing children in learning to read

Jean Palmer

Introduction

My work in training teachers of deaf children, as well as my connection with reading research undertaken during the past six years in the Department of Audiology and Education of the Deaf at Manchester University, has led me to think that an understanding of some of the problems which deaf children experience in learning to read can help us to appreciate some of the difficulties of children who do not suffer from this handicap. For, strange as it may seem, the greatest problem that deaf children encounter in learning to read is not that of decoding; their chief problem seems to be that of understanding the great variety of language structures used in even the most carefully devised of readers designed for hearing children. Obviously, mastering the mechanics of reading is important and it is extremely difficult, but the deaf child's retardation in both language and experience presents a far greater problem.

What is the linguistic retardation of deaf children? Many lay people, unfortunately, refer to deaf children as being 'deaf and dumb'. This is not true; a deaf child is not a dumb child. Yet without very special help the deaf child does not learn to talk, merely because he is unable to acquire speech and language as normally hearing people do, i.e. by hearing other people talking. Language is a skill which most people acquire naturally. The young hearing child generally learns to talk without paying a great deal of conscious attention to the task, just because he is in an environment where he hears people talking. The hearing child, when he enters school at the age of five, can speak in sentences and is able to use and understand quite complex spoken English. He has a sufficiently good knowledge of the *system* of his native language to enable him to *use* it. What he cannot do is describe how he formulates sentences. In fact, quite an early step in learning to talk is learning to use automatically the forms and arrangements that are part of normal English usage. With people of normal hearing, these patterns are so thoroughly and naturally acquired in early childhood that even the majority of adults would find it difficult to analyze these forms. Yet language, which most people use so easily without paying a great deal of attention to what they are doing, is one of the most intricate of all systems of human behaviour.

It is only when faced with the challenge of trying to impose on deaf children structures that normal people learn so easily, but which many of the deaf find so tremendously difficult, that one becomes aware of the vast complexities of the thing we call language. (I think I am correct in saying that the computer has not yet been invented which can produce language.)

It is interesting to see each year students who are training to be teachers of the deaf becoming increasingly aware of the subtleties of their native language as they learn to deal with deaf children. In fact, only today a group of students, all of whom are qualified teachers and some of whom have a considerable amount of teaching experience, commented (after some of them had tried to teach groups of profoundly deaf children and had realized that they had used language that was too complex) that they had never been so conscious of language before. For the first time they realized that the same words were being used in different ways when the meaning only became clear through use of context for example: find a *stick*. *Stick* the square . . . ; draw round . . . (which did not mean draw a circle). They realized that 'Stir it all up' was confusing for a deaf child even though, or perhaps because the child knew the meanings of all the words in isolation.

Most teachers of the deaf believe that language for deaf children needs to be simplified and structured to some extent wherever possible, but this simplification is a task which we can only do adequately if we ourselves have a good grasp of language and the way it works.

Language and meaning

Let us examine some of the ways in which language, in this case the English language, works to enable speakers to convey the most subtle of meanings, the most complicated of thoughts. According to Quirk (1962), the first thing to note is that a language has at least two important dimensions. The first of these is the word-stock, also known as the vocabulary or lexis; in other words, our total collection of names for things. Words are so predominant in language that it is tempting to think that there is nothing else to consider. But a language cannot work with words alone. A group of words like 'man', 'go', 'think', 'girl', do not tell us much until a second dimension of language is added— grammar. With the addition of grammar, these four words can be made to tell us something, for example; 'The man thought the girls had gone.' In this sentence grammar has done three things. First, it has arranged the words in a particular order, making clear who did the thinking and who the going. Second, grammar has contributed *tense* by the alteration of 'think' to 'thought', and *number* by the addition of *s* to 'girl'. Thirdly, grammar has added some additional words, 'the', 'that', 'the' and 'had'. This statement need not be confusing if it is remembered that English has two kinds of words—lexical words and grammatical words. (An easy way of differentiating between the two is to say that the grammatical words have 'less meaning'; they are 'empty' words.) Sometimes these grammatical words are referred to as function words; they are the vital signals which reveal the type of connection that is to be understood between the lexical words. These signals are difficult for deaf children and probably for some hearing children too.

The grammar of language is learned naturally by people with normal hearing during the early stages of childhood. Of course, grammatical mistakes are still made by children at the primary stage of education. An example might be 'John and me buyed an ice-cream.' The sentence is incorrect but it communicates its meaning adequately. In fact, it reveals how the child is using the language system. In time such mistakes are eliminated and the child uses structures exactly as the adult does. He develops a feeling for what is right. Eventually, familiarity with normal English structure leads us to recognize Lewis Carroll's:

'Twas brillig and the slithy toves
Did gyre and gimble in the wabe.

as a basically English utterance, though a fairly meaningless one. Most of the words in this quotation are nonsensical yet we recognize them as adjectives, nouns, verbs etc. On the other hand, the foreigner's 'What it is?' is composed of a collection of meaningful words in which the structure is strange and unnatural.

Cherry (1957) emulated Carroll to some extent and produced the following sentence: 'The ventious crapests pouted raditally.' Again, we recognize an adjective, a noun, a verb and an adverb—to use but one form of grammatical analysis. Cherry had the audacity to translate his sentence into French: 'Les crapêts ventieux pontaient raditallement', and it still sounded quite acceptable.

The point is that most people develop unconsciously a knowledge of structure and it is the relative lack of this knowledge in the deaf child which contributes so much to his problems in reading. It may be true that some hearing children who have this knowledge as regards *oral* language, find it more difficult to deal with the printed word if their attention is focused too much on decoding.

Normally, people understand sentences because of their awareness of two things—first, the structure signals and the ways they operate; second, an awareness of the meaning of the words. Normally the words and the structure are noticed together. It is not enough to know the meaning of the main words. It has been said, though perhaps this is something of an exaggeration, that it is possible to understand the meaning of all the words in a language and yet not to understand a single utterance in that language. Perhaps the interrelationship of words and structure can be made clearer by referring to some of the work of Gleason (1965). He takes a Punjabi sentence and translates the lexical items, while leaving the structural features untouched. The following is an example of such a sentence: '*mere* friend *ne* washerman *nu* stream *kol* walk-*de* see-*a* uncle *nal*.' It is obvious that the sentence is about a friend, a washerman, a stream, an uncle, and the acts of walking and seeing. Yet the meaning is not very clear. There is doubt about *who* is walking and *who* is seeing. It is therefore not enough to understand the main words, one needs to grasp the relationship of the words, the structure. (Fully translated, the sentence reads: 'My friend saw the washerman walking with uncle near the stream.')

Words, therefore, are not the only thing that matter in language, and teaching words is not teaching language. To quote from Derrick (1966):

> There is a danger that, because language is apparently made up of words, the learner or teacher will confuse *words* with *language*. Teaching language does not consist simply of teaching words, any more than learning language consists of learning just words. The teacher of English as a second language has to teach grammar in action. The teacher will in fact find it most useful to think of grammar in terms of structure—the way words and forms of words are used together to convey meaning.

Specific language difficulties of deaf children
To return to deaf children; most workers in the field of deaf education would agree that many of these children find difficulty with structure. Their sentences commonly consist of a collection of words. Does the deaf child's 'Me play ball' mean, 'I am playing ball'? Or does it mean, 'I want to play with that ball', or 'I played with my ball yesterday'? It would seem fair to assume that for many deaf children, reading with full understanding is as impossible as it was for us with the Punjabi sentence. The deaf child may know the meaning of the main words he is likely to come across in the early books of published reading schemes, yet lack the knowledge of the particular meaning carried by those words in the structure in which they are used. This is not merely a hypothesis: to quote from a Scottish Education Department Report (1950):

> The difficulties of construction are as great at least as those of vocabulary. The deaf child who knows the meaning of 'up', 'straight' and 'sit' does not thereby know the meaning of 'Sit up straight.'

Research results obtained by Redgate (1964) showed that in a representative sample of 144 deaf children aged eight to ten years, 76 per cent could respond correctly when presented with very simple written commands. However, when using the *same simple vocabulary,* these commands were slightly restructured by the substitution of a different preposition or the introduction of a negative, only 32–36 per cent of these children could respond correctly. Various less common sentence structures, still using very simple vocabulary, were understood by as few as 1–13 per cent of these deaf children. Yet these varieties of sentence structures are to be found in reading books designed for hearing children which deaf children are also expected to use.

In 1961 I administered the Neale Analysis of Reading Ability to 54 children, aged 12 years to 16 years 9 months, in the secondary department of a big school for the deaf. Other children in the age group were not tested because it was known that they would not be able to score at all. Although the sample tested contained a large proportion of partially hearing children, the mean reading age in the group was 7 years 6 months, and 33 per cent of the pupils attained a level of less than 7 years. (A recent study conducted on 698 deaf children in 23 schools for the deaf shows that sixteen year olds are, on average, only six months ahead of nine year olds in reading, and are still below the eight year reading level.)

The linguistic difficulties experienced by the deaf child which I have outlined are not, unfortunately, the only sources of his problems. Also important is his lack of experience, and this is a problem that he may share with the many thousands of children who suffer from deprivation of one kind or another. Reading is not merely a thought-getting process. To quote from Smith and Dechant (1962): 'The mind must function in the reading process'; 'Neither printed page nor orally spoken words transmit meaning. The essence of meaning comes from the reader's fund of experience. Reading includes thinking as well as understanding'; and 'The author does not really convey ideas to the reader; he merely stimulates him to construct them out of his own experience.' Very often the deaf child has not the requisite experience to bring to the printed page. Similarly, many hearing children may not have the requisite firsthand experience which would seem to be essential at an early stage.

The research project I referred to earlier was concerned partly with a comparison between the use of i t a and t o with deaf children and partly with an evaluation of a published reading scheme. Its findings are, in the main, outside the scope of this paper. Yet certain aspects of the project, related to children's language and to reading schemes in common use in normal schools, are of interest here.

The choice of a suitable reading scheme for the experiment was no easy task. Obviously the scheme chosen had to be published in both i t a and t o. Twenty-two different reading schemes were studied in depth in terms of the methods used, that is phonic or look-and-say, the amount and kinds of reading material supplied, the style of language used (with attention being paid to sentence structure, tenses used, whether the language was natural or 'English English', the interest level, the print, layout, illustrations, vocabulary gradient and so on). One interesting point to emerge was that many of the schemes which claim to have a carefully controlled introduction of new vocabulary in fact fall far short of this! The repetition of vocabulary once it has been introduced is not consistent. The McKee scheme (McKee *et al* 1956) was finally chosen because it was considered to have the fewest disadvantages. Even so, the research team doubted whether it would really meet the needs of deaf children.

It is probably worth mentioning that throughout the experiment teachers compiled record cards of each child's progress. These records should prove invaluable to anyone designing reading materials for severely linguistically deprived children.

The research results seem to indicate that if deaf children are to master the English language and read well, there must be a carefully controlled introduction and reinforcement of language patterns — controlled and reinforced to a greater extent than is found in most materials at present produced. There must also be an attempt to limit the language in first readers to that already met by the children in other situations. Preferably, some language used in books would be based on language actually used by children. In this way it is hoped that deaf children might be enabled to progress beyond the current 7 to 8 year reading age plateau. It would seem reasonable to assume that while deaf children are working through the first readers of a conventional scheme, their difficulties are accumulating, though this does not become apparent until later when progress seems to be halted. A much firmer grounding in early reading skills, through greater control of structure, would seem to be required. Yet reading materials are so often analyzed according to the frequency with which the words are repeated on successive pages. If experts in the field of teaching reading to hearing children are becoming increasingly concerned about the attention which should be paid to control of structure, how much more important it is that this should be a concern for teachers of the handicapped.

Language difficulties of hearing children
Many of the difficulties relating to the structure of language which prove to be obstacles to deaf children who are trying to learn to read are also applicable, although in less severe forms, to children of normal hearing. They are particularly relevant to the linguistically deprived child, whether he comes from a linguistically impoverished English-speaking home or from a home in which English is not the native language. Accordingly, the conclusions drawn about the language deficiencies of deaf children, as well as the criticisms made about the language used in many books used for beginning reading, can help to

point the way to improved reading teaching for children who are not deaf.

The following points might be particularly helpful in this respect:

1 More attention than hitherto should be given to the careful and controlled introduction of linguistic structures in reading schemes.
2 Ideas involved in early reading material should be within the experience of the child.
3 Consideration should be given to the increase in difficulty encountered between consecutive books in a reading scheme— perhaps by use of such techniques as the cloze procedure.
4 Attempts should be made to develop in teachers a greater awareness of the way their language works.

References

CHERRY, C. (1957) *On Human Communications* New York: Wiley, Chapman and Hall
DERRICK, J. (1966) *Teaching English to Immigrants* London: Longmans
GLEASON, H. A. (1965) *Linguistics and English Grammar* New York: Holt, Rinehart and Winston
McKEE, P. *et al* (1956) *The McKee Readers* London: Nelson
QUIRK, R. (1962) *The Use of English* London: Longmans
REDGATE, G. W. (1964) *Diagnostic Tests of Reading Ability for Deaf Children* Unpublished M.Ed. thesis University of Manchester
SCOTTISH EDUCATION DEPARTMENT (1950) *Report*
SMITH, H. P. and DECHANT, E. B. (1962) *Psychology in Teaching Reading* New Jersey: Prentice Hall

21 The English Colour Code programmed reading course

David V. Moseley

Research background

A survey of 1,254 children, carried out in 1967, revealed that the following symptoms were characteristic of retarded readers:

1 inability to blend three or more phonemes
2 limited awareness of single-phoneme differences between words
3 poor visual analysis of figures consisting of three or more elements

At least 75 per cent of retarded nine year olds had one or more of these difficulties although very few (5 per cent) had all three.

These results influenced the design of a remedial reading and spelling programme, recently published by the National Society for Mentally Handicapped Children. If phoneme-grapheme relations were made explicit by auditory prompts and visual cues, it was thought that the majority of slow learners would be able to make the necessary links.

This rationale led the author to experiment with colour-coded grapheme tiles. As Lee (1960) has shown, consonants are much more regular in spelling than vowels. It was not necessary, therefore, to use separate colours for consonant sounds. The English Colour Code consists of fifteen colour-cues used for vowel symbols, with the exception of neutral vowels. The name of each colour includes the appropriate vowel sound, e.g. red *e* (short vowel), green *e* (long vowel). An essential point was that every possible combination of letters used for vowel sounds was included, and a single grapheme tile always stood for a single sound. The complete set of consonant and vowel graphemes was used for word-building, with the teacher providing the necessary items and giving phonic prompts as required. For example, if a pupil wanted to build the word 'launch', the teacher supplied him with the following symbols: au n l ch. The pupil would work out the correct order, and perhaps copy the word.

The grapheme tiles were used for six months by twenty-nine children (aged 7–10 years) entering remedial groups. The children were selected from a considerably larger pool of entrants, on the grounds that they performed badly in blending and discriminating sounds or in copying designs. At the end of the six-month period, the average improvement in word recognition was twenty-one months on the Burt test, and this was accompanied by improved blending scores.

While these results were encouraging, the procedure necessarily involved one-to-one teaching. However, if the teacher's prompts and feedback were recorded on tape, and printed worksheets were supplied, the student would be able to work without close supervision. But would separate graphemes be recognized as such in printed words, in the same way as before, when separate tiles were used? Before proceeding to publication, it was important to determine by experimental means whether coloured vowel symbols and various other typographical cues simplified the decoding process.

Five versions of the same *ar* worksheet were randomly distributed among 290 normal eleven year olds. Sentences were read out on tape, and missing letters and words filled in to phonic dictation. No mention was made of the different graphic cues, which included colour, as well as fine, bold, and italic type. Comparison of pre- and post-test spelling scores showed that the scarlet *ar* was not confusing, but that both fine and italic type gave poorer results than no cues at all. However, bold type helped to reduce errors in polysyllables by 61 per cent, although it was not effective when used as a cue for neutral vowels. In fact, all special cues used for neutral vowels and silent letters tended to confuse rather than clarify. For a more detailed account of this research, see Moseley (1969a). In the published version of the worksheets, colour and bold type are the only cues which have been retained.

A duplicated version of the complete course was used by ten backward secondary children for a period of seventeen weeks. The phonic prompts were supplied by a teacher, not by a tape recorder. In addition, a second group of eight children followed the same course, with recorded instruction played back by the (Edison's Responsive Environment) Talking Typewriter. Both groups showed substantial gains in reading, spelling, phoneme-blending, and spatial analysis. As with junior children, it was very unlikely for a pupil to exceed a seven year level of attainment if he were unable to blend four phonemes reliably. Full details of programme content are given in a report by Moseley (1969b). The strong emphasis on phoneme-blending, first as a listening skill, and then linked with precise visual analysis of word structure, appears to be fully justified. So, too, does the claim that recorded phonic instruction can to a great extent take the place of the live teacher.

Application

The course has undergone two extensive revisions since the duplicated version was compiled. Each type of exercise has been tried out both at the Centre for Learning Disabilities and in schools. While some parts of the course are specially intended for teenagers, the scheme is suitable for any pupil of eight years or more who can make sense of a phonic approach. This will exclude some educationally subnormal children who have inadequate powers of analysis or generalization.

As writing plays an important part in the course, a spelling test rather than a reading test should be used to decide where a student should begin. Spelling scores are sometimes significantly lower than reading scores, but the reverse is almost never true. A table of spelling ages and recommended starting points, covering attainment levels between five and nine years, is given in the manual.

If a tape recorder and headphones are available, the course may be used in a normal classroom as well as in a small group setting. Additional sets of worksheets may be purchased, so that more than one pupil can follow the same tape. If a tape recorder is not available, the teacher can present the material from duplicated notes.

The length of study periods will vary according to age and ability, but will probably be between fifteen and thirty minutes. It is not intended that a complete programme (or even a complete page) should always be worked through in a single session. The slowest rate of working is likely to be one programme per week. This allows three or four sessions per week for supplementary exercises and activities which will ensure enough repetition at each stage of learning. When the student shows his completed worksheet to the teacher, and reads out certain sections, the teacher decides how much followup work is needed. Some suggestions are given in the manual, and many other useful ideas have been put forward by Jackson (1971).

The worksheets are nonexpendable. They may be cleaned with a damp cloth, but before doing this the student should enter the words he has written in his own 'spelling dictionary'. He will then have lists for revision and for rapid reference during free-writing. He should be encouraged to add new words on his own initiative. A colour-coded reference system is described in the manual.

Progress tests are given at three key points in the course. If a student does not reach the levels indicated, he should not be allowed to proceed.

Stages of learning
The practice of 'sounding out' never fails to attract criticism from holists. And yet the ability to blend phonemes is the most important single correlate of word-recognition (once a basic sight vocabulary has been acquired). Blending can fail to occur for a number of reasons, among which are the following:

1 poor auditory discrimination
2 indistinct articulation
3 limited memory for a sequence of sounds

All three defects can be trained by audio-vocal practice.

Additional visual and association processes are involved in decoding the printed word. Immediate recognition of two and three-letter graphemes becomes very important at a reading age of seven plus. Another essential development is flexibility in assigning sound-values to graphemes. In fluent readers these processes are automatic, although even fluent readers analyze new words subvocally, usually in syllable units.

It is obviously better for a child to rely on rapid subvocal analysis of a new monosyllable than to 'sound it out aloud' with grunts and groans. However, good subvocal habits are best acquired by listening to the voices of competent models. Quiet conditions are essential. A headset shuts out unwanted background noise.

The first five programmes are concerned with letter recognition, initial consonant sounds and short vowel sounds. No prior awareness of serial position is needed. No initial consonant blends are given in the examples for auditory discrimination, so the single consonant sounds may be as salient as possible. Many phonic programmes make the mistake of asking for responses to first, middle and final sounds at too early a stage. As Carver (1970) has shown, children do not normally master sequential aspects of decoding, including auditory discrimination of initial multiple consonants, before they reach an attainment age of $6\frac{1}{2}$–7 years.

More than 100 written responses are made in each programme, and the print size has been chosen to match the handwriting of a young child. The first side of each sheet deals with a group of five letters, which have dissimilar shapes and sounds. On the 'rhyme side' the range of letters to be recognized and written includes those which have been studied in earlier programmes. Here the student writes whole words and also copies simple sentences. A total of forty words is used. If both the letters and the words are to be thoroughly learned, supplementary exercises and games will be needed. Some of these should be designed to help make reliable discriminations between very similar sounds (e.g. m/n) or very similar shapes (e.g. i/j).

The next stage (programmes 6–10) gives a great deal of emphasis to the serial aspects of words and sentences. Both whole-word and phonic exercises are used. While more than seventy common words are learned without analysis, at least three times as many are shown to make sense phonically. Important sight words are taught in groups of four. The student has to put a mark beside the appropriate word whenever he hears it in a story. Frequent pauses are made so that the student can rehearse the phrase or sentence he has just heard. This trains him to try out various possible solutions, without forgetting the context in which a word occurred. It is most important that concentration on single words or sounds should not preclude listening for meaning.

The aim of the picture exercises in these programmes is to promote rapid blending of phonemes as a listening skill, and to link the dictation of sounds with visual scanning. The sounds are articulated at the rate of two per second. At this speed, the burden on immediate memory is greatly reduced and closure is easily achieved. The only motor response required is underlining one of two words, most of which differ by the omission or addition of a letter. If the sequence of sounds is rehearsed, the only visual aspect of the exercise is scanning the words and determining how many graphemes are present. This visual analysis is facilitated by the use of extra bold type to indicate graphemes of two or more letters.

Context clues are included in the phonic dictation exercises which follow. Here the student is asked to write in the letters as he hears the sounds. In each case he knows which word he is writing, and as the rate of dictation is slow he should be able to anticipate each sound subvocally. Attention is drawn to all letter positions in four-phoneme words. At first, the student has to write in only one or two letters per word but this is gradually extended to a maximum of four. At this level he may begin to analyze initial or final consonant combinations as single units. However, he is not yet expected to decode new words with any degree of fluency.

On the 'story side' of each programme, the student applies what he has learned in previous exercises. He listens to an episode featuring Ted and his friends and then writes in most of the words, which he can find in an alphabetical reference list at the top of the sheet. At each point the preceding words are read out on the tape, so the student can look back at what he has just written and keep the context in mind. The few words he does not have to write are those which are outside the sight vocabulary and grapheme patterns with which he is already familiar.

The structure of programmes 11–20 is constant, and at this stage the pupil learns how to decode words of three or four phonemes, including those with consonant digraphs and long vowels. Colour-coding facilitates the immediate recognition of vowel digraphs, and once a particular spelling pattern has been studied, it should be recognized without the aid of colour. Only one new combination of letters (qu) is introduced in these programmes; otherwise they serve to consolidate the spelling patterns which occur in programmes 7–10.

Throughout the course, the words to be written include only those spelling patterns which have been previously studied, together with one new pattern from programmes 20 onwards. There are also some sentences for the pupil to read, where the same restrictions apply. New demands are made on the student every three or four lines. Most of the sentences on the sheets include words with missing letters, which are filled in to phonic dictation. Sometimes the word is illustrated by cartoon-style pictures, and recorded sound effects are provided where appropriate. The student has to listen to the phonemes very carefully in order to get the full meaning of each sentence. After time has been given for him to complete the word, it is then spoken normally on the tape, and the student copies it at the side of the sheet. Dashes indicate the number of letters, and the position of digraphs is indicated by the usual cues of bold print for consonants and colour for vowels. Phonic dictation is used for words which include the particular grapheme which is being studied. All the other words written by the student are excluded from analysis.

Each programme includes thirty or more examples of a particular spelling pattern. The words are taken from a 5000 word source list, compiled by the author from seven well known vocabulary and spelling lists. It is clearly not possible to provide enough repetition of individual words for learning to take place on a word-by-word basis. There has to be generalization on the basis of grapheme-patterns if the pupil is to progress beyond a reading repertoire of more than about 200 words. The worksheets are designed to familiarize the student with the full range of graphemes in a gradual progression. The order in which new graphemes are introduced is determined by frequency counts (number of different words rather than occurrence in continuous text), but some concessions have been made to the normal practice of teaching certain patterns in groups.

The teacher should provide ample opportunities for reinforcement of new words after the student has completed each programme. Games and exercises should be available requiring discrimination between short and long vowels, and including some of the more difficult consonant combinations such as *spr* and *str*. After programme 20, reading will come to play a major part in providing reinforcement, particularly if a phonically graded scheme is used. Most words will be read without hesitation, subvocal phonic analysis being used for those patterns which are as yet not fully automatic.

Increasingly, the whole syllable becomes the basic unit for word-building, and to prepare for this, extra bold print is introduced at programme 21 for cueing syllables which are stressed in speech. Separate phoneme cues are phased out, and dropped altogether after programme 35. The grapheme patterns studied towards the end of the course are of relatively low frequency, and include most combinations with silent letters. An attempt should be made in followup work to learn most of the examples.

A supplementary spelling course entitled *Syllable Study* concludes the programme. This is suitable for older and more intelligent students. It covers some rather complicated spelling rules, and teaches the meaning of common prefixes and suffixes.

References

CARVER, C. (1970) *A Group or Individual Word Recognition Test* (Manual of Instructions) London: University of London Press

JACKSON, S. (1971) *Get Reading Right* (Handbook) Glasgow: Gibson

LEE, W. R. (1960) *Spelling Irregularity and Reading Difficulty in English* Occasional Publication no 2 Slough: National Foundation for Educational Research

MOSELEY, D. V. (1969a) Graphic cues for spelling in *Education*, May 14th

MOSELEY, D. V. (1969b) The Talking Typwriter and remedial teaching in a secondary school in *Remedial Education* 4, 196–202

22 Reading failure: a re-examination

John E. Merritt

Introduction

There have been many studies over the years which have shown a relationship between some neurological, perceptual, emotional, sociological or other factors and reading disability. An admirable review of studies of this kind is to be found in Gredler (1971). There is, however, a major problem in interpreting studies of the kind he describes: *in the case of every factor that is supposed to contribute to reading disability we can find a child who should be at risk who can read perfectly well.* In other words, it is no great problem to find a child who is emotionally disturbed, ESN, perceptually impaired or socially disadvantaged who can read tolerably well, even though children in these categories tend to be below average readers or even severely backward. How then do these various influences tend to affect some children, but not others?

I would like to discuss two concepts which, in my view, may be rather important in helping us to understand how this comes about. The two concepts to which I refer are *error factors* and *reading neurosis*.

Error factors

Error factor theory was developed by Harlow (1959) to account for the way in which human beings and animals learn to make discriminations and also how they 'learn to learn'. In initial learning to read, it is necessary for children to discriminate between the sounds of speech, and to discriminate letters and words. It is also necessary for them to learn how to learn new words which they encounter in print. What light may error factor theory throw on this?

First, what is error factor theory? According to this theory, a particular discrimination can only be learned if the correct general response is already in the response repertoire. Obviously, a child cannot discriminate red if he is colour-blind. Similarly, he cannot respond to length if he cannot judge size and distance, or to position if he cannot perceive body-object relationships, and so on. So much is obvious.

The critical point that Harlow emphasized, however, is that in learning to make a new discrimination in a particular situation the child, or animal, must *select* from his repertoire of responses that response which is *appropriate* in the new situation.

M

An important element in the child's selection is the preference he has for the various responses already in his repertoire. If, for example, you want a child to respond to 'twoness' the child may have a preference for 'redness'. Your verbal prompting may, for a variety of reasons, go over his head. And if you want him to attend to volume, as in a Piaget-type experiment, the child may prefer to respond to length.

The examples, of course, are endless, so we must group them in some way if we are going to talk about them sensibly.

Harlow suggested that four error factors were of particular importance: stimulus perseveration; differential cues; response shift; and position preference.

Stimulus perseveration

This refers to a tendency to persist in those responses to a stimulus which are based on preferences as in the examples given above. The preferences may be innate, as in the rat's preference for darkness; on the other hand, they may be the result of previous learning, as when a child taught to read by sounding separate letters says 'wu-a-su' for 'was' or 'tu-hu-e' for 'the'.

If opportunities for learning the correct response are plentiful such errors tend gradually to disappear. Sometimes they persist. This depends to some extent on the treatment the child receives each time he makes a response and we can see how in considering the next error factor.

Differential cue

We can easily make it quite clear to a child that he is correct in making a particular response. For example, we can show our approval when he says the word on the card we show him. But it is less easy to make sure that the child is responding to the relevant features of the printed word. If, for example, he is responding to a flash card, he may be responding to any one of a number of cues when giving the right word. He might be responding simply to word length, or to a dirty mark, or a tear on the card. He might be responding to the relative size of the word against the area of the background. If there are a number of words he might be responding to the position of the word in relation to other words. Some children will do almost anything rather than read!

The influence of this differential cue factor has been found to be a highly persistent source of errors. We can easily see why if we look at the effects of rewarding a correct response in a rather erratic fashion—a procedure known as 'intermittent reinforcement'. If we are constant in rewarding or reinforcing a correct response, the incorrect responses soon drop out and learning is fairly rapid. If on the other hand we are rather erratic in reinforcing a response, that response tends to become relatively fixated and highly resistant to change. Now, if the child is responding to a stimulus for the wrong reason, then in terms of *his* perception he will be receiving intermittent reinforcement.

Consider, for example, the case where a child is required to learn a fairly small number of words. They may occur as the first sentence in a reading scheme, as a set of words on a flash card, or as a block of words on a chart. Let us suppose that the child responds to position. He may possibly think that he is correct when he gives a particular word because it is the first word on the line, the third word shown to him, or the word in the top left-hand corner. He is bound to be right occasionally by chance alone. If he adds another cue, i.e. word length, he will be wrong less often. In terms of *his* perception he is then receiving intermittent reinforcement for responding to position and word length instead of shape. He will, therefore, become even more strongly fixated in responding to a cue that is either wrong, or inadequate. Many children confuse 'here', 'there', 'this', and so on—typical first words in sentences in reading primers. And many children confuse words like 'on', 'do', 'to,' 'is' and so on—typical flash card or lotto words. Much of this may well be accounted for in terms of the intermittent reinforcement of differential cues—the classic route to error fixation.

Response shift
Children, like animals, tend to be unpredictable, even when there seem to be good grounds for us to expect them to be consistent. Even when they have achieved a high level of performance on a task, making no mistakes, they will often shift quite unexpectedly and make a 'foolish' error. Harlow (1959) explains this in terms of an exploratory drive, and reports that it seems difficult to suppress.

But when a child produces a response shift of this kind and makes a 'silly' mistake, what is the typical response of the teacher of an overlarge class at the end of a tiring day? Hopefully, one may say that the teacher is usually tolerant. But it is hard to be tolerant when tired—particularly when faced with behaviour that seems to be at the least perverse and at the worst provocative.

It would be some help, at least, if the teacher knew that such behaviour is not necessarily blameworthy—that it is in some cases beyond the child's control. If we don't feel that a child is necessarily blameworthy, we often find it easier to deal with his behaviour with wisdom and good nature instead of inadvisedly and with impatience.

Position preferences
This is a special case of stimulus preservation. The source of position preference is often 'handedness', something that occurs in animals as well as man. But these are relatively unimportant sources of error in man, and the notion that handedness itself is an important factor in reading failure seems to be largely discredited (Clark 1970).

A complication: the suppression of a suppression

In general, Harlow's position is that one does not positively learn a 'new' response. What happens, rather, is that a number of responses that already existed are suppressed. Thus, in learning to recognize a letter we may learn, for example, not to attend to colour, line thickness, position, background detail or figure-ground relationships. We may then respond primarily to shape—a response tendency we possessed in the first place.

But let us consider the response to orientation—a very important factor in reading. For the first five years of our lives we have been learning to treat orientation as an error factor in identifying objects (Vernon 1957, Merritt 1970a). But nearly half the letters of the alphabet can only be distinguished from other letters by responding to their orientation. In the case of the following letters we must decide what they are by noting whether they are placed facing left or right, or one way up or the other: b-d-p-q; u-n; h-y; f-t.

The same argument applies to sequence. For example a child does not think of his train as being different merely because he switches the position of a couple of the carriages, or if he runs his train across from right to left instead of from left to right. It is still the same train. However a response to sequence is certainly in his repertoire in some circumstances. He soon learns that to be last in a queue is not very rewarding. What he does learn is to ignore sequence as a means of *recognizing* objects. That is to say, having learned to suppress his responses to orientation as an important factor in recognizing objects, he must now suppress that suppression. Little wonder that he is confused when he has to learn that 'was' is now 'saw', 'on' is not 'no', 'goal' is not 'gaol' and so on.

But there is worse to come. I have said that he has to suppress his suppression of response to sequence when looking at letters. He has got to do the same in order to learn to read sequences of words from left to right. But then he has to learn *not* to use a position response as a means of identifying words i.e. he must learn to recognize a whole word by its letters, not by its position in relation to other words.

If you find this confusing then what about the child? Just imagine trying to programme a computer to follow those instructions. And if you find this confusing you clearly do not understand an important element in the learning task. If *you* do not understand it then the child must be learning in spite of your teaching—not because of it. What a marvellous brain even the ESN child must have!

Let us return for a moment to the opening theme: if this orientation problem owes so much to learning, what do we gain by stressing the neurological aspect? If a child's difficulty with orientation does owe something to a neurological deficit of some kind we certainly cannot operate on his brain. Whatever may have predisposed the child to experience difficulty, the remedial problem consists of developing the appropriate learning sets. This is where more attention is really needed both for practical and theoretical reasons.

Interaction of errors

Now let us consider the sum of all these factors. If we had one hundred per cent control over the learning situation for any child, we could, arguably, get rid of the error factors fairly efficiently. But we do not have so much control, nor anything like it. By chance alone some children will happen to be exposed to a better array of learning situations than others.

Perhaps this point could be emphasized by means of an illustration. During the last war, a 'buzz bomb' attack was launched on London and certain districts were badly hit. In the second, third, and subsequent waves of bombing, certain districts which had already suffered severe damage were hit again and again. It was then rumoured that the bombs were being deliberately directed at certain targets.

A bit of careful analysis was enough to show that this was not the case. If a limited number of bombs are directed in a certain general direction then, by chance, they will tend to scatter and not all districts will be hit in the first wave. In the next wave, each district already hit is just as likely to be hit or missed as any other district. The same applies to subsequent waves. Until rather a large number of bombs have been launched, therefore, there will be quite a number of districts which, by chance, receive far more than their fair share. And, of course, some will receive none.

Now let us relate this to the learning situation and consider the reinforcement of errors occurring in a similar way. It must be remembered that we are talking about what *the child* perceives as reinforcement and what *the child* perceives as the response that is being reinforced. As the reinforcements don't occur very frequently, those that do occur will tend to be spread rather unevenly between children and rather unevenly within the total number of responses that any individual child makes. Some will occur in such a way that learning is facilitated. Others will tend to reinforce errors in the manner described above. Some children will be very lucky. Some will be very fortunate. And many will be moderately lucky and moderately unlucky. Hence, even if all children were equal in all respects at the outset, their performances would tend to vary quite appreciably over a period of time.

But of course all children are not identical at the outset. Some are bright and others are less bright, some have minor perceptual lags and others have some degree of emotional disturbance.

A child with one or more minor handicaps may be lucky. He may get the reinforcements he needs just at the optimal moments. He may then become quite a good reader. Another child may just happen to suffer a pattern of reinforcements which fixates a number of errors in critical areas. Being in any case at risk he suffers even more than the average child.

When a number of separate factors can all affect a situation, they usually interact. Thus, if we apply both water and fertilizer to soil, the water will influence growth, the fertilizer will influence growth, and some combinations of water and fertilizer will influence growth to a much greater extent than can be accounted for in terms of the separate effects. The interaction effects of all the factors affecting reading almost certainly operate in this way. The child with two defects is thus thrice handicapped.

Cumulative effects

In reading, as in mathematics, failure tends to be cumulative. If a child fails in certain elementary skills he will make little progress until the failure is remedial. If he is lucky, he may encounter a teacher with a good insight into the reading process who can help him. Or he may eventually realize how to help himself. Many children are not so fortunate and they build up a ballast of errors that sinks them as far as educational achievement is concerned. Again, there is this rather frightening element of sheer chance. And the consequences of being unlucky are disastrous.

Reading neurosis

I should like to draw your attention to a theory I presented at a UKRA Conference in Nottingham (Merritt 1970b). At that time I proposed that the term 'reading neurosis' should be used in a rather specific way. I made this proposal within the context of a different kind of debate and it got lost in the general furore that surrounded that particular issue. I should like, therefore, to restate the points I made.

The story really starts with Pavlov, or more strictly, with Shenger-Krestovnikova in 1914. A dog was trained to salivate when a luminous circle was projected on a screen. This was achieved by projecting the circle immediately prior to feeding. The circle, by the process known as 'conditioning', came to mean 'grub up'. Once this was achieved, an ellipse was occasionally presented but this was not followed by food. The dog then salivated when it saw the circle but did not salivate when it saw the ellipse. The shape of the ellipse was then changed by stages until it was almost that of a circle. There came a point at which discrimination ceased to improve and actually got worse over a period of three weeks. At this stage the dog clearly did not know whether it was on its head or its elbow—if we may paraphrase a colloquialism!

The whole behaviour of the dog underwent a sharp change. The dog, previously a docile animal, began to squeal in its stand, struggled in its harness, bit through some of the apparatus, and barked violently when taken into the experiment room. Later investigations reported signs of anxiety such as whining and trembling, a breakdown of the learning already achieved, and a very much delayed response to the stimulus. A refusal to eat in the experiment room was reported by Dworkin and yawning and drowsiness were reported by Muncie and Gantt. Among the symptoms observed in a wide range of researches summarized by Hilgard and Marquis (1964) were the following:

1 hyperirritability
2 resistance to entering the learning situation
3 motor abnormalities, tics and tremors
4 changes in social behaviour, including refusal to join the flock, and symptoms of 'suspicion' and 'aggressiveness'
5 inability to resist making incorrect responses
6 loss of the ability to delay a response
7 autonomic symptoms including abnormalities of respiration, eliminative functions and heart action.

In a related set of experiments it is reported by Liddell (Hilgard and Marquis 1964) that experimental neurosis in sheep were very persistent, lasting for thirteen years or more.

Masserman (1950) reported the following symptoms which were observed in cats when they were punished for making a response which had previously been rewarded:

1 restlessness and agitation or, sometimes, passivity
2 fear responses—trembling, cowering, hiding, attempting to escape from the learning situation
3 'compulsively' stereotyped behaviour
4 regression to earlier patterns of behaviour

I would add that experimental neurosis is often fairly specific, i.e. it is possible for it to be closely related to the task situation and for behaviour to be otherwise fairly normal.

The dominant element in these experiments appears to be the necessity of making an overly difficult discrimination. There is then a clash between a tendency to respond and a tendency not to respond. Sometimes the tendency not to respond arises because punishment is introduced. Sometimes it arises merely because the response is not rewarded—which is really rather extraordinary. Evidently, we do not need to punish children to induce stress—as the sensitive teacher well knows.

Let us consider the earlier analysis of learning in terms of error factors. The subject, according to Harlow, is required to suppress responses already in his repertoire—some of them the result of earlier learning. If the discriminations to be made are rather crude, or rather obvious, it would seem that the suppression of the wrong responses presents no great problem. Very often, however, the discrimination is neither crude nor obvious. For example in the case of the development of number concepts, children with limited preparatory experience find the concepts difficult to attain. They do not appreciate which responses to suppress in order to respond to the very abstract numerical properties of the stimuli. Little wonder that so many develop 'number shock'. Indeed, there are very many otherwise normal adults who have the greatest difficulty in dealing with numbers, particularly under stress, as a consequence of early learning difficulties.

Does it not seem likely that there is a relationship between this sort of difficulty and the experimental neurosis induced in animals? In both cases there has been some initial learning and this has broken down when the discriminations have proved too difficult, too confusing. In both cases there is often a tendency to become anxious in the task situation. In both cases there is a strong tendency to avoid the situation altogether and to try to escape once it occurs—struggling, in the case of the animal, and making excuses for doing something else, being uncooperative, or being cooperative but engaging in distracting behaviour, in the case of the child. In both cases there may be a tendency to regress to earlier behaviour patterns. And in both cases there is often a breakdown of earlier learning. The child who seemed to have mastered a concept yesterday seems to have forgotten it today.

In both cases, stereotyped behaviour may occur. In maths, for example, the child may go through meaningless mechanical rituals without the slightest hope of solving the problem presented. Eliminative disorders, too, may occur in both situations. Bed-wetting and soiling are often equally likely to be due to other causes. However, they are a regressive type of behaviour and may well be precipitated by the stress of learning failure.

I have chosen the example of maths deliberately. From our point of view, in maths the material is quite clear and unambiguous. It is far from unambiguous to the child.

I need hardly add that reading presents much greater difficulties. The ambiguities are built-in. Letter orientation and letter sequence call for the suppression of well-established learning sets. For example, a response to single letters has to be suppressed in the case of digraphs. Another feature is that single letters can stand for many sounds— often sounds that are normally represented by digraphs, and so on. If asked deliberately to design a situation for trying to induce experimental neurosis, one could scarcely do better than use the beginning reading situation as a model. Indeed, the only consolation in all this is that the presence of a teacher who is warm in manner and methodical in approach makes an appreciable difference. This may be linked with the observation of Liddell (1954) that lambs are less likely to become neurotic in experimental situations when the ewe is present.

Of course it may possibly be the case that some cognitive disability, not reflected in IQ tests, accounts for the seemingly normal children who fail to make satisfactory progress, as Vernon (op.cit.) suggests. As she says, a multitude of minor causes may hit such children particularly badly. Such a disability would be hard to demonstrate, however, and the arguments based on the evidence presented here do seem rather impelling. They are impelling enough, in my view, to justify a considerable amount of attention by those who are actively engaged in research in this field.

Conclusions

I have argued that neurological hypotheses about causes of reading disability do not take us very far. Perhaps we might qualify this by adding 'except in very severe cases'. Such cases, I would suggest, are few. For most children who are diagnosed as 'dyslexic' or as having 'severe reading disability' we can find some children with similar disabilities who can read. What I have suggested, therefore, is that certain children may certainly be regarded as 'at risk' on the grounds of a variety of handicaps. But I have argued that it is a combination of circumstances in learning situations which may by chance act together to impair learning ability in ways indicated by error factor theory. The effects of these hazards are cumulative.

In addition I have suggested that they can occur in such a way as to induce a very persistent and severe learning disability—reading neurosis—a highly specific disability which may or may not transfer as a *neurotic* response to other learning situations. It does, of course, affect learning in other areas in which reading is required.

In my opinion these vagaries of the learning situation could well account for the 20 per cent or so of our children who are inadequate as readers. If this is the case we may regard beginning reading as a process akin to the slaughter of innocents rather than the exposure of the inadequates.

I am sure that teachers would appreciate more help in trying to understand the learning problems and possible modes of treatment of these unfortunates, and would prefer less emphasis on factors they could not conceivably control and which serve, largely, to justify our own failures.

References

CLARK, M. M. (1970) *Reading difficulties in schools* Harmondsworth: Penguin

GREDLER, G. R. (1971) Severe reading disability—some important correlates in Merritt, J. E. (ed.), *Reading and the curriculum* London: Ward Lock Educational

HARLOW, H. F. (1959) Learning set and error factor theory in Koch, S. (ed.) *Psychology: A study of a science* vol. II New York: McGraw-Hill

HILGARD, E. R. and MARQUIS, D. G. (1961) *Conditioning and Learning* London: Methuen

LIDDELL, H. S. (1954) Conditioning and emotions in *Scientific American* 190, 48–57

MASSERMAN, J. H. (1950) Experimental neuroses in *Scientific American* March

MERRITT, J. E. (1970a) Reading skills re-examined in STONES, E. (ed.) *Readings in Educational Psychology — Learning and Teaching* London: Methuen

MERRITT, J. E. (1970b) An evaluation of the research report on the British experiment with i t a in Daniels, J. C. (ed.) *Reading: Problems and Perspectives* United Kingdom Reading Association

VERNON, M. D. (1957) *Backwardness in Reading* Cambridge: Cambridge University Press

Part five The teachers of reading

23 Training the teachers of reading

Margaret M. Clark

Introduction

This study group for lecturers in colleges of education and university departments of education consisted of six sessions which were conducted on discussion lines and not as a series of presented papers. Each speaker provided a brief written summary of the main points he wished to develop in the ten minutes allocated to him. Within the general theme of 'Training the teachers of reading', present practice in a selection of English and Scottish colleges was discussed, as were some developments in teacher training in the United States. The use of video tapes in the training of teachers both here and in the States was considered. One session of the course was devoted to the role of in-service training, with contributions from speakers from outside the colleges of education. Possible and desirable changes in the training of teachers of reading both here and in the States were considered in the final session.

Present practice

Christopher Walker from Mather College, Manchester, has just completed a study of the present situation in training the teachers of reading in colleges in the Manchester area. He claimed that apart from practical work associated with infant method, little attention seems to have been paid in the colleges to the teaching of reading until the last three or four years. He found that the colleges were now establishing a common basic compulsory course in reading for all their students, with a further development planned towards differentiated courses for infant, junior and secondary levels. The major emphasis in junior courses, where these existed, was on achievement of mechanical competence and on remedial work, without a full awareness of the importance of acquisition of the higher skills for the child with basic competence. It appeared that a considerable extension in the time allocated to reading within college courses was planned. The colleges, aware of past inadequacies, were already extending and coordinating courses in the teaching of reading directed towards the needs of children at different stages in their school career.

John Ball described the present courses in reading at Homerton College, Cambridge, a college with 630 female students and approximately equal numbers training for primary and secondary schools. An introductory course is taken by all students in the first year linked with observation in the schools during teaching practice. Students are asked to analyze schemes and methods for themselves, and assess the value of different types of apparatus. In their third year all students have further courses, emphasizing the developmental nature of the reading process, recent developments in the teaching of reading and linguistic approaches to the teaching of reading. Diagnosis and treatment of severe reading difficulties is also included and visiting speakers are invited to participate on this and other topics.

Alastair Hendry of Craigie College of Education, Ayr, described the teaching of reading at Craigie College, where 739 female and 57 male students are in training for primary teaching. In this college the teaching of reading is shared between the education, English and psychology departments, with time allocated to the subject in each year of the college course. The coordination of the work in reading is ensured by the Reading Committee, and the newly developed Reading Centre serves as a focus for the work on reading. This centre is available both to students in training and to serving teachers in the area.

Three levels of work have emerged:

1 departmental—tutors from a department working with a group of students on specific topics
2 student level—students working in groups or individually on a variety of assignments
3 pupil level—facilities are provided for work with children from local schools.

By bringing together tutors and serving teachers, the Reading Centre is providing vital feedback on the effectiveness of the college courses on the teaching of reading.

Clare Ferguson of Notre Dame College, Glasgow, discussed the training of 1,135 female and 212 male students for primary and secondary teaching in Roman Catholic Schools. Notre Dame, like Craigie College, has recently opened a Reading Centre where teachers and students have the opportunity of examining reading schemes and available materials. The involvement of a number of Notre Dame students in a project involving experience with individual preschool children and their families, has brought home in a way which might not otherwise have been possible the real language and experience deficits of some of the children with whom they will deal as teachers, and has proved an invaluable fund upon which students and the tutors can draw in bringing home the reality of this situation.

In-service training

This topic was the subject for one of the sessions and also featured in the contributions by Evelyn and George Spache who described their courses in Florida where, by the coordination of training of specialists in the area, who in turn trained groups of teachers, with their own work as consultants in the schools, it was possible to make a considerable impact on reading practice.

Gwen Bray, in introducing the session on in-service training, emphasized the need of all teachers for refresher courses, and the time to step back and look critically, at some time in the course of their professional duties. Ideally, representatives from colleges of education, teachers centres, local authority advisors and headteachers need to meet and establish needs and priorities within an area. The wide variety of methods and reading materials to be found in schools, makes it essential for teachers to be adaptable in their approach. A wider range of teachers may wish to benefit from in-service training courses and their needs may be met most successfully by different types of courses. The problems presented by different school environments, types of organization, the contrasting needs of able and disadvantaged children, adequate recording of children's progress, may all be necessary topics for in-service work to extend the possibilities after pre-service training. Pre-service training, though it can create an awareness of needs and problems, cannot, no matter how successfully organized, provide all the answers and it is to meet these demands, which become apparent only in practice, as well as the needs for refresher courses, that in-service training must be developed.

Betty Boyle and Gilbert Heley, in describing the development of local courses in south-west Hertfordshire, emphasized the importance of the role which the local UKRA council played in that development. An in-service organizer was appointed in the area, who encouraged the continuance and development of UKRA activities, and visits by groups of teachers were arranged to schools using different methods of teaching reading and meetings for a group of teachers concerned with slow learners were initiated. Two courses were described—the first planned by two heads of infant schools; the second, a workshop, took place in the local teachers centre during school hours for a full day over five successive weeks. A detailed syllabus and notes from these courses was provided for the benefit of the members of the group.

Christine Dickson from Edinburgh questioned whether the teachers centres were taking over some of the functions of colleges and institutes of education, and she expressed concern at the communication gap between the colleges and the schools. Compulsory day courses for probationer teachers with feedback from the classroom and discussions with a number of tutor-teacher teams was one proposal. It was also stressed that in-service courses on the teaching of reading should emphasize the continuity of the teaching of reading throughout the schools. In-service courses in remedial work were recommended not only for prospective remedial teachers but also for class teachers. It was stressed that training the teachers of reading is a continuous and developmental process, and that in-service training has a leading role to play as a natural development from initial training and should bring together expertise from all areas of the educational scene from college and classroom.

The uses of audio-visual aids

Betty Ruth Raygor described the versatility of the portable video tape recorder used in Hamline University in Minnesota. The compactness of the equipment meant little disturbance of the normal classroom scene. The use of video tapes to produce records for observational training, illustration of various teaching methods, organization of a lesson and various types of classroom management were discussed. Video tapes were also providing valuable material on the use of diagnostic reading tests and informal reading tests. Finally, the students learnt a great deal from viewing video tapes of their own experiences in classrooms using a variety of techniques.

Neville Collins of ETV described with video taped examples the background to the TV series *Learning to Read* which has been prepared for use in colleges and departments of education as a result of collaboration between the Institute of Education of London University, several of its constituent colleges and the mobile VTR section of the ILEA ETV Service, with the ETV liaison officer acting as coordinator The television recordings are designed to form part of a range of audio-visual material including full background notes, colour slides and sound recordings. These items in the package were considered an essential component of the method which was designed to be as flexible as possible so that each college could integrate it into its courses in reading. As far as the television series was concerned, these principles dictated the decision to provide largely unedited examples of classroom activity. This also determined the absence of commentary which might have mitigated against the versatility of the materials. Tutors in the colleges selected the schools used in the series and when a recording was completed, it was viewed by the working party who judged its suitability for the series.

This interesting cooperative venture, which is still in progress, led to discussions on a wide range of topics including the extent to which video taped materials could compensate for deficiencies in teaching practice; the appropriate stage in training at which to use such illustrative material; whether its use could be individualized and also more technical matters of types of recording and playback equipment required for such programmes.

A look ahead

In the final session Alastair Milne stressed college lecturers' need for support and stimulation, and suggested that sabbatical leave with attendance at staff colleges should be considered. Communication not only within but between colleges of education was felt to be of importance. The structure of the present courses was questioned and it was suggested that without lengthening the total course, a two-year training could be followed by one year in teaching before completing the final year, with a greater role given to school tutors.

Miriam Balmuth, in describing the trends in the United States, mentioned the effects of a sudden change from acute teacher shortage to an excess of teachers with a consequent raising of the standards which could be demanded—a possibility in this country in the near future. The national 'Right to Read' programme described in chapter 2, with the vast sums of money placed at its disposal and the planned training of ten million tutors (not teachers), would clearly have considerable impact in the next few years. In general, greater community involvement in school matters was becoming apparent with, for example, tutors from the community being used in the classroom to assist in communication with minority groups. This was resulting in teachers having to be trained to work with paraprofessionals. In Great Britain considerable opposition has been raised to any suggestion that teachers should be supported in the classroom by any form of paraprofessional, whether parent or auxiliary, with any form of teaching duties. The relief felt by some of the young teachers in the States at the presence of another adult in the classroom is worth considering in future discussions on this vexed topic. The development of 'areas of competencies' necessary for teachers to be accredited in certain parts of the States was another interesting development and the possibility that UKRA might consider planning such areas of competencies in the teaching of reading was a thought-provoking note on which to close, or rather adjourn, the course.

The contributions of the main speakers and the lively discussions of the participants in this course led almost inevitably, after the formal closing of the conference, to a reconvening of the group as a working party of UKRA, under the chairmanship of John Ball. It will develop the themes raised at the course and will provide tangible evidence from the lecturers themselves that not only are they concerned with the training of teachers of reading, but that they also have a fund of expertise already within the colleges available to assist others wishing to extend their courses. It was clear from this course that in many colleges there is both the determination and the professional expertise required to instil in students an appreciation of the importance of reading as a developmental process, as well as to stimulate them with a desire to enrich their skills and increase their expertise as teachers of reading.

Joyce M. Morris

Grow old along with me!
The best is yet to be,
The last of life, for which the first was made:

I first read these three lines by Rabbi Ben Ezra (alias Robert Browning) as a teenager, when circumstances beyond my control were making me into a future teacher instead of the research scientist I had always longed to be. Such can be the power of print on the receptive mind that they consoled me then as no spoken words had been able to do. What is more, they have continued to comfort me at times of tribulation in a professional life devoted, in one way or another, to helping fight for the cause of literacy.

The lasting effect of Browning's message is not simply because it appeals to a romantic sense of personal destiny, or to a temperament naturally forward-looking. Experience has shown that growing older not only can, but does, bring increasing happiness in terms of hopes fulfilled and ideas brought to fruition. Twelve years ago, for example, I first urged that a reading (or language arts) centre should be established in London. But my plea fell either on deaf ears or ears tuned only to appeals for the beginning of experimentation with the initial teaching alphabet. Disappointed, yet undaunted, I subsequently seized every opportunity to promote this idea and, to my great joy, on 30th September, 1971 it was my proud privilege officially to open London's Centre for Language in Primary Education. (This centre, incidentally, has been set up by the ILEA to help raise literacy standards in its own schools, and should not be confused with the *proposed* Reading Development Institute at national level.)

Thus ideas, dreams, visions—call them what you will—are the seedlings of realities. But only if they are well-nurtured and the climate is right. Undoubtedly, the very existence of UKRA has helped to create an educational climate in which the ILEA accepted the 'centre' concept as did Reading University earlier and several colleges of education. Doubtless too, without the untiring efforts of UKRA members, we should not be rejoicing about other significant events such as the recent award by Liverpool University of the first-ever diploma in the teaching of reading.

N

Impediments to progress

However, as you will probably have guessed from the preamble, my purpose is rather like the proverbial school report which begins 'Has tried hard with commendable results' and continues '*but*, must try harder or else . . .' Indeed, what I should really like to do is start a revolution, albeit a peaceful one. Its basic aim would be to overthrow the tyrants preserving a status quo which prevents most children being given the best possible opportunities to learn to read and write as effectively as their potential for literacy will allow. I am referring of course to the triumvirate of impediments to progress—Ignorance, Confusion and Fear.

These tyrants have many guises. They hide behind the mask of administrative and financial problems when slowing down the achievement of universal nursery education and a drastic reduction in the average size of infant classes. Yet these two reforms are far more important than raising the school leaving age to sixteen; for the early years of childhood are vital for the development of linguistic competence on which educational progress largely depends.

Another guise for Ignorance, Confusion and Fear is commonly known as 'passing the buck'. When university departments and colleges of education are criticized for the literacy standards and literacy teaching of some of their products, they tend to blame the secondary schools who, in turn, blame the primary schools. The buck used to stop at the bottom of the pecking order, i.e. with the reception class teachers, but in recent years it has gone outside the school to parents of the community at large. Admittedly research generally confirms a close association between literacy problems and home backgrounds which might be described as 'linguistically' or 'culturally deprived'. But when are we going to stop producing parents who cannot do otherwise than continue the chain of linguistic or cultural deprivation? Surely after a hundred years of compulsory education, Britain's teaching profession as a whole should recognize that the acquisition of literacy involves complex, developmental processes. Hence, almost all its members from university professors to nursery school teachers are responsible for the results achieved.

The guise which I, as a consultant, have been most frequently allowed to penetrate, especially during the last three years of literacy 'drives', is the one which exasperates me most. This justifies certain ineffective practices on the grounds that they could be classed, at a pinch, as 'language experience', 'progressive', 'liberal-minded', in the 'Piagetian manner' and so on. It is a facade which cannot be destroyed quickly on a widespread scale unless many more educationists have the courage to appear reactionary in print as well as speech. It is likely to persist as long as inspectors and advisers hope that pseudo-modern practices will develop into the real thing if only the confidence of the teachers concerned is not undermined by adverse comment. But what I find so exasperating about the situation is that it need never have arisen. All that was necessary when the progressive education movement and the knowledge explosion began to affect the training of teachers, was the commonsense to recognize the following obvious facts:

1 The more child-centred the curriculum, the more knowledge, clarity of purpose and organizational ability the teacher requires to make it work.
2 It is not enough for 'progressive' teachers to understand the development of children and how they learn: they must understand the nature of what children have to learn especially to become effective, mature listeners, speakers, readers and writers.
3 British teachers, whatever their educational philosophy, need a thorough knowledge of how language works in general and the English language in particular. This should also include an understanding of relationships between speech and print, the uses of language and so on.

The contribution of linguistics
Facts 1 and 2 are now generally accepted though, alas, too late to have influenced the pre-service training of the majority of serving teachers. As for the third fact, its implications have yet to be widely recognized. This is probably because four years ago, the Plowden Report (Central Advisory Council 1967) made rather lukewarm observations about the contribution of linguistics. For instance, paragraph 611 states:

The growth of the study of linguistics, with its interest in describing and analyzing how language works, the differences between written and spoken language and the influence of language on children's thought and mental development will no doubt come to be reflected in teachers' courses and in classroom techniques.

My proposed revolution would turn this tepid forecast into a certainty, using television and other mass media to carry out a massive training programme for all concerned with the development of language arts from nursery to university level inclusive. Failing this, I hope the provision of a comprehensive, multimedia language arts course in 1973 for Open University students will go a considerable way to achieving the same goal that less ambitious courses are now working towards. I also hope that the forthcoming report on the government-sponsored inquiry into teacher training will not only recommend a course in linguistics for all teachers of English, but will do so as strongly as I did in my published evidence for the inquiry (Morris 1970).

Explicit knowledge of language

Meanwhile, let me hasten to say, I don't believe that if all teachers had appropriate linguistic knowledge and could apply it, our literacy problems would be solved. Nor do I think linguisticians should lay down the law about language teaching any more than experts in psychology and other disciplines contributing to educational theory and practice. However, I am convinced that future progress depends very much on recognizing that our teachers need far more than an 'operational' knowledge of the English language and the processes of listening, speaking, reading and writing.

As is stressed in papers 1 (Doughty 1968) and 2 (Hasan and Lushington 1968) of the recent series called *Programme in Linguistics and English Teaching*, there is a vital distinction between having knowledge *of* one's language and having knowledge *about* it. Teachers naturally have the first kind, but most of them have not acquired the second, i.e. the kind of 'explicit' knowledge which takes the facts of language into account and provides a fully self-consistent description. Moreover, this holds true for university graduates in English who are usually responsible for the school and college English courses of prospective teachers. In consequence, as Hasan and Lushington point out, a self-perpetuating vicious circle exists which can only be broken if the teaching of 'explicit' knowledge of language forms a substantial part of the student teacher's training.

Pending the report on teacher training referred to earlier, it is useless to speculate whether, and if so when, this particular vicious circle will be broken. Even if it is, and as soon as possible, there remains a gigantic task of in-service training to accomplish. Several strategies for tackling it from the new language centre in the London area have already been formulated. Not surprisingly, in view of the dearth of educationists with 'explicit' linguistic knowledge, priority will be given to training experienced teachers as future leaders of the movement using this kind of knowledge to improve literacy teaching.

Misunderstandings eradicated and prevented

These measures would help to eradicate common misunderstandings from the minds of practising teachers and prevent student teachers from acquiring them. In so far as educational writers are or have been teachers, they would also assist in solving another major problem. This is the high proportion of publications advertised as *for, about* or *relevant to* the learning and teaching of literacy, which reveal their authors to be very much in the grip of the tyrannical trio, Ignorance, Confusion and Fear.

It would be invidious to give evidence for this conclusion by singling out publications by name. In any case, so many have unwittingly helped to spread misunderstandings, and often sheer nonsense, that the validity of the conclusion may readily be checked using the following examples.

First, sheer nonsense is illustrated by 'reading is a *natural* ability, activity or process'. This statement and variations conveying the same dogma may be found over and over again in manuals to reading schemes and guides for parents as well as teachers. The authors have obviously been influenced by the philosophical concept of 'naturalness', so much so, they cannot see how ridiculous their statement is, or how disastrous its effects on parents worried about their nonreading children and on teachers prone to put their faith in learning to read by 'osmosis' in a 'rich' reading environment.

Second, misunderstandings about relationships between speech and print are frequently encountered especially in the publications of language experience enthusiasts. Definitions like 'reading is no more than talk written down' are both incorrect and misleading. They lead, for instance, to the notion that the language children normally speak is the easiest material through which to teach them to read and write. Yet as leading British linguisticians such as Halliday, McIntosh and Strevens (1966) have pointed out, this is clearly not true: 'quite apart from the inconsistencies and omissions of our orthography, no one has yet recorded and analyzed enough of the speech of children to be able to simulate it in writing.'

Third, educational writers rightly stress the importance of motivation of literacy learning and of teachers making every stage a 'meaningful' experience for the learner. But they tend to use hackneyed phrases like 'reading for meaning from the beginning', as though it was possible for beginning readers to get 'literal' or 'real-life' meaning directly from print. In other words, far too many appear either ignorant of or indifferent to the alphabetic nature of our spelling system. Notable exceptions, of course, are those who write in an informed manner about i t a and signalling systems using colour or diacritical marks.

Fourth, the incorrect use of technical terms such as 'phonetic' is so common as to demonstrate amply a general lack of professionalism even among recent publications.

These are but a few examples from a collection started years ago when it became obvious to me that writing reviews for publication was too much of a strain to do more than one at long intervals and even then to select carefully. How difficult it is to give one's honest opinion in print about a publication with little to commend it, knowing full well that your comments will hurt another well-intentioned human being! How equally difficult it is to be an educational writer oneself, knowing full well that the tyrannical trio of Ignorance, Confusion and Fear are still very much a part of one's own professional life, and likely to remain so to the end of it!

I can solve my own problems, at least partially, by studying hard and by publishing comparatively little in relation to my peers in experience.

I can make a contribution by speaking plainly about what needs to be done, and by helping train future leaders to ensure that it is done. But only a concerted effort on the part of everyone in authority who cares about the cause of literacy will bring about the radical changes that are urgently needed.

Minimum standards for professional training

In my view, the time has come for UKRA to follow the precedent of IRA by publishing guides to minimum standards for the professional training of teachers of literacy and specialists in this field. This at least would make clear to the educational world the amount and kind of knowledge required to raise literacy standards in the United Kingdom.

Part of this required knowledge will be the subject of my contribution to the study group on 'The early stages of reading and the language arts'. Briefly, it consists of the 'explicit' knowledge of language which my recent experience of conducting in-service courses suggests is often most sadly lacking even amongst headteachers, inspectors and college lecturers. First, for example, a knowledge of the phonological and visible systems of English with special reference to phoneme-grapheme relationships, since an understanding of them is basic to effective phonic instruction. Second, what every normal child has achieved in speech development by the age of five or six as summarized on page 91 of *The Deaf Child* by Whetnall and Fry (1971). This, by the way, should go some way to dispelling prevalent misconceptions about the 'analytic' and 'rule-learning' language abilities of reception class children.

The best is yet to be

Hopefully these two examples will suffice to indicate the nature of the knowledge I believe future generations of student teachers should be given as a matter of course. Hopefully, too, I shall live to see the day when this comes to pass.

Meanwhile, let me conclude as I began by recalling Rabbi Ben Ezra. He reminds us, 'How good it is to live and learn'; hence I trust you will understand my special interest in overthrowing the forces of ignorance. He also encourages us to do what has been my basic message: 'Strive, and hold cheap the strain.' Finally, he promises that 'The best is yet to be'.

For us as UKRA members, the *best* means the time when all children in the United Kingdom are assured of the *best* possible opportunities to become as literate as their potential allows. Assuredly that time will come, and more quickly by our strivings. So please, let us not grow too old as an association before it does.

Bibliography

CENTRAL ADVISORY CENTRE FOR EDUCATION (1967) *Children and Their Primary Schools* (The Plowden Report) London: HMSO

DOUGHTY, P. S. (1968) Paper 1 The relevance of linguistics for the teacher of English in *Programme in Linguistics and English Teaching* London: Longmans

HALLIDAY, M. A. K., McINTOSH, A., and STREVENS, P. (1966) *The Linguistic Sciences and Language Teaching* London: Longmans

HASAN, R. and LUSHINGTON, S. (1968) Paper 2 The subject-matter of English in *Programme in Linguistics and English Teaching* London: Longmans

MORRIS, J. M. (1970) *Teacher Training: Teaching of Reading* Minutes of evidence taken before the Select Committee on Education and Science (Subcommittee B) London: HMSO

WHETNALL, E., and FRY, D. B. (1971) *The Deaf Child* London: Heinemann

Part six Reading research

25 Reading research in England and Wales

Elizabeth J. Goodacre

There is no central institution in this country with responsibility for guiding, coordinating and disseminating the results of investigations and experiments in the teaching of reading. Several national bodies have taken an interest in reading and related areas of study, but not on a sustained basis. These are the National Foundation for Educational Research in England and Wales, the Schools Council, and the National Children's Bureau.

The NFER is currently undertaking a national survey of the reading attainment of eleven and fifteen year olds, which includes the study of the influence of bilingualism in Wales on the teaching of reading. The NFER's main period of sustained reading research was during 1953–63 when the Foundation carried out a reading research programme, which concentrated on the factors in the school situation affecting children's reading progress. Dr Joyce Morris wrote two reports (1959, 1966) on standards and progress in the primary school based on work in Kent, while the writer produced two reports on teaching infants to learn to read using data collected in London schools. The research programme concentrated on the importance of environmental factors on the reading process; Dr Morris's work emphasized the effects of inadequate teacher training and experience and the unequal distribution of materials and facilities for good and poor readers, while the writer's research (1967, 1968) explored the dimension of teachers' attitudes to pupils of differing home background, particularly in regard to the relationship between teachers' attitudes and expectations and pupils' level of reading achievement. The last report based on this reading research by Cane and Chanan, is to be published in the autumn, some twelve years after the data was originally collected. This last report deals with the problems of analyzing the elements in the teaching, the school and the child's home background which contribute to success in reading in a small group of schools in London, from what could be described as educational priority areas (EPAs).

The common link between all these reports is the importance attached to factors in the school situation. At the time the research programme was instigated it was considered a valuable field of study which would redress the balance in research. Previously, much of the reading research being carried out concentrated on perceptual and constitutional differences between pupils in relation to their reading progress. The research programme reflected the then current interest in environmental rather than hereditary factors.

The Schools Council's most recent report for 1969/70 lists seven reading projects. Probably the best known of these are the independent evaluation of i t a (Warburton and Southgate 1969) and the programme in linguistics and English teaching originally initiated by the Nuffield Foundation, which has produced the infant language programme called *Breakthrough to Literacy* (Mackay *et al* 1970), and its related reading materials. The other Schools Council projects include a review of postwar research and experiments, concentrating mainly on the function of books for young nonreaders, and the factors involved in children's success or failure at the learning to read stage; a study of children as readers, being carried out by the National Association for the Teaching of English, which involves teacher groups examining the problem of whether children's literature can be taught; an investigation into children's reading habits being carried out by the Sheffield Institute of Education, which is studying the amount of children's reading and how their preferences change at different ages.

The impression is that the attention of the Schools Council is now being directed away from the initial stages of learning to read, and towards the exploration of how proficiency in reading skill can be not only maintained but improved, so that children can use it for their own enjoyment and interest. This is a very commendable aim, but it must be remembered that the Council's evaluation of i t a (1969) clearly stated not only the desirability of further research into the use of i t a in schools, but also the 'urgent need for the construction of suitable tests of reading for children aged five to eleven'. In the i t a Report the late Professor Warburton, in his evaluation of the various studies into the effectiveness of i t a, clarified a number of the factors which had bedevilled much of the reading research of the previous decade. His analysis also clearly showed that doubt must be cast upon the reliability of research where insufficient resources are being devoted to improving the accuracy and relevancy of the measuring devices commonly in use. Reading this Report one is left with the overwhelming impression of a rapidly developing field of study—dare I say science— where researchers are not only groping to form hypotheses but at the same time trying to examine and define the criteria of 'success', 'progress', etc as well as designing and evolving relevant means of measurement. In reading research in this country, one of the most important problems seems to be that it is not generally realized that research must be sustained in order for results to be collated and knowledge to be cumulative; or, to put it simply, one must walk before one runs!

Before leaving the work of the Schools Council, mention should be made of the Research and Development Project in Compensatory Education based on the University College of Swansea, which is also one of the Council's projects. As part of their programme for developing techniques for the early identification of infant children in need of such education, the project's team has reexamined the concept of 'reading readiness' and analyzed the published tests available for use at this stage of children's progress (Chazan 1970). Their work also included a study of the use of the 'tell a story' test as a means of determining readiness, and the development of a test of phonic skills (Occasional Paper No 2; 1969). The Project's programme will end next year.

The National Children's Bureau (previously known as The National Bureau for Cooperation in Child Care) has studied children's reading progress as part of its national child development project (Pringle et al 1966). Some five hundred seriously backward readers were selected from the children in the national project and studied in greater detail. The results of this study should be available in the very near future but again, as with the NFER results, there is a considerable lapse of time between the collection of raw data on which the findings are based and the publication of these findings in report form.

Occasionally the Department of Education and Science finances research. For instance, it gave assistance to J. K. Jones (1967) in his experiment into the effectiveness of his Colour Story Reading, a system using a colour code intended to simplify the early stages in learning to read. A Reading Research Unit was established at the University of London Institute of Education with the support of the then Ministry of Education in 1961, under the supervision of Professor Downing. This Unit carried out the main i t a experiments, and also several subsidiary experiments involving the use of i t a. The Unit was able to continue with a grant from the Ford Foundation but finally closed in 1967. The following year a course on 'The psychology of literacy' was offered as an MA option subject at the Institute. Several students completed this course and carried out studies including those of the attitudes of users and nonusers to i t a, young children's understanding of the concepts involved in learning to read, and the use of reading apparatus in infant schools. However, this option subject will not be made available after the present academic year.

At the present time, higher degree students can carry out reading research within the faculty departments of English, social or educational psychology at different universities, and diploma students in the university institutes in certain circumstances offer theses on reading research as part of their work. For instance in the past year studies at the Cambridge Institute of Education have included an investigation of the relationship between 'higher order' skills in reading and language development, the prediction of reading failure in the infant school, and an analysis of the reading miscues made by children of the same reading age.

This brief description of the range and the scope of reading research suggests that it is being carried out by researchers in universities, colleges of education and certain national education bodies. Because there is no central institution with responsibility for coordinating, guiding and disseminating results, it is difficult to know either the extent or the quality of the research which exists. Certainly the research is not cumulative, sometimes because of poor communication between workers in the field but more often because of the tendency for the larger national bodies to discontinue interesting lines of development after initial and sometimes superficial exploration. It seems that a tradition is being established of initiating research programmes which last just long enough for the research workers involved to be acquainted with the problems of criteria and measurement before the projects are disbanded. This may be one way of training research workers, but it seems a short-sighted policy for determining priorities and accumulating evidence in this particular field of knowledge. When results are produced, their style often makes them 'unreadable' for the classroom teacher. What is perhaps less easily remedied is the effect of the delay between collecting the data and reporting the findings. Such delay lessens the impact of the insights and findings put forward in these reports, so that their results and suggestions appear obvious to the classroom teacher who loses faith in the relevancy of research to her current problems. In the writer's experience, the delay between data collection and publication is usually due to a number of factors, rather than a single cause. For instance, there may be

1 uneconomic use of experienced personnel with appropriate teaching reading experience
2 poor costing of technical assistance
3 inadequate estimating of the time involved in field work (e.g. going back to test absentees, visiting schools on 'convenient' days) and in analysis of results and report preparation
4 reading projects may be given a low priority in the queue for scarce resources and facilities (e.g. computer time etc).

The shortage of personnel combined with the paucity of financial resources available for reading research, results in work which often appears to be of limited value to the classroom teacher, particularly if the implications are not clearly made, while the academic critic feels it lacks the appropriate scientific rigour.

In this context, the findings of a recent survey of LEAs carried out by the Centre for the Teaching of Reading, at Reading is interesting (Goodacre 1971). The survey was on the subject of local authority provision for reading, and included a question on whether the LEA knew of any reading research being undertaken in their area. A similar survey had been carried out by Dr Joyce Morris in 1960, for the NFER, so it was hoped that it would be possible to make a ten year comparison.

The questionnaire went to all county and borough LEA.'s in England and Wales. The level of cooperation in 1960 was 93 per cent; in 1970 it was 80 per cent.

The following tables show the percentage of authorities reporting research by type of LEA in 1970, and the ten year comparison figures.

Reading research (1970)

Research	Yes	Q.Yes	No	No inform.	Total
County	32	9	57	2	100/N47
Borough	32	0	64	4	100/N80

Ten year comparison - reading research

Research	Yes	Q.Yes	No	No inform.	Total
1970	32	3	62	3	100/127
1960	12	7	80	1	100/139

In the 1970 survey, four LEA's had plans for research in connection with surveys of reading attainment in the near future, and these were coded as qualified affirmative answers. Of those answering yes, several described more than one research study. LEAs mentioned work done by teachers for higher degrees, by school psychologists or remedial staff, or schools and teachers taking part in projects being carried out by national bodies, (five LEAs mentioned Schools Council or NFER projects). Some twenty-two LEAs referred to studies or investigations which were primarily at the instigation of the School Psychological or Remedial Service. These included:

1 *Survey studies* Limited survey of the reading ages of some 500 pupils transferring from primary to secondary schools. It is intended to repeat the survey when these pupils are in their last year at school.

2 *Test construction* An attempt is being made to standardize a group reading test for screening purposes in the county. Satisfactory progress is being made with this.

3 *Backwardness* Cross-laterality and neurological impairment and its effects on reading performance.

4 *Reading materials* Senior educational psychologist is conducting an

evaluation of Breakthrough to Literacy in five infant schools, each containing matched experimental and control classes.

5 *New approaches* Two schools are carrying out comparative experiments using traditional methods and materials, and newly developed audio-visual equipment—especially the Language Master (Bell and Howell) and the Talking Page (Rank Audio-Visual).

The ten year comparison showed significantly more LEAs able to report research in their areas. It must be remembered that some of the projects reported were either researches being undertaken by national bodies (e.g. Schools Council, Nuffield, NATE, Compensatory Education etc) or related to the work of the School Psychological or Remedial Services. These national bodies and the School Services had expanded both their work and their influence; it was therefore to be expected that the LEAs would be aware of these developments to some extent. Also, the proportion of LEAs reporting research ten years earlier had been comparatively small, so that even a moderate increase in research would have appeared as a significant increase.

The studies described in the 1970 questionnaire data have been listed and the Centre for the Teaching of Reading would like to use this information as the basis for compiling a register or index system of current reading research, which could be made available to research workers located in this country or visiting researchers and educationists. This listing of current reading research projects already shows that certain LEAs are concerned about tackling reading problems early in the child's primary schooling and have either instigated 'screening' surveys at top infant or first year junior level, or are proposing to do so. The information (from those LEAs who have conducted such tests) on their survey programme and organization, as well as their experience of particular tests, could be of value to the LEAs interested in the value of 'screening' surveys if this information were pooled and generally made available to a wider audience. Similarly, several LEAs were involved in studies of the relationship of cross-laterality and reading backwardness, and the collating of such information could be of considerable value to other research workers concerned with backwardness factors. Certainly, this list of current research at the local authority level provides evidence of the need for a central body with responsibility for coordinating, collating and disseminating the results of such research if it is to reach a wider audience. If indeed there is an increase in the amount of reading research being undertaken by LEA personnel, then the need for this type of central research 'clearing house' is even more imperative to avoid work being unnecessarily duplicated and research workers' efforts largely wasted. Reading through the research list compiled for the Centre for the Teaching of Reading, the writer can but conclude that the priorities in this country, as Weintraub wrote in his report for the American ERIC/CRIER project on reading research trends and needs are

... better instruments than now exist to assess reading and reading related skills, unique new approaches to research problems, a concerted attack on worthwhile problems that are researchable, and an effort to collect data over longer periods of time.

References

ERIC/CRIER Newsletter (1970) A new ERIC/CRIER project develops a systematic approach to more analytic, interpretive treatment of information vol. 5 (1), December

GOODACRE, E. J. (1967) *Reading in Infant Classes* Slough: NFER

GOODACRE, E. J. (1968) *Teachers and their Pupils' Home Background* Slough: NFER

GOODACRE, E. J. (1971) *Provision for Reading: An investigation into the facilities provided by LEAs in England and Wales* University of Reading School of Education

JONES, J. K. (1967) *Colour Story Reading: A Research Report* London: Nelson

MACKAY, D., THOMPSON, B. and SCHAUB, P. (1970) *Breakthrough to Literacy* London: Longmans

MORRIS, J. M. (1959) *Reading in the Primary School* London: Newnes

MORRIS, J. M. (1966) *Standards and Progress in Reading* Slough: NFER

PRINGLE, M. L. K., BUTLER, N. R. and DAVIE, R. (1966) *11,000 Seven Year Olds* London: Longmans

UNIVERSITY COLLEGE OF SWANSEA DEPARTMENT OF EDUCATION (1969) *Children at Risk* Occasional Publication No. 2. Schools Council Research Project in Compensatory Education

CHAZAN, M. (1970) *Reading Readiness* University College of Swansea Faculty of Education

WARBURTON, F. W. and SOUTHGATE, V. (1969) *i t a: An independent evaluation* Edinburgh: Chambers and London: Murray

26 Class size, pupil characteristics and reading attainment

Alan Little, Christine Mabey and Jennifer Russell

The desirability of reducing class sizes in our primary schools is one of the few educational topics on which there is widespread agreement amongst professionals, administrators, politicians and parents. One reason for this consensus is, perhaps, that this is one factor which it is relatively simple to change (given adequate numbers of teachers, money to pay them, the classrooms or sufficient space to accommodate them) and the change is directly observable. Yet there has been comparatively little recent research on the link between class size and the attainment of young children. Furthermore the majority of investigations have indicated that class size does not in itself appear to be an important factor in influencing the speed of learning (Thouless 1969).

There are three fairly recent English studies to which reference should first be made. In chronological order they are; first, the investigations of Joyce Morris in Kent during 1954–1957, reported in *Reading in the Primary School* and *Standards and Progress in Reading* (Morris 1959, 1966); second, the investigation by Stephen Wiseman in Manchester in 1964, reported in volume II of the Plowden Report (HMSO 1967); third, the National Child Development Survey which covered the whole of Britain—the part with which we are concerned is the survey of the children in 1965 when they were seven years old (Davie 1970).

Morris found that there was a tendency for children in large classes in top infants and juniors to have better reading attainments. She suggested that the reasons for this were partly the urban/rural difference (larger schools are in the towns, large classes are found in large schools) and also the policy of putting the less able children in smaller classes. As part of the evidence presented to the Plowden Committee, Wiseman considered children in a 25 per cent sample of Manchester primary schools (controlling for school size, type and socio-economic level). Although these children were 10 + at the time of his investigation, he had available test results throughout the junior school. He found a small but positive association between size of class and educational attainment (holding parental occupation constant); in other words the larger the class, the better the reading.

The National Child Development Survey is a study of a complete cohort of children born in one week in 1958. The children were traced again in 1965 when they were seven years of age and amongst other measures the relationship of class size to reading attainment at the end of infant school was considered. Even taking account of school size, length of schooling, parental interest and occupation, it was still the case that the children in larger classes had higher attainments. Davie suggested that this was partly due to the difference between urban and rural schools and also that 'small' was not small enough— that is, classes might have to be as small as 20–25 before attainment was improved. The researches of Marklund in Sweden has particular relevance in this context (Yates 1966). He considered attainment of thirteen year olds, both in a national sample and from south Stockholm, examining class sizes of 16–20, 21–25, 26–30, 31–35. Attainment was highest in the classes of 26–30 and lowest in the classes of 21–25 and when classes were combined, the attainment in classes of 26–35 was significantly higher than that in classes of 16–25. He concluded that a reduction in class size would not *in itself* lead to improved attainments especially as having made 281 different comparisons between the class sizes, all but 59 were not significant (and of these 37 favoured the larger classes and 22 the smaller).

A certain amount of fresh evidence is available from a literacy survey covering all the ILEA junior and junior-infant schools. The testing took place in October 1968 when all children in the authority's schools born between 2nd September 1959 and 1st September 1960 were given a sentence completion reading test. The test was designed by the National Foundation for Educational Research for their streaming project: it has two parallel versions, SRA and SRB. SRA was used in this study. In the followup study of the same cohort immediately prior to transfer to secondary schooling (i.e. summer 1971) SRB was used. Further information relating to the children's backgrounds and educational experience was also collected. The aspects that concern us here are the size of the classes that the children were in at the time of the survey (normally pupils at the beginning of the second year juniors), the children's countries of origin, the occupational status of the fathers or guardians, as well as the teachers' knowledge and judgment of the homes and the children. Furthermore, we had access to an index of the educational priority ranking of the school which provides some idea of the social and physical problems affecting the schools in comparison with the rest of the authority.

Our first finding was striking: there was an increase of reading attainment with increase in class size—from a mean reading quotient of 90.7 in classes of 30 or under to 100.5 in classes of over 40. However, many of the children in smaller classes were those whom head-teachers thought required special help (though not necessarily a remedial class). Also in London more of the denominational schools have large classes, and these schools have higher mean reading scores (99.2 in Roman Catholic schools and 96.9 in Church of England schools compared with 94.3 in county schools). In addition children who were reported as having had some remedial help in the school they were attending at the time of survey tended to be in smaller classes. Further, the LEA has a policy of allocating more resources (including teachers) to schools in most need. We therefore propose to look more closely at certain of the characteristics of pupils in classes of 31–34 and of 35–40 pupils and to exclude from the analysis children who had any specific remedial help with reading during the previous 14 months, whether in remedial classes, withdrawn groups or individual remedial help. However, it must be pointed out that although class sizes of 31–34 are probably realistic current improvements on existing sizes, they may not be sufficiently small to have significant impact on pupil performance. What these results may indicate is the likely results of current policy in primary school staffing. In our sample the mean size of the 31–34 group was 32.4 pupils, and of the 35–40 group, 37.5 pupils; a difference of 5 pupils or a 14 per cent reduction.

As it is ILEA policy to allocate more resources to the schools considered to be most in need, that is schools with a high EPA ranking, we compared schools of similar ranking on an EPA index. We found small but consistent differences favouring classes of 35–40. For example, in the most disadvantaged areas the mean reading quotient of pupils in classes of 31–34 was 93.4, compared with 94.1 in classes of 35–40. Figures for schools in the most privileged areas were 102.4 and 104.2.

Table 1

Reading scores and percentage of children in classes of different sizes and in schools of different EPA ranks

EPA *rank*	*Class size*			
	31–34 RQ	%	35–40 RQ	%
1–99	93.4	11.6	94.1	6.3
100–299	94.8	18.9	96.5	19.3
300–599	99.1	36.5	99.5	30.6
600–875	102.4	32.9	104.2	43.8
N	(98.7)	3,783	(100.6)	11,826

It can be seen from Table 1 that the smaller classes tend to be in schools of higher rank but the marginal difference in attainment in favour of the larger classes still occurs. We next considered the kinds of pupils in the schools—the proportion of immigrants and the proportion of children from lower socioeconomic backgrounds. The

O

same tendency for the children in the larger classes to have a higher mean reading score irrespective of nationality or social class emerges.

Table 2

Reading scores and percentages of children in classes of different sizes

| Nationality | Class size | | | |
	31–34 RQ	%	35–40 RQ	%
Nonimmigrant	99.7	86.1	101.6	87.1
Immigrant	92.4	13.9	94.7	12.9
N	(98.7)	3,764	(100.7)	11,814

| Social class | Class size | | | |
	31–34 RQ	%	35–40 RQ	%
Nonmanual	104.6	24.8	105.9	29.9
Manual	96.8	75.2	98.5	70.1
N	(98.7)	3,764	(100.7)	11,814

From Table 2 it can be seen that the differences are small but consistent and favour the larger classes. Probably the safest conclusion is that reduction of class size on the scale currently envisaged may have little impact on reading.

In themselves nationality and social class are rather unsatisfactory ways of categorizing children and their families. In our survey (in an attempt to assess the support the children had from their families) the teachers were asked if they considered the homes to be culturally stimulating, if they felt the parents were interested in the children's education, and whether or not parents had discussed their child's education with the teacher. When class background was controlled, sixteen comparisons were made between small (30–34) and large (35–40) classes; all the differences were small and all favoured the larger classes. As a detailed example, Table 3 gives the results for cultural stimulus of the home.

Table 3

Reading scores and percentages of children of different social class in classes of different size according to cultural stimulus of the home as this was rated by the teacher

Nonmanual   *Class size*

	31–34		35–40	
	RQ	%	RQ	%
Stimulating	111.3	41.2	111.5	42.5
Average	101.0	50.2	103.5	49.7
Unstimulating	94.9	8.6	95.9	7.8
N		859		3,254

Manual   *Class size*

	31–34		35–40	
	RQ	%	RQ	%
Stimulating	106.6	11.0	108.1	10.8
Average	98.9	55.3	100.2	62.9
Unstimulating	90.3	33.7	91.9	26.3
N		2,545		7,301

But the main reason for reproducing this table is to contrast the impact of cultural stimulus with reduction of class size. The difference in the mean reading score of children from stimulating and unstimulating home backgrounds is a year and a half or more (15–17 points). Contrast that with the differences between 'small' and 'large' classes which although real are very small; in most cases there is less than two points between the mean reading scores of the two class sizes under consideration. In other words, although we have found an almost consistent difference in favour of the larger class size, this difference is perhaps educationally insignificant. The indications from our evidence are that for these class sizes, one of which is over the target number of 35 and the other (31–34) within the range of realistic short-run improvements in class sizes, the actual class size in itself is not the most important factor in reading performance. More important influences would seem to be pupil characteristics, the homes they come from and the support they receive.

Conclusions
Our main findings have been that little or no differences exist between the reading standards of children in relatively small classes compared with those in larger ones and even when social class, length of education, immigrant status and the educational priority status of the schools are controlled, little difference can be found. If anything,

children in large classes do marginally better than their counterparts in smaller ones. Given the extent to which this conflicts not only with professional opinion but also with lay views on the desirability of smaller classes, some mention of the limitations of the analysis is necessary. Only one measure of educational performance has been used (a group test of reading). Had other tests of reading been used, or other tests of basic skills (numeracy) or tests of personality skills and development, different results might have been obtained. Furthermore, the measure was used at a single age—an age after the basic skill of reading has normally been acquired. Perhaps had the tests (or similar ones) been used during the period of learning to read (infants and first year juniors) different results might have been forthcoming. Obviously the full force of these points is made when taken together: testing various skills covering the full range of the curriculum at successive ages. However, Wiseman had available information on different attainments at successive ages and still found the attainment to be slightly superior in the larger classes. These results suggest that we ought to begin collecting more information on basic skill performance, resource inputs, and teaching strategy before placing the priority upon reduction of class size as current educational policy implies.

A further note of caution must be sounded. In this paper we have assumed that all teachers are equally effective, the only variable being the numbers of pupils in their classes. This is obviously naive, and might well be a factor in producing the results we have found. For example, internal school policies might result in the deployment of the weaker and younger teachers with smaller groups and the more experienced and skilled teachers being given the larger teaching groups. A parallel policy could be the allocation of more advanced readers to the relatively larger classes and less advanced to the smaller ones. Both of these points assume that there are considerable variations of class sizes within schools (i.e. some below and some above 35 in terms of our present analysis).

But in 45 per cent of ILEA junior schools such differentiality was impossible because the school had only one class in the relevant age range. In another 35 per cent of schools there was no difference in the sizes of parallel classes or a difference of one or two pupils. Eight out of ten schools did not make use of improved staffing ratios to create relatively large and small teaching groups. In fact, in schools that had the opportunity to have parallel classes in the same age band only one in eight had a difference of six or more pupils and at least a third of these would have been eliminated from our analysis. But there are possible arguments consistent both with our findings and the desire to reduce class size in the hope that it will affect pupil performance. However, they open an area of discussion that is seldom mentioned in the debate about class sizes and the need for more teachers, which is deployment of these teachers within the school and the deployment of teacher time and teaching strategy within the classroom. American research on the 'more effective school' suggested that for the first couple of years, a drastic reduction in class size in the early years of elementary school produced no improvement in pupil performance, largely because teachers taught smaller groups in exactly the same way as they had been teaching the larger groups, and with the same effect (or lack of it). This observation suggests that thought should be given to ways of using improved pupil-teacher ratios and not restricted to pressuring for their reduction and, allied to this, ways of teaching pupils from different home backgrounds, different motivations etc.

But how far need classes be reduced to improve performance? This paper has examined the types of reductions that are likely in primary schools in the near future. Perhaps significant improvements in performance will only be achieved with even more drastic reductions (classes of 15, 20 or 25). Our lack of relationship might be because the reductions we have examined, although currently politically relevant, are not educationally significant. In principle this is a strong argument and obviously should be seen in relation to the deployment of teachers and the changed teaching strategy mentioned above. It also raises an even more profound organizational question: given the current impracticality of teaching groups of 15 or 20 in primary schools throughout the day, how far can team teaching, family grouping, integrated day, create such teaching situations for part of the teaching day by staff deployment? There is the obvious danger of small group situations within large classes being used as an alternative to improvements in pupil-teacher ratio; this is not what is wanted. The strain of teaching large groups of children is probably considerable (and perhaps the best argument for smaller classes is reduction of that strain) but what we are suggesting is that smaller teaching groups can be achieved by organizational changes within the classroom; also one of the reasons why the existing reduction in class sizes has not produced improved pupil performance, has been the failure to modify teaching practice in such a way as to utilize the possibilities of existing class sizes.

What then is our main argument? Reduction of class sizes on the scale currently envisaged, i.e. primary classes of 30–35, may not directly improve pupil performance, in so far as this has been measured by reading skills. Paradoxically our evidence shows that it might be linked with lower performance—a finding which is consistent not only with previous English educational research but also Scandinavian research. The solution is not simply more teachers. Some thought and consideration must be given to how the educational opportunities offered (at considerable human expense) in smaller teaching groups can be utilized, and how much smaller groups can be contrived within existing staffing ratios. Briefly, staff utilization and deployment should be given as much professional attention as staff numbers.

Finally, the magnitude of the differences found in the scores of children coming from interested and stimulating homes and the scores of children from unstimulating and uninterested homes, surely suggest that the social and psychological factors are of greater immediate significance than the types of reductions in class size we are currently envisaging. Perhaps the best way to utilize and deploy improved staffing ratios would be to attempt to influence parental interest and involvement, and pupils' attitude towards work and school rather than reduce class sizes. However, as Bernstein and Davies have pointed out, this may be a sociologically naive recommendation because such attitudes and relationships are the consequences of other aspects of the structure of a complex industrial society unamenable to change through education.

References

BERNSTEIN, B. and DAVIES, B. (1969) Some sociological comments on Plowden in Peters, R. S. (ed.) *Perspectives on Plowden* London: Routledge and Kegan Paul

DAVIE, R. (1970) *The Child, the School and the Home*—Unpublished paper presented to the British Association

MARKLUND, S. (1962) Scholastic attainment as related to size and homogeneity of classes Abstracted by the author in Yates, A. (ed.) (1966) *Grouping in Education* Hamburg: UNESCO Institute for Education, 248–250

MORRIS, J. M. (1959) *Reading in the Primary School* London: Newnes

MORRIS, J. M. (1966) *Standards and Progress in Reading* Slough: NFER

THOULESS, R. H. (1969) *Map of Educational Research* Slough: NFER

WISEMAN, S. (1967) The Manchester Survey in *Children and their Primary Schools, Volume II*, Appendix 9 London: HMSO

27 Reading difficulties in schools

Margaret M. Clark

This paper is concerned with the implications for the classroom and for future research of an investigation into the nature and magnitude of the problem of severe reading difficulties in schools. The research itself has been published elsewhere (Clark 1970, 1971) but has not been reported at a conference of the United Kingdom Reading Association.

Research workers have the responsibility both to communicate their findings intelligibly, to others and to draw the practical implications from their research themselves; otherwise they leave their findings open to misinterpretation. This is the justification for the present paper based upon work which has already appeared in print. Since the research will be reasonably familiar, a brief outline only will be given.

The aim of the research was to determine how many children of average intelligence have prolonged, severe difficulty in learning to read. The research began in 1966 at a time when there was controversy about the extent of this problem; anything from one to ten per cent of children of average intelligence with normal motivation, adequate teaching and without defects of vision or hearing were claimed to suffer from 'word blindness' or 'dyslexia'. The Scottish Education Department agreed to finance the research over a period of two years and the county of Dunbarton in the west of Scotland was selected for the study.

The research was in three phases. In the first stage, all children attending school in the county who were born between 1st April and 31st August 1959, were tested. This group of 1,544 children in 70 schools had all started school at the same time, and had been at school for two years. All the children in that group who had not attained independent reading skill after two years at school were retained for further investigation, whatever their level of intelligence. These 230 children, 15 per cent of the original group, were tested again after three years at school. For the final stage of the research, both intelligence *and* reading level influenced the selection. All the children who had been lacking in independent reading skill when first seen at seven years of age and who were of average intelligence, were tested again at nine years of age.

To summarize:
Stage 1 All children born between 1st April 1959 and 31st September

1959 attending schools in the county, 1,544 children (791 boys, 753 girls), were tested after two years at school.

Stage 2 All children with no independent reading skill at seven years of age (RQ 85 or less) were retested after three years at school; 230 children (138 boys, 92 girls).

Stage 3 All children from Stage 2 who were of average intelligence (defined as at least IQ 90 + on WISC) were tested again at nine years of age, 165 children (106 boys, 59 girls).

The testing throughout the research was individual and the only children lost to the study during the research were those who left the county.

In this paper the implications of the findings of the first and second stages of the research will be considered together and followed by a brief study of the implications of the final stage.

1 *The community study of reading difficulties*

There were two aims in studying all the children in the county born within the chosen five months. The first aim was to select those children who were still experiencing difficulty with the mechanics of reading at the age of seven; the second aim was to obtain up to date information on some of the features which have been claimed to have associations with reading progress and thus provide information against which clinic cases could later be assessed. Each of these aspects will be considered briefly.

About 15 per cent of this age group of children in the county in 1967 were without any independent reading skill after two years at school. It is important to bear in mind that a percentage like that may oversimplify the problem as it masks the much higher percentages in some schools and areas and the rarity of such children in others. An identical level of reading failure will present different problems both for the teacher and for the individual child, and perhaps requires different remedies, depending on whether the child is an isolated instance in that school or one of many with similar problems in a single class. Before discussing the implications of these findings in general terms, it is important to consider whether these results are likely to have been specific to that year or to that county. Evidence from other sources would suggest that this problem still has to be faced within the county and that a problem of at least as great magnitude must be faced elsewhere.

A minimum standard in reading within a few years of starting school is still required with modern approaches, which perhaps even increase the need for independent study. Once a child has reached a certain level of reading competence, the reading tasks required by projects for example, will increase both his skill and his motivation; below that level they may only cause frustration. Clearly it is important to identify early those children who have not reached such a minimum level and treat them appropriately. There is ample evidence from this research and elsewhere that such children are not always either treated or even identified. Two issues for the members of this Association are when and how screening should take place and when and in what form intervention should take place. Evidence of the long-term effectiveness of remedial work has been disappointing and so it seems important that classroom intervention and teacher training, and not merely remedial teaching in the traditional sense, come within this brief.

It is important to accept realistically the present educational system and plan immediate action within it. At present in this country, children who have failed to learn to read by seven or eight years of age are likely to be at a severe and permanent disadvantage. However, it is essential to look beyond this. The tenor of the present argument is not that the ideal is necessary for all children to reach a higher level of mechanical reading ability as early as possible. It is important that an association such as UKRA, while paying attention to the needs of the children and the teachers within the present educational system, considers also the wider issues: to what extent does failure to make progress in reading result from circumstances which place a child in a group reading situation at a time which is inopportune for him? Unfortunately, in the British school system as in others, there are some learning situations which are presented when the majority are ready and should a particular child not be ready at that time, his opportunity has passed. The age of starting school, the organization of schools (separate infant schools, change at the end of primary schools etc), the organization within schools, and even the sex of the teachers may all be important variables as also may be the type of training which teachers have received which has led to certain expectations.

The second main aim in the community aspect of the study was to obtain up to date information on characteristics of the children or school with possible association with reading progress against which clinic cases could later be assessed. Several of these findings have general interest.

First, many children still confused right and left in themselves or other people at seven years of age, whether or not they were backward in reading. Only one quarter of the children were by then free of such confusion even in a task with five simple items.

Second, only about one third of the children had the ability to copy a diamond to an acceptable standard by the age of seven.

When these two findings on a sample of 1,544 children are taken together, the occurrence of reversals of letters and letter order in words should not come as a surprise. Further, it seems important that steps be taken to assist these children to appreciate that order and direction are important for reading and writing. Concern, but not surprise, should greet the appearance of poorly coordinated letters and reversals, concern on the part of the teacher to suit her classroom practice to the needs of the children. Problems of coordination and direction are not confined to clinic cases.

Third, one in ten of the children was found to be left-handed and one in three left-eyed. No association was found between left-handedness or left-eyedness and reading progress. It seems unfortunate that so much publicity has led parents of left-handed children to anticipate reading and spelling difficulty and to assume a causal relationship between this and the left-handedness or eyedness. It is time teachers and college lecturers stopped alerting parents to a characteristic for which there is no evidence of causal relationship with reading progress in normal children; this finding is not confined to this survey but is also that of many other large scale surveys. This negative finding has been quoted not only for its own sake but also as an illustration of the importance of paying attention not only to the positive but also the negative findings of research.

Much attention has been centred on staff changes within schools and the problems that this creates in providing continuity of instruction. In this study the absences of the children in their first two years at school, and also their changes of school, were recorded. One quarter of the children had changed school at least once during their first two years at school; as many children moved into the county as had moved within the county. A uniform approach to the teaching of reading throughout the county would not therefore have been a complete solution to this. Again from other evidence, it would seem that these are not problems peculiar to this area. Frequent absence in the first two years and changes of school on the part of the children, together with rapid turnover of staff in primary schools, make it essential that systematic recording of children's progress in reading be developed. Only then can the best use be made of the diversity of approaches which are to be found in the schools in this country. Many teachers feel that informal recording of children's progress is sufficient for their needs. This may be so within the individual classroom, though even there it is questionable if it is sufficient. It is certainly not adequate for efficient teaching of children who have a great deal of absence, a succession of teachers, or several changes of school. Here again is an important task for UKRA who should set up a working party to devise a record card or check list of the subskills of reading for use by teachers in recording progress. If the information this card contained were positive in its structure, it could be sent with any child who changed school. It need not limit the freedom of any teacher to develop her own approach to reading but would give her an immediate picture of the strengths and weaknesses of the children in her class. The schools in this country have been slow to adopt systematic assessment of reading progress and the type of short attainment tests available in this country have tended to make teachers distrustful of testing devices in general. Here is a task for the colleges of education in their pre- and in-service training, to encourage teachers to see that the use of more systematic recording devices need not cramp teaching, but make it more efficient and more diagnostically related to the individual children in the class.

Prolonged difficulty in children of average intelligence
The children who will be considered now are those nineteen children who had been without any independent reading skill at seven years of age, who were of average intelligence, and who were found still to be severely backward in reading (two or more years backward on the Neale Analysis of Reading Ability) at nine years of age. Thus in this county the maximum size of this particular problem of children of average intelligence with prolonged severe reading difficulties, from whatever cause, was just over one per cent. The following points emerged in connection with this group:

1 the majority of this group were boys (15 boys, 4 girls)
2 only one child had all three IQs above 100 on the WISC; nine had only their performance IQ above 90, while verbal IQ was below 90
3 speech defects and poor auditory discriminations were common in this group
4 poor visuo-motor coordination was shown by many of the children
5 there was little evidence of active assistance on the part of the parents, though the parents were not negative in their attitude to the school. Most of the children had little reading material except that provided by the school.

Prolonged difficulties with reading and spelling were thus found to be a severe problem for a number of children with intelligence in the average range, though none were of high intelligence, and their disability was intensifying rather than disappearing with the passage of time. These children were unable to read for enjoyment or information or to produce intelligible written communication. The absence of any severely backward readers of very high intelligence in the present study does not indicate that no such children exist. The press and television have recently highlighted the problems of children with specific reading difficulty, dyslexia or 'word blindness'. Misunderstanding has often arisen from differences in the use of the terms by neurologists, psychologists and educationists. The aim of this research was not to prove either the presence or the absence of 'dyslexia'; it was to assess the extent to which this kind of severe difficulty is the business not so much of the expert in the clinic, but of the classroom teacher. Though such cases may be met rarely by any particular teacher during her teaching career, she should nevertheless be equipped to identify them and seek specialist guidance which should be available. In general the difficulties of these children were not specific to the problem of deciphering words on a printed page; rather they appeared to require assistance over a wider range of activities. The striking finding was the *diversity* of disabilities and *not* an underlying pattern common to the group which could have provided a basis for one single remedial method for all these children. This was true even in a group selected from a single community where the initial approach to the teaching of reading, the structure of the schools and even the home background, had many similarities which would not have been apparent in a more widely selected group.

Frequent short periods of instruction, alone or in small groups, linked with classroom followup by a teacher who has been made aware of the approach which is being tried, is not only the most economical but probably the most efficient way of dealing with the majority of children with reading difficulties. This requires teachers trained in a wide variety of skills in reading and sensitive to the needs of their individual children, together with specialists with an appreciation of the importance of the role of the class teacher. Only with mutual respect and understanding between the various disciplines involved in the teaching of reading can any real progress be made. It is to be hoped that an association such as UKRA which brings together classroom teachers, remedial teachers, college lecturers and psychologists both from this country and the United States may help to develop not only an increase in the requisite skills within each area of expertise but also an appreciation of the contribution of others.

References
CLARK, M. M. (1970) *Reading Difficulties in Schools* Harmondsworth: Penguin
CLARK, M. M. (1971) Severe reading difficulty: A community study in *British Journal of Educational Psychology* 14, 14–18

Contributors

BALMUTH, Miriam, B.A., M.S., Ph.D.
Associate Professor, Department of Curriculum and Teaching, Hunter College of the City University of New York

BAMBERGER, Richard, Ph.D
Professor and Director of The International Institute for Children's and Juvenile Literature, Vienna

BRACKEN, Dorothy Kendall, A.B., M.A., Ph.D.
Director, The Reading Clinic, Southern Methodist University, Dallas, Texas Past President of IRA

CLARK, Margaret M., M.A., Ed.B., Ph.D.
Senior Lecturer in Psychology, University of Strathclyde, Glasgow President-Elect of UKRA (1970–71)

CORLETT, Margery
Principal Lecturer in Education, Padgate College of Education, Warrington

DOWNING, John A., B.A., Ph.D., A.B.P.s.S.
Professor of Education, University of Victoria, British Columbia Past President of UKRA

GOODACRE, Elizabeth J., B.Sc., Ph.D.
Tutor to the Psychology of Literacy Course, Institute of Education, University of London

HASLAM, Audrey, D.A.S.E.
Senior Lecturer in Education, John Dalton Faculty of Technology, Manchester Polytechnic

HUUS, Helen, B.A., M.A., Ph.D.
Professor of Education, University of Missouri—Kansas City Past President of IRA

LITTLE, Alan, Ph.D.
Research and Statistics Group, Inner London Education Authority

MABEY, Christine
Research and Statistics Group, Inner London Education Authority

MCCULLOUGH, Constance, A.B., M.S., Ph.D.
Professor of Education, San Francisco State College, California

MERRITT, John E., B.A., A.B.Ps.S.
Professor of Educational Studies, The Open University Past President of UKRA

MONROE, Marion, A.B., M.A., Ph.D.
Authorship staff of Scott Foresman and Company, Illinois

MORRIS, Joyce M., B.A., Ph.D.
Language Arts Consultant, London Past President of UKRA

MORRIS, Ronald, M.A.
Senior Staff Tutor in Secondary Education, University of Newcastle upon Tyne

MOSELEY, David V., M.A.
Educational Psychologist, Director of Centre for Learning Disabilities (National Society for Mentally Handicapped Children), London

MOYLE, Donald, M.A., L.C.P., L.T.C.L.
Senior Lecturer in Education, Edge Hill College of Education, Ormskirk

PALMER, Jean, B.A.
Lecturer in Education of the Deaf, Department of Audiology and Education of the Deaf, University of Manchester

PUGH, Anthony K., B.A.
Fellow in Reading Efficiency, University of Leeds

PUMFREY, Peter D., M.Ed., Dip.Ch.Psych., D.E.P., A.B.Ps.S.
Lecturer in Education, Child Study Centre, Department of Education, University of Manchester

RAYGOR, Alton L., A.B., M.A., Ph.D.
Professor of Educational Psychology and Coordinator of Reading and Study Skills Centre, University of Minnesota

ROBERTS, Geoffrey R., M.A.
Lecturer in Education, Department of Education, University of Manchester

ROBINSON, H. Alan, B.A., M.S., Ed.D.
Professor of Reading, Hofstra University, New York Past President of IRA

RUSSELL, Jennifer, B.A.
Research and Statistics Group, Inner London Education Authority

SMITH, Helen K., Ph.D.
Associate Professor of Education, University of Miami

SOUTHGATE, Vera, B.Com., Dip.Psych., M.A.
Lecturer in Curriculum Studies, School of Education, University of Manchester President of UKRA (1970-71)